# Beyond Functionalism

# Beyond Functionalism

*Attitudes toward*
*International Organization*
*in Norway*
*and the United States*

By
ROBERT E. RIGGS
and I. JOSTEIN MYKLETUN

University of Minnesota Press
Minneapolis

Universitetsforlaget
Oslo

105922

© The Norwegian Research Council for
Science and the Humanities 1979
(Norges almenvitenskapelige forskningsråd)
Section B. 12.48.75.001T

Cover design by: Oddvar Wold

ISBN 82-00-01866-0 (Universitetsforlaget)

**Library of Congress Cataloging in Publication Data**

Riggs, Robert Edwon, 1927–
Beyond Functionalism

Includes bibliographical references and
index.
1. International relations–Research.
2. International organization
3. United States – Foreign relations – 1945 –
4. Norway – Foreign relations – 1945 –
I. Mykletun, Jostein I., joint author.
II. Title.
JX1291.R54    327'.07'2    79-11306
ISBN 0-8166-0898-9

Published simultaneously in
Norway by Universitetsforlaget and in
the United States of America by
University of Minnesota Press.

Printed in Norway by
Tangen-Trykk, Drammen

*To our parents*

# Acknowledgments

In conducting this study the authors have received financial assistance from institutions in both Norway and the United States. We gratefully acknowledge research support from the Norwegian Research Council for Science and the Humanities, U.S. Government National Endowment for the Humanities Grant RO-8812-76-400, the University of Minnesota Office of International Programs, Møre and Romsdal Regional College, and the J. Reuben Clark Law School of Brigham Young University. The Norwegian Research Council also financed the publication of this volume. Although the study would not have been possible without their financial assistance, the opinions expressed herein are not necessarily those of the grantors. Any deficiencies in the final product are of course the sole responsibility of the authors.

We also wish to acknowledge research assistance provided at various stages of the project by James Chamberlain, Barbara Chisholm, Nguyen Cao Dam, Eldar Grønfur, Ole Håvard Hansen, Mitchel Joelson, Timothy King, Nathan Kirk, B. Carol Pierce, Lynn Schumann, and Per Sætre. Needless to say, the many government officials who responded to questionnaires and granted personal interviews deserve our special thanks.

Provo, January 1979            Molde/Oslo, January 1979
Robert E. Riggs              I. Jostein Mykletun

# Contents

# I. The Functionalist Premise

Can international functionalism be put to an empirical test? 'It is, in a way, invidious,' says one commentator, 'to subject something as impressionistic, speculative and idealistic as this to rigorous criticism, reformulating it as a coherent theory of international change for the purpose of "testing" it.'[1] The man has a point. David Mitrany and his intellectual forebears did not formulate a 'theory' in any scientific sense, and certainly not in the mold of modern behavioral science. Their ideas were not intended to be tested by meticulous application of data analysis techniques now associated with social science research.

In a larger sense, however, international functionalism was meant to be tested against the unfolding witness of history. The reformer and the advocate challenge the world to try their 'theories' and see if the predicted consequences do not follow. At some point in time historical judgment will be passed – a kind of test that functionalists surely anticipated. Viewed in this light the attempt to verify or disconfirm the tenets of functionalism by systematic ordering of historical facts is entirely appropriate. If the reformulation and operationalizing of concepts is done fairly, preserving the essential character of the original, no injustice is done by subjecting functionalism to rigorous analysis. History in its due time will render inexorable judgment upon the functionalist premise, including those elements that cannot presently be weighed and measured. In the meantime there is no good intellectual reason for not attempting to measure what we can to see how well the pieces fit the pattern. Indeed, the intrinsic importance of the subject makes such an attempt almost imperative.

The purpose of the present study is to make that attempt in a limited but important area of functionalist thought. We will examine in detail the proposition that national government officials who become personally involved with the activities of international organizations will develop attitudes more favorable to international cooperation. This is by no means the only assumption underpinning the functionalist dynamic, but, for practical purposes, some narrowing of focus is necessary. A body of thought as wide-ranging as functionalism cannot be analyzed in its entirety within the scope of a monograph such as this.

11

Given the need to limit the scope of the inquiry, there are persuasive reasons for making participant attitudes the focus of analysis. The relevant concepts can be readily reduced to variables which are susceptible to measurement and yet remain faithful to the original concept. This is essential if good, testable propositions are to be framed. Furthermore, data on attitudes – the dependent variable – are relatively inexpensive to gather in sufficient quantity to make meaningful generalization possible. Such a research focus also enables us to take advantage of a well-developed body of literature on attitude change, including several prior studies dealing with attitudes of international organization participants. Most important, perhaps, is the intimate relationship of attitude change to the substance of functionalist thought. Individual learning is central to the functionalist conception of the institutional growth process at the international level, and attitude change is an important part of the learning supposed to occur. If the predicted attitude change can be demonstrated, in some reasonably inferrable cause and effect relationship, the functionalist theory of institutional development gains credibility. If the predicted change is not apparent, serious questions may be raised regarding its viability as empirical theory.

This study will examine the individual learning process as expressed in attitudes of government officials in Norway and the United States. From this comparative perspective we will draw conclusions about the validity of the functionalist premise. The details of the research design are set forth in chapter 2, and the data are presented in chapters 3-5. Before proceeding to the research, however, we must provide in the following pages an appropriate theoretical context. This will be done by presenting an overview of Mitrany's functionalism and a survey of previous studies dealing with attitude change through exposure to international organizations.

## Mitrany's Functionalism

Functionalism in its international context is generally identified with the writings of David Mitrany.[2] Mitrany, of course, was not the first of the international functionalists. Distinctively functionalist concepts are found in the works of Reinsch, Salter, and Woolf, written more than a half-century ago.[3] One need look no farther than the title of Simeon E. Baldwin's essay on 'The International Congresses and Conferences of the Last Century as Forces Working Toward the Solidarity of the World,' published in 1907, to observe that functionalist ideas had begun to emerge in the very early years of this century.[4] But it was Mitrany's pamphlet, A Working Peace System, first published in 1943, that provided the mother lode to which seekers after functionalist truth have perpetually returned.[5]

Mitrany's tract was diffusely organized, at times repetitious, and replete with broad generalities captured in arresting phrases. '(T)he problem of our times is not how to keep the nations peacefully apart, but how to bring them actively together.'[6] 'Society will develop by our living it, not by policing it.'[7] 'Sovereignty cannot in fact be transferred effectively through a formula, only through a function.'[8] 'Promissory covenants and charters may remain a headstone to unfulfilled good intentions, but the functional way is action itself.'[9]

Through all the verbiage, nevertheless, the basic message was clear: governments should begin cooperation now in specific functional areas where a recognized need for international cooperation exists. Don't worry if troublesome questions of military security or territorial boundaries remain unresolved; start where states have recognizable common interests in problem solving. This might be in such matters as shipping, river and rail transportation, international air transport, refugees, disease control, communication. Let cooperation fan out from there as new areas of common interest among groups of states emerge. The functional way is to proceed 'by means of a natural selection, binding together those interests which are common, where they are common, and to the extent to which they are common'.[10]

The beneficent result of such action would be two fold. First, it would solve problems that desperately needed solution. Second, it would eventually create a better and more peaceful international society. In Mitrany's words, 'Every activity organized in that way would be a layer of peaceful life; and a sufficient addition of them would create increasingly deep and wide strata of peace – not the forbidding peace of an alliance, but one that would suffuse the world with a fertile mingling of common endeavor and achievement.'[11]

Mitrany's functionalism caught on because it was, to use an overworked expression, an idea whose time had come. A host of intergovernmental agencies (IGOs), most of them of a functional nature, were to spring into being in the years following World War II. From 1945 to 1950, according to the tabulation presented by Wallace and Singer, some forty-eight new IGOs were established, representing an increase during a six-year period of more than 50 % in the total number of IGOs in existence. The trend continued virtually unabated during the succeeding decade with 58 new IGOs created from 1951 to 1960.[12] Governmental officials had obviously seen what Mitrany had seen – that certain kinds of international problems could best be handled by the creation of functional international organizations. Moreover, the apparent striking success of the European Community offered convincing evidence that functional cooperation on a regional basis could be practical and workable.

The argument that functional cooperation is linked with world peace also came to be widely accepted and reiterated in the political arena. This popularization of an idea was not much of Mitrany's doing – it just seemed, to many people bent on avoiding the mistakes of past generations, an obvious lesson from history. The idea also had utility as a rationale for publicly justifying and defending the creation of a host of functional international agencies. Not only would the new agencies help solve particular problems, they would also help build the structure of peace. This functionalist tenet had clearly attained the status of political orthodoxy when it began to appear in the Charters and constitutional documents of the new international organizations that were being created.[13]

International developments of recent years have provided a somewhat less congenial setting for the functionalist idea to flourish. The European Community, while still viable, has seen a slow-down in the pace of integration. Other regional unions spawned in hope of emulating EC successes have generally proved disappointing. At the global level, evidences of bureaucratic ossification and elephantiasis within existing functional agencies have drawn criticism from member states. The 'politicization' of functional agencies has posed a practical challenge to the assumption that organization of cooperation along functional lines could effectively insulate such activities from the political conflicts of the day. And with the growing numbers and assertiveness of developing countries, there has been a shift in the dominant ideology of many intergovernmental organizations from functionalism to 'developmental functionalism' or simply 'developmentalism'. This change has brought decreasing emphasis upon functional cooperation as the road to peace and increasing emphasis on the economic development of poorer countries.[14]

On the other hand, functionalists can take comfort from some aspects of the changing environment. The East-West cleavage that once dominated the global scene is being overshadowed by the North-South cleavage, which makes the approach of functionalism appear somehow more relevant to many emerging issues than the politics of alliances and balance of power. The growing preoccupation with resource shortages and environmental overload, while presenting numerous highly charged political issues, gives rise to new and pressing needs for functional cooperation. And the fact remains that functional links between nations continue to proliferate. From 1960 to 1972, by one count, the number of intergovernmental organizations increased from 154 to 280.[15] Transgovernmental relations – that is, less formal contacts be-

14

tween bureaucrats of different countries concerned with similar specialized functions within their own governments – have also expanded mightily.[16] Of still greater magnitude is the growth of transnational contacts among private groups and individuals in a wide variety of economic and social activities.[17] The focus of this study is upon intergovernmental rather than nongovernmental functional cooperation. Mitrany, to a large extent, shares this emphasis. But functionalists have also stressed the importance of private international ties in building a global community, and this aspect of the changing international system must surely give them aid and comfort.

A felicitously phrased idea energetically articulated in a favorable environment may be a recipe for popularization, but not necessarily for academic respectability. Mitrany's functionalism has achieved that as well, because his ideas were underpinned by an incomplete and inchoate but nevertheless intellectually provocative theory of international behavior.[18]

Mitrany's functionalism embodies a set of partially articulated assumptions about how international institutions come into being, expand and proliferate. Put in simplest terms functional cooperation arises in response to perceived 'needs' that cannot be met by governments acting individually.[19] In speaking of needs, Mitrany tends to emphasize the objective conditions that create global interdependencies. At times he almost suggests that the conditions themselves are sufficient to generate the functional response.[20] But his advocacy of functionalism as a strategy clearly implies another crucial variable – the capacity of national leaders to perceive the need for functional cooperation and persuade their governments to act in ways that maximize the chance of success. Presumably this will mean concentrating on specific functional areas of relative noncontroversiality where common interests among states are easiest to identify.[21] The form of any new functional organization will flow naturally from the function. As Mitrany puts it,'. . . activities would be selected specifically and organized separately – each according to its nature, to the conditions under which it has to operate, and to the needs of the moment'.[22] Ideally, these functional bodies 'would be executive agencies with autonomous tasks and powers; they would not merely discuss but would do things for the community . . . .'.[23]

As thus far recounted, functionalist theory predicts the autonomous appearance of international organizations in specific functional areas as needs develop and as common interests are perceived by national leaders. But the process does not stop there. Once a functional organization is established, additional forces for institutional growth and development are set in motion. In explaining this process, Mitrany sometimes appeals to an organismic analogy by which one function is 'left to generate others gradually, like the functional subdivision of organic cells'.[24] The analogy is intended more as an illustration than a precise description of a process, however. Upon careful examination, the new forces appear to be the product of individual and social learning, not some inscrutable organic growth process.[25] Because the functional approach works, it provides a model for application to new areas through expanding the functions of existing organizations or creating new functional organizations. This may be called the 'demonstration effect' of functionalist practice. At the individual level, the learning process brings attitude change. People who participate in functional activities, or at least enjoy their benefits, become supportive of expanded functional cooperation. Mitrany is quite explicit about the fact of attitude change in his allusions to the breeding of a 'new conscience',[26] the development of 'common habits and interests'[27] and the growth of 'a collectivity of functional loyalties'.[28]

The impetus for functional growth comes from perceived needs subsequently reinforced by individual and social learning. The shape and scope of the institutional arrangements likewise evolve through reaction to needs and learning from experience. This pragmatic process is known as 'technical self-determination'. Mitrany describes it with undisguised approbation:

> Here we discover a cardinal virtue of the functional method – what one might call the virtue of technical self-determination. The functional *dimensions,* as we have seen, determine themselves. In a like manner the function determines its appropriate *organs.* It also reveals through practice the nature of the action required under the given conditions, and in that way the *powers* needed by the respective authority. The function, one might say, determines the executive instrument suitable for its proper activity, and by the same process provides a need for the reform of the instrument at every stage.[29]

This analysis necessarily rests on an assumption that manifest need and low controversiality will permit political leaders to leave the running of functional organizations to experts and professionals, who will then be able to respond primarily to questions of technical efficiency in performing the function.[30]

We should emphasize that the process of functional growth and development does not depend on assumptions of national or individual altruism. The process feeds on the self-interest of the actors. Functional organizations emerge as common interests are perceived. Functional agencies expand and proliferate because interests are served.

16

This undoubtedly assumes an enlightened self-interest, capable of anticipating benefits from cooperative and mutually rewarding activity. Self-interest expressed in aggression and fierce, zero-sum competition would of course be disruptive of a functional system. Mitrany recognizes that limits on the process are imposed by 'political maturity', which is perhaps another way of referring to the capacity to pursue a course of enlightened self-interest.[31] Nevertheless, interest – not altruism – is the presumed motivating force that fuels the functionalist process.

And where does it all end? Mitrany is much more concerned with immediate prospects than final goal states, but his analysis clearly portends that the organization – and reorganization – of international life on a functional basis will continue indefinitely as needs are perceived and responded to. At appropriate junctures necessary coordinative machinery will evolve, like the machinery of specific institutions, through the processes of need recognition and response, learning and technical self-determination.

Mitrany speculates that this might proceed by stages, beginning with coordination of a group of related functions – various forms of transport or communication perhaps. As the need becomes manifest, second-stage coordination among several groups of functional agencies may be introduced. A third stage would involve coordination of the 'working functional agencies' with any international planning agencies such as, for example, an advisory international development commission. Overall coordination, finally, could be provided by some broadly representative Assembly designed to 'discuss and ventilate general policies', without actually having authority to prescribe.[32] The logical ultimate is a global government of interlocking functional units. Mitrany pointedly rejects coercive governmental powers for the overall coordinating body, but the several functional agencies presumably would have the powers necessary to perform their functions; and a functional agency for international security, if such were created, would look quite governmental.[33]

In addition to a rudimentary theory of institutional growth at the international level, functionalism also asserts a linkage between functionalist practice and world peace. The principal link is the functional contribution to building a world community.[34] Proceeding activity by activity, functionalist practice blankets the world with successive layers of peaceful life. Active cooperation – 'doing things together in workshop and market place' –[35] lays a concrete foundation of shared interests and cooperative habits. Simultaneously, individual learning brings reorientation of attitudes and the growth of a sense of community. Functionalism thus provides both the behavioral and attitudi-

17

nal components of world community which in turn lays the basis for world peace. Ideally, Mitrany adds, 'in the measure in which such peace-building activities develop and succeed, one might hope that the mere prevention of conflict, crucial as that may be, would in time fall to a subordinate place in the scheme of international things, while we would turn to what are the real tasks of our common society – the conquest of poverty and of disease and of ignorance'.[36]

Closely related to the growth of world community as a foundation for peace is the diminished significance of the territorial state. Mitrany does not present a well-developed theory of the causes of war, but the nation-state system appears again and again as the chief malefactor.[37] A territorially organized world, in Mitrany's thinking, is inherently incapable of dealing with problems that cut across territorial boundaries.[38] Moreover, the system engenders a competitiveness that itself breeds conflict and war, and no amount of boundary shifting that leaves the basic system still intact can make any significant difference. In Mitrany's words,

> Any political reorganization into separate units must sooner or later produce the same effects; any international system that is to usher in a new world must produce the opposite effect of subduing political division. As far as one can see, there are only two ways of achieving that end. One would be through a world state which would wipe out political divisions forcibly; the other is the way discussed in these pages, which would rather overlay political divisions with a spreading web of international activities and agencies, in which and through which the interests and life of all the nations would be gradually integrated.[39]

If the state system bears in itself the seeds of conflict, it is also strongly entrenched. The genius of functionalism lies in avoiding the risks of frontal assault, seeking instead to erode the system around the edges by transferring only a slice of sovereignty at a time and concentrating in areas that are non-threatening to political leaders. This will eventually 'make changes of frontiers unnecessary by making frontiers meaningless through the continuous development of common activities and interests across them'.[40]

Implicit in the case against the state system is an assumption about the causes of war that suggests a third functionalist contribution to peace. The state system inhibits an effective attack on the economic and social ills that afflict mankind. These unsolved problems, in turn, generate frustrations that may find their outlet in tension-provoking international conduct. To alleviate those problems is to reduce the

18

prospect of war. 'Give the people a moderate sufficiency of what they need and ought to have,' says Mitrany, 'and they will keep the peace.'[41] By providing a framework for solving problems on a global basis, functional cooperation helps to reduce the tensions that lead to war.

Building a world community, diminishing the importance of the territorial state, and alleviating some of the root causes of international tensions are the most immediate functional contributions to peace. In time, however, other controls over conflict may emerge. Functional organizations may acquire the capacity to wield economic sanctions by denying services and benefits to an aggressor.[42] The system itself may come to embody a built-in form of economic deterrence as states refrain from violent conflict to avoid the costs involved in disrupting the fabric of functional cooperation. Finally, the system of interlocking functional units ultimately can provide a governmental apparatus for the global community. The last may be the least important contribution, however, since world government would be simply the capstone set on the edifice of a world community. Creating the community is the important part; government follows eventually as a logical extension of the community, and only to the extent that it is needed.[43]

Functionalism is, on its face, a very attractive doctrine. Inis L. Claude, Jr., more perceptively than most critics, has identified the multifaceted appeals of functionalism. To the practical-minded person it recommends 'the logical course of taking up the less difficult jobs first, in preparation for tackling the harder ones.' It appeals to the humanitarian idealism of the pacifist and the international do-gooder, while exploiting the national self-interest of political leaders who want to acquire new benefits for their peoples. To conservatives 'it may appear as an organic, naturalistic, evolutionary approach to world organization', while the liberal can applaud its 'application of the welfare state philosophy to the international sphere'.[44] 'Lastly,' says Claude,

> Functionalism has all the earmarks of a profound and sophisticated approach to the problem of war. To those who are weary of superficial approaches, it justifies itself by burrowing deep under the surface of reality to find the roots of the problem. To those whose skepticism is excited by panaceas, it offers the appeal of a system which prescribes specific treatment for the primary ills from which war derives, instead of a cheap patent remedy for the secondary symptoms of human society's malaise. Functionalism seems to emerge from the diagnostic clinic, not the drug counter, of the internationalist movement.[45]

Still, in the absence of systematic evidence, one must admit that much support for functionalism rests on a simple 'gut feeling' that somehow it is a good idea. Donald P. Warwick in explaining his own affinity for the transnational variant of functionalism willingly conceded this when he said,

> Most of us who write in this area are convinced that transnational contacts have benign effects on the prospects for world peace, but much of this conviction is derived from sources other than empirical evidence. The only way in which we can know whether our beliefs have any basis in fact is through a more extensive program of research. The efforts to date have been tantalizing, but hardly satisfying.[46]

The same can be said of international functionalism generally.[47]

## Critiques by Haas and Sewell

To agree with Warwick that research on functionalism has been 'tantalizing but hardly satisfying' is not to say that nothing of significance has been done. One can scarcely talk about Mitrany's functionalism without also taking account of the work of Ernst B. Haas and James P. Sewell. Haas is the originator of the 'neo-functionalist' concept, which has achieved its most characteristic expression in studies of regional integration.[48] Neo-functionalists are concerned primarily with the role of intergovernmental and supranational institutions in the integrative process. They ask how institutions under given conditions lead – or fail to lead – to higher levels of integrative behavior. As contrasted with functionalism, neo-functionalism is more self-consciously rooted in social science theory, more concerned with the detailed elaboration of explanatory variables, including political variables, and more systematic in examining the process by which economic cooperation spills over into the political sphere.[49]

Not all neo-functionalists acknowledge their debt to Mitrany, but Haas does. In his massive study of the International Labor Organization,[50] Haas explicitly reformulates functionalist doctrines in a 'neo-functionalist' mold. The Haas model is much more attuned to the politics of the integrative process than was prior functionalist doctrine. Mitrany saw international functional cooperation as proceeding from a foundation of perceived need and harmony of interests, upon which technocrats could build community through quiet problem solving. Haas, on the contrary, depicts international integration as 'resulting from an institutionalized pattern of interest politics, played out within

20

existing international organizations.'[51] For Haas, functional cooperation implies no necessary harmony of interests – just a series of demands and compromises, with sufficient authority delegated to the institutions to make the compromises workable. Thus, the 'political' is not and cannot be separated from the 'functional', and power is not separated from welfare.

Haas also argues that the learning of integrative habits and the transference of loyalties are not a necessary or certain result of functional cooperation. Mitrany, of course, recognizes that the integrative process is limited by the political maturity of participants. But he assumes that functionalist ventures will generally be successful and, by appealing to the self-interest of the actors, will in fact tend to generate increased support for international cooperation. Haas is much more guarded in his prediction that positive affect and loyalty transfers will occur. In particular Haas sees experts or technocrats contributing to integration only to the extent that they can draw support for their cooperative ventures from various national constituencies – an obviously political process. Thus, even if individual learning occurs, the consequences for further integration may be slight unless the actors concerned have the political sensitivity, contacts and skills to persuade domestic decision-makers to take the necessary actions. Haas concludes, nevertheless, that his modified version of functionalism may have some utility in explaining the growth of international institutions and the processes of international integration.[52]

Sewell's study of World Bank agencies presents a more focused and less wide-ranging attempt to explicate functionalism. In further contrast to Haas, he attempts to test some of the central theses of functionalism on their own terms, without extensive reformulation. In the application of functionalist concepts to a study of UN programs financing economic development, Sewell finds organizational growth and task expansion as predicted, but generally not for the reasons postulated by functionalism. He grants that functionalism sheds light on the growth process, but argues that the 'functionalist interpretation neither brings nor encourages a grasp of the context or the specificities of these developments. It enfolds everything in a vague formula: need, functional response, modified need, functionally modified response.'[53] Sewell suggests that the vagueness might be overcome by 'grafting on additional variables'. This would add the needed dimension of specificity to functionalist theory by stating more precisely the conditions under which the predicted functionalist reordering of human attitudes and behavior is likely to occur.

There is, however, a more fundamental defect in functionalist thinking stemming from 'inadequate consideration of the nature and operation of politics.'[54] Where functionalism predicts task expansion and institutional growth through technical self-determination in a setting of relative non-controversiality, Sewell, like Haas, finds institutional growth to be a product of political bargaining and compromise. 'Needs' are better understood as 'demands', and their 'satisfaction' is 'a question of the partial and temporary resolution of conflict through distinctly political procedures.' The new institutions that emerge from this process are "not so much organs in a nascent world community as new instrumentalities born of the play of international politics.'[55] Nor, indeed, are functionalist institutions insulated even from the play of domestic politics. National policy on international issues seldom emerges without friction among political parties, interest groups, governmental agencies, and political leaders. Presumably this failure to take account of the political context could also be remedied by grafting on additional political variables. But the remedy might require such a fundamental alteration of functionalist assumptions as to make the theory unrecognizable.

Haas and Sewell both find much to contradict and modify in traditional functionalism; yet both glean from it useful insights into the growth processes of international institutions. Their works also underline the need for more systematic analysis of the tenets of functionalism. Each writer tackles the whole corpus of functionalist thought and each produces a conceptually rich analysis, massively illustrated and buttressed by a careful case study. But their theoretical propositions remain largely speculative because they are not subjected to the test of systematic sampling and analysis of many cases. This is not to criticize Haas or Sewell for not doing more but only to suggest that further progress in the criticism and development of functionalist theory will require other studies of narrower conceptual focus and a broader data base.

## International Organization and Attitude Change

One area in which promising work has already been done is that of attitudes and attitudinal change. We earlier identified the learning of cooperative habits and attitudes as a central feature of Mitrany's theory of functional development. Without specifying conditions or qualifications, Mitrany simply asserts that participants and beneficiaries of functional activities are likely to develop attitudes favorable to further international cooperation. Since Mitrany was not writing in a rigorously scientific tradition, a reasonable interpretation would suggest that he was predicting attitudinal change as a general rule but not necessarily laying down an inflexible law applicable to every case.

22

105922

Haas, with some qualifications, explicitly adopts the concept of learning as expressed in the application of past experience to new functional contexts and in the reorientation of attitudes to reflect altered perceptions of interest.[56] Sewell is more reluctant to concede the occurrence of any significant attitude change,[57] but he presents little evidence that is directly relevant one way or the other.[58]

There is additional empirical work more specifically focused on attitudinal change resulting from personal contact with international organization.[59] Some of this research has been done with reference to the functionalist model, and some not. One of the earliest is B. E. Matecki's study of the establishment of the International Finance Corporation.[60] Matecki's purpose is to explore the impact of international organization on the foreign economic policy of the United States, not to test functionalist theory. Documentary evidence and interviews with participants form the basis of a careful case study, which finds that international organization influenced United States policy by shaping participant attitudes. On this point Matecki is quite emphatic:

> Though we cannot document our contention otherwise, the interviews that we had with a number of U.S. representatives on various United Nations bodies led us to the belief that the reshaping of their thinking and outlook, directly attributable to their contacts with the United Nations, was far more responsible for conditioning their final position on IFC than mere expediency.
>
> This reshaping of the thinking and outlook of U.S. representatives on U.N. bodies was profound. It took two forms. It imparted a sympathetic attitude to the problem of economic development of under-developed countries and the demands presented upon the United States in this connection to those who previously had not had such an attitude. It also reinforced such sympathetic feelings among those who had had them before. In all cases, its effects proved to be great and they were particularly pronounced among businessmen assigned to U. S. delegations.[61]

Matecki has written the only book-length case study, of which we are aware, designed to show that international organizations have a substantial effect on important national policy decisions. But numerous other writers who have observed or interviewed participants in international meetings have reached similar conclusions about change of attitudes. Benjamin Cohen, himself a participant, wrote in 1951 that the United Nations

> has caused American policy to be formulated with greater con-

23

sciousness of wider interests which may profoundly affect American interests and which the United States as a world power cannot wholly ignore. The United Nations has broadened the scope of American foreign policy and made it more quickly conscious of and responsive to the effects of its own foreign policy on world public opinion.[62]

Haas in his study of the ILO suggests that direct contact with international agencies may influence the beliefs of individuals and groups,[63] although not always in a positive direction. Lindberg is more emphatic in his finding that European Community participants, particularly 'at ,the level of high policy makers and civil servants', developed a greater 'community-mindedness' through their involvement in joint problem solving.[64] In a comparative study of European Assemblies, Kenneth Lindsay similarly concludes: 'There is no doubt that the experience of working in European assemblies has enlarged the outlook of individual members, created a European pressure group in many parliaments, and made parliaments more aware of the problems of Europe.'[65] J. J. Fens likewise asserts that delegates to the Assembly of the Western European Union had learned to view the problem of defense 'in a genuine Western perspective'.[66] Lindberg and Scheingold's landmark study of patterns of change in the European Community also finds evidence that participants in the EC policy-making process develop more supportive attitudes toward the Community.[67]

Most of the studies just cited are not concerned with the validation of functionalist theory, but all share the conclusion that participation in international organizations tends to promote a larger community-mindedness in the participants. Measurement of attitude change is not a central focus of any of these studies, however, and none of them makes use of techniques for the systematic study of attitudes. Their conclusions, therefore, must be compared with the findings of other scholars who have undertaken more systematically to ascertain the attitudinal effects of participation in international organizations.

A pioneer in this area, Chadwick F. Alger, administered a structured interview schedule to twenty-five UN delegates of varying nationality before and after their participation in the 1959 regular session of the UN General Assembly. The number of respondents was small, and apparently they were selected on the basis of availability rather than as a random sample of the delegates. The study had the strengths of the before-and-after interview design, however, and it focused directly on the problem of attitude change. Alger found strong evidence of cognitive change. Through participation the respondents learned something about the workings of the United Nations, the nature of the issues, and the views of other countries. To a lesser extent the data suggested that the experience may also have changed 'the delegate's affective map of the world – i.e., his designation of which nations are the "good guys" and which are the "bad guys".'[68] But Alger agreed with the findings of an earlier study of foreign travel that the change was 'not in the adoption of internationalist or liberal attitudes, but in their greater awareness of considerations lying outside their own immediate environment.'[69]

Data obtained by Harold K. Jacobson from a mailed questionnaire survey of delgates to the ITU Plenipotentiary Conference in 1965 also bears directly on the question of attitude change.[70] Jacobson did not use a pre and post test research design, but he was able to distinguish between delegates who had never previously attended an ITU meeting and those who had, a form of static group comparison. Presumably the latter group would in their responses show the effects of the prior experience as an international organization participant. As expected, the findings showed the more experienced group to have a better, more sophisticated grasp of international organization processes and issues. However, the more experienced delegates tended to regard the ITU and its activities as less important to their country than did the first time attenders.[71] This may be viewed as a cognitive effect – a more realistic appreciation of the ITU and its functions – but it may have some affective content as well. In any event, it runs somewhat counter to the functionalist thesis that participation brings increased support for functional activities.

Two studies of participation in European regional parliamentary assemblies by Bonham and Kerr, respectively, further substantiate the proposition that cognitive changes occur, but they provide no support for the thesis that participants become more favorable toward the institutions of international cooperation. Bonham's object was 'to examine the relationship between participation in regional parliamentary assemblies and attitudes toward political integration.'[72] His study is based on interviews of parliamentarians from Norway, Denmark and Sweden who had attended sessions of the Nordic Council or the Consultative Assembly to the Council of Europe. For a control group, he interviewed a random sample of parliamentarians from the same countries who had not participated in either regional body.[73] The results of the survey at first blush appeared to contain inconsistencies. Delegates to the Consultative Assembly were somewhat more favorable to European and Nordic integration than were members of the control group; but, on three of four attitudinal dimensions tapped by Bonham, delegates to the Nordic Council were less favorable to integration than the control group. Probing deeper, Bonham concluded that the group differences were due to the recruitment process rather than to the experience of participation in a regional assembly. The Consultative Assembly group was more favorable because its members were recruited on the basis of their interest in Europe, and their linguistic ability, which suggests a greater initial predisposition to favor regional integration. For participation in the Nordic Council, experience and parliamentary status tended to be important criteria, which meant that Nordic Council participants were older on the average than the other two groups. With the age factor controlled, differences between the Nordic Council group and the control group almost disappeared. Direct response to questions about the effects of the experience appeared to confirm the proposition that attitude change had been minimal. Only 11 % admitted that they had become more favorable toward European integration, while the others referred mainly to their increased knowledge about European affairs. 'A small minority said that it had no effect or a negative effect on their outlook.'[74]

Kerr, using a research design broadly similar to that of Bonham, interviewed German and French delegates to the parliament of the European Community (the 'European Parliament') as well as a randomly selected sample of 73 French and German parliamentarians who had never been members of an international parliamentary assembly.[75] His avowed purpose was to examine the functionalist theory of attitude change in the light of the European Parliament experience. Kerr's interview schedule was specifically designed to distinguish between the cognitive and the affective components of individual attitudes. The cognitive component he defined as 'what a person knows about an object, how he perceives it, and how central the object is to his beliefs', whereas the affective component represents 'liking or disliking', approval or disapproval of the object or some of its attributes.[76]

Within this framework, Kerr's findings were generally consistent with those of Jacobson and Bonham: participation had pronounced cognitive affects but no discernible impact on the affective component of parliamentarians' attitudes toward European integration. The cognitive effects were evidenced by greater information about European integration, much greater reliance on European as opposed to national sources of information, increased capacity to make fine distinctions in defining issues and stating preferences, and a larger interest in European unification issues. In attempting to measure affective change, Kerr found – as Bonham had – that delegates to the Parliament were significantly more favorable to European integration than non-delegates. But when he controlled for the effect of self-selection, the 'differences in overall level of support' for integration 'virtually disappeared'.[77] The 'self-recruits' among the delegates scored about the

26

same on most of the unification dimensions as did persons identified as 'potential volunteers' among the non-delegates; and the party-recruited delegates scored roughly the same as the 'non-volunteer' non-delegates. Furthermore, in contrast to measures of cognitive change, length of membership in the European Parliament had only a weak and statistically insignificant relationship to positive attitudes toward integration. In fact, the best predictor of respondent attitudes toward European integration was party affiliation.[78]

A recent study by Karns examines attitude change in U.S. Congressmen resulting from participation in international meetings.[79] Karns is unconcerned with functionalist claims, but his central hypothesis that 'participation in interparliamentary group meetings is associated with increased support for international involvement' might well have been drawn from functionalist literature. He measures attitude change by means of an internationalism-isolationism score derived from voting records on foreign policy issues for each Congressman and Senator before and after attending international meetings. This is supplemented by a number of personal interviews. The results give some aid and comfort to functionalists – but not much. The participants are shown to be, on the average, somewhat more internationalist in voting behavior after attending the meetings than before, although the differences are not statistically significant in most cases. More significant is the convergence of attitudes toward a common norm – the isolationists becoming less isolationist and the internationalists becoming less internationalist. Attitude change also appeared to be significantly related to the participant's domestic reference groups. Democrats and liberals (as measured by ADA and COPE ratings) were more prone to change in an internationalist direction or, if already very internationalist, to exhibit only a slight falling away. Republicans and conservatives, by contrast, experienced more change in an isolationist direction or, alternatively, less than average movement away from a previously isolationist position. Karns explains the observed change by reference to theories of cognitive consistency.

All of the empirical studies discussed above are concerned with attitudes of parliamentarians and other political/diplomatic representatives to international meetings.[80] At least three additional studies have focussed on attitude change in European national civil servants who served as seconded members of the European Community bureaucracy, as participants in EC working groups, or as staff members of national permanent delegations to the European Community. All are based on more or less systematic personal interview and, with respect to the nature of attitude change, the results are mixed. Lawrence Scheinman and Werner Feld[81] report that 10 of 24 interviewees of varying nationalities admitted to having 'adopted a more "European" orientation' as a result of their experience as seconded Eurocrats or participants in working groups and national delegations.[82] Scheinman and Feld recognize the existence of countervailing pressures in support of national goals and viewpoints, and they see the process of socialization to European norms as proceeding 'only haltingly'. Nevertheless, they conclude that participation does tend to blunt the most nationalistic responses to Community policies and bring a 'partial assimilation' that 'is likely to advance the European cause.'[83] Smith, on the contrary, found that 48 Dutch respondents had not become more 'Europeanized' through service as Eurocrats or other contact with the Community.[84] The chief attitudinal effect was increased 'realism' about the future of European integration. Smith's interviewees possessed a 'highly developed "European" outlook' both before and after the experience, however, which is consistent with official Dutch policies toward the Community, and there is no indication that service with the EC made them less European.[85]

A third study, by Pendergast, entailed interviews with 24 officials serving as staff members of the French and Italian permanent delegations to the European Community.[86] The interview responses, according to Pendergast, revealed an 'almost total absence of increased support for integration.'[87] There must have been a substantial amount of initial support for the Community, however, because all respondents 'shared a commitment to succeed in the task of common policy elaboration'; virtually all 'favored the expansion of Community competence'; and a majority supported direct, popular election of the European Parliament and abolition of the Council veto.[88]

The empirical studies just examined are in general agreement on the cognitive effects of participation in international organizations. Participants become more aware, informed, and interested in international affairs. With respect to affective change, the evidence is much less conclusive. Bonham, Kerr, and Jacobsen find that the participant's 'affective map of the world' is not changed much, at least not in ways that reflect support for international cooperation and integration. Alger presents evidence that raises at least the possibility of positive affective change, but his findings of expanded knowledge and awareness, i.e., cognitive change, are much more pronounced. Karns finds a slight overall change in the direction predicted by functionalist theory and significant change in both directions when party, ideology, and isolationism-internationalism are controlled. The studies probing the attitudes of government officials below the level of political-diplomatic representation do not make a strong case for or against the growth of supportive attitudes. Change apparently occurs in both directions, which suggests that the effects of exposure to international organizations are mediated by interaction with other variables.

The preceding discussion has identified the principal elements of Mitrany's functionalism, briefly summarized the critiques offered by Haas and Sewell, and examined existing literature on the subject of attitude change as a result of exposure to international organizations. From this discussion it is apparent that: (1) the learning of cooperative attitudes is a key assumption in functionalist thought; and (2) the empirical basis for this assumption, as thus far explored, has at best been demonstrated only ambiguously and inconclusively. Against this background we may now present our own research on attitude change in Norway and the United States.

# II. Testing the Premise

Although the purpose of this study is to put functionalism to an empirical test, we are not using a testing ground that is in all respects ideal. This is particularly true of the portion of the study that focusses upon the experience of national legislators as UN delegates. Mitrany regards the UN General Assembly as a 'political' rather than a 'functional' organization; and as functional actors he has in mind persons with the status of experts or specialists working in their respective technical, relatively non-controversial fields. In contrast national legislators have highly politicized roles within their own governments. Their dealings with international organizations, such as UN, tend to be of a short-term, temporary nature. As delegates to international organizations they play primarily a generalist's role, not a specialist's role.

There is, nevertheless, ample justification for studying the attitudes of legislators. Although functionalists tend to focus on the expert as actor, there is no theoretical reason why learning – including the learning of positive attitudes toward international organization – should be limited to subject matter specialists. Indeed, if national policies are to become more accommodative to multilateral cooperation, the attitudes of those who make the policies ultimately must be influenced. We may accept, for hypothesis, that politicization of a role reduces the chances of positive attitude change in the actor but not, surely, that politicization is totally disabling. By any sensible definition of politics, all roles are politicized to a degree – just some more than others.

The use of data on legislators, as well as on civil servants (who undoubtedly are closer to the Mitrany notion of a functional actor), has some positive advantages. Comparison of different types of participants in international organizations enables us to draw conclusions about the effect of role politicization upon the participant's propensity to develop favorable attitudes toward international cooperation. Furthermore, if we find attitude change in the predicted direction among both types of participants, there is an even stronger case to be made for the presumed impact of participation.

The choice of the UN General Assembly as a forum of participation follows from the decision to include parliamentarians as a category of functional actor. It is the only intergovernmental organization, other than interparliamentary meetings, in which significant numbers of legislators from both countries have participated. The General Assembly is not a typical functional organization. It is multi-functional rather than uni-functional (the ideal type). It is not concerned solely with economic, technical, and social-welfare activities – although these are certainly part of its domain. Political non-controversiality is supposed to be part of the setting in which the functionalist dynamic works best, while controversiality tends to be the hallmark of the General Assembly. In all these respects the UN General Assembly may be one of the least favorable fora in which to test the functionalist premise. This tends to 'stack the deck' against confirmation of functionalist theory, assuming that learning of positive attitudes occurs more readily in a unifunctional, welfare-oriented, politically non-controversial setting. On the other hand, a finding of predicted change would be all the more convincing. If positive affect flows from experience as a General Assembly delegate, a fortiori, it should occur in a more 'ideal' functional setting.

There is of course the possibility that the General Assembly differs from allegedly typical functional organizations more in theory than in practice. All intergovernmental organizations are multifunctional in some sense of the word. No one has ever operationalized the concept of 'function' to the point of clearly distinguishing where one function (with all its sub-functions) ends and another function begins. Furthermore all international organizations are 'political' at least in the sense of involving competing claims by contending groups; and hence all involve some degree of controversiality. Mitrany says international organizations are 'functional' if their activities center on '. . . the development of the common or cooperative interests of the peoples in areas which lie outside, or on the margin of the usual play of politics.'[1] In our view such international organizations are hard to come by.[2] Conversely, we do not know of any major international organizations which do not at least marginally involve some 'functional' activities. If the line between 'political' and 'functional' organizations is in practice so hard to draw, objections to treating the General Assembly as a functional organization for purposes of testing the learning hypothesis may lose some of their weight.

## Design for Research

The design used for carrying out the greater part of the research is one described by Campbell and Stanley as a 'static group comparison'.[3] It involves making comparisons between groups of research subjects, in this case people, on the basis of observations taken at a single point in time. The subjects are assigned to a 'test group' or a 'control group', depending on whether they have been exposed to certain stimuli, and the observer looks for differences between the groups that by hypothesis may be attributable to the difference in experience which was the basis of the group assignment. The absence of a time dimension means that the design cannot measure change directly; it merely measures differences between two static groups. It does, however, permit inferences that the group differences, if any, may be related to the presence or absence of the stimuli. In sum, as Campbell and Stanley succinctly put it, 'This is a design in which a group which has experienced X is compared with one which has not, for the purpose of establishing the effect of X.'[4]

As applied to our investigation, the research subjects are government officials in Norway and the United States who responded to a mailed questionnaire soliciting their views on the United Nations and other aspects of multilateral cooperation. The sample includes professional grade civil servants in both countries, as well as members of Congress and of the Norwegian parliament. In the analysis the responses of civil servants and parliamentarians are examined separately for each country.

For the parliamentarians, two pairs of test and control groups were formed. One pair consisted of legislators who had been delegates to the UN (test group) and those who had not (control group); the other pair differentiated legislative delegates to international organizations other than the UN General Assembly (test group) from non-delegates to such organizations (control group).[5]

The rationale for these groupings is straightforward: a person who attends international meetings has been exposed to certain stimuli which others have not been exposed to. These include new information, personal interaction with other nations' representatives, and exposure to group norms of international organizations. Such stimuli, we assume, will be associated with a learning experience of the delegated legislator. And we hypothesize that this learning experience will cause the members of the test groups to develop perceptions and attitudes toward the international activities more favorable than those of the members of the control groups.

The civil servants likewise were assigned to test and control groups, in this case including three rather than two pairs. The distinguishing criteria were, respectively, (1) whether or not the person had participated in international meetings and conferences; (2) whether or not the person's work task involved international organization matters; and (3) whether or not the person had dealt with international organization matters in some previous governmental position. Our assumptions concerning the effects of international organization on civil servants are the same as those expressed for the legislators. That is, if the hypothesized group differences appear, we would draw from this the inference that attitudes had in fact been changed by exposure to the activities of international organizations.

Such an inference is subject to qualifications which become immediately apparent when it is recast in 'if-then' form. Strictly speaking, we can say only that *if* there are no variables operating on the test and control groups, other than the international organization experience, and *if* the groups are otherwise equivalent, *then* the group differences are caused by that experience. This is another way of saying that both groups must be hypothesized as isolated from all extraneous environmental factors for such a causal statement to be made. It is superflous to note that this assumption grossly oversimplifies reality. As Blalock notes:

> It is because of this hypothetical nature of causal laws that they can never be tested empirically, in the strictest sense of the word. Since it will always be possible that some unknown forces may be operating to disturb a given causal relationship, or to lead us to believe a causal relationship exists when in fact it does not, the only way we can make causal inferences at all is to make simplifying assumptions about such disturbing influences.[6]

The problem of simplifying assumptions applies in some degree to nearly all research, both experimental and non-experimental. But with a design such as ours, which is at best quasi-experimental, special problems are posed by the relative absence of experimental controls. With a static group comparison there simply is 'no formal means of certifying that the groups would have been equivalent had it not been for the X.'[7] In truly experimental research, the random assignment of subjects to groups provides a significant control for differences in background characteristics of the subjects. With the static group design we can only identify certain respondent characteristics which might be assumed to affect attitudes and attempt to introduce statistical controls for those characteristics. Such controls have been introduced with respect to such matters as sex, age, education, and residence abroad.[8] But this tells us nothing about other background or environmental conditions that might conceivably help explain group differences. The inability to control for all possible background factors does not thereby render invalid all causal inferences from the data. Far from it. But it

33

does mean that inferences must be qualified by the recognition that other causal factors may also be operative.

Indeed, one background variable has been of special concern because of its potential for distorting our findings and the difficulty of developing adequate controls. This is the self-selection factor, which exists to the extent that our test group subjects have purposely sought exposure to the stimuli. That is, people attending international organization meetings or dealing with international organization activities in their work may have actively solicited such appointments; and they may have sought the appointment because of pre-existing favorable attitudes toward multilateral cooperation. The self-selection factor is very important because of the static nature of our design. We tap the attitudes of the test and control group members at a single point in time and thus cannot measure the overtime effect of participation on attitudes. This means, in effect, that possible differences between the groups may be due to self-selection by members of the test groups rather than to the experience with the international organization.

For the civil servant groups, we have tried to attack this problem by conducting an *indirect* test of the validity of our inferences. This is done by taking account of the duration or magnitude of exposure to international organization activities. If the difference between test and control groups increases with the degree of exposure, we have a rather convincing empirical basis for inferring that the difference is attributable to the exposure rather than self-selection. Hyman clarifies the underlying rationale for this assertion:

> . . . if the experience was actually selected on the basis of an initial trait or attitude, then we would expect no difference in the attitude between respondents [within the test group], no matter what the length of experience . . . *Only if the attitude were a developmental product of experience, would it change with the magnitude of experience.*[9]

Data bearing on duration or magnitude of exposure are supplied by responses to the questionnaires. Each official was asked to specify (a) the duration of his public career, (b) the number of international organization meetings he had attended, and (c) the amount of work time in his current position devoted to matters directly related to international organizations. Thus if we find that respondents with the greatest exposure to international activities display the most favorable attitudes toward international cooperation, we have reason to conclude that exposure rather than self-selection produces the attitude differential.[10]

With respect to the national legislators, the control problems are of a somewhat different nature because we are not able to perform an internal validity test based on the duration or magnitude of the international experience. If a statistically significant number of legislators had been UN delegates more than once, such a test could have been conducted. But in fact, only two legislators who responded to the questionnaire had been delegated twice. We have, however, attempted to establish other controls for the self-recruitment factor. Chapters three and four give details on the control procedures used for the two national groups of legislators. Our findings suggest that for the Norway group of parliamentary delegates the self-recruitment factor does not present a serious design problem. In the case of U.S. Congressmen, self-recruitment is more in evidence, but an additional set of data has been used to compensate for this weakness in design application. These data are derived from content analysis of speeches relating to the United Nations appearing in the *Congressional Record*. Comparing speeches by each Congressman before and after his period of service at the UN provides a direct measurement of change. This eliminates the inference that attitudes tapped subsequent to the UN experience reflect only the persistence of attitudes held prior thereto by a self-selected group of participants.

Methodologically, the static group comparison design may be less than ideal for our purposes. But so are the available alternatives. A controlled experiment in which human subjects are exposed to the experimental treatment, while being shielded from the effects of all extraneous variables, is obviously impossible. A before-and-after design using repeated interviews with the same subjects is a practical possibility, but such a project must necessarily focus on a single event or experience from which the 'before' and 'after' time periods are to be calculated.[11] There is no obvious way to operationalize the 'before' stage when dealing with government officials whose work relates to a variety of different international organization activities. And if repeated interviews are to be conducted with a large number of officials, research costs mount substantially. Under these circumstances we have opted for static group comparison as a reasonably reliable means of testing the functionalist premise, while keeping within resource limitations.

*The data*
The main body of our data derive from responses to questionnaires mailed to national parliamentarians (congressmen) and civil servants. Both the Norway and the United States questionnaires include state-

35

ments about the UN or about values and policy positions that have been subject to controversy in the UN. Most of the statements in the various questionnaires are parallel, although a few were altered to fit the respective political contexts in the two countries. The questionnaire sent to U.S. civil servants probes a few additional dimensions of international cooperation, while the questionnaires directed to both groups of legislators contain items permitting them to assess their experience as UN delegates. Respondents in both countries were asked to choose from a five-point scale (strongly agree, agree, undecided, disagree, strongly diagree) the response closest to their own attitudes on each item. In addition, the respondents were asked to specify the magnitude of their past and present dealings with international organizations, as well as to provide information about various background characteristics, such as education and travel experience.

Both questionnaires were mailed in 1974. Synchronizing the mailings enabled the various respondents to react to the statements in the same international time context.

In Norway all national legislators received the questionnaire; in the United States the questionnaire was sent to a 50 % sample of each house of Congress. The sample of Norwegian civil servants included all professional grade officials in the government departments of Commerce, Foreign Aid, and Foreign Affairs. In the United States we sampled a broad cross-section of professional grade officials in nine executive departments (Department of Agriculture, Commerce, HEW, Housing and Urban Development, Interior, Labour, State, Transportation, and the Treasury). Both survey strategies were successful in obtaining responses from officials with varying amounts of experience with international organizations. Further details on the two mailed surveys are provided in Chapters three and four respectively.

Data from the mailed questionnaires were supplemented by personal interviews with a number of legislators and other government officials from both countries. The interviewees were not selected as a statistically representative sample, nor were the interviews designed to serve as a quantitative measure of attitudes toward international organization. Rather the objective was to acquire additional insights from personal anecdotal information, which a standardized mailed questionnaire hardly invites. Information from these interviews was found useful in interpreting our questionnaire data.

In addition to the mailed surveys and personal interviews, the attitudes of U.S. legislators were further explored through a systematic content analysis of speeches appearing in the *Congressional Record*. The strength of this approach, detailed in chapter four, is its dynamic characteristic. It provides a direct measure of attitude change based on

36

comparison of delegates' attitudes before and after their UN experience.

Content analysis of Norwegian parliamentary addresses was not undertaken, primarily because foreign relations speeches in the Storting commonly reflect party positions rather than the speakers' personal political views. Analysis of speech content might give some clue to shifts in party positions but could not be a very useful measure of individual attitude change. With so little potential payoff, it did not seem prudent to invest the rather considerable resources such a task would demand. In any event the nature of our mailed survey among Norwegian parliamentarians did not reveal a need for conducting a content analysis of speeches. The number of questionnaire responses was very high, and evenly distributed for delegates and non-delegates; and the self-recruitment factor was much less pronounced among Norwegian legislators than among United States legislators.

## Hypotheses to be tested

The survey instrument was designed to test a number of specific propositions deduced from functionalist assumptions about learning and attitude change. Our emphasis was placed on the affective (preference or liking) component of participant attitudes rather than the cognitive (knowledge) component.[12] Questionnaire items undoubtedly touch both dimensions, but they were designed primarily to tap the former.

Not all questionnaire items probe the same type of affect, however. Some are more explicitly evaluative than others. Two examples will illustrate the distinction:

Item 1. The UN, and what the organization in principle stands for, represents the most important 'cornerstone' in Norway's foreign policy.

Item 2. Norway ought to be generally more involved in the work of the UN.

While both items clearly tap an affective dimension, Item 2 is more explicitly a statement of preference than Item 1. Item 1 is in the form of a statement of fact rather than of preference, but a respondent who agrees with the statement is very likely to be communicating by implication a generally favorable view of the UN. To further clarify the distinction, attitudes evoked by Item 1 reflect the respondents' general evaluation of the UN and related matters, while attitudes associated with Item 2 bear on willingness to make an explicit commitment to action as a concrete expression of favorable evaluation. The implicitly evaluative responses will hereafter be designated Type 1 attitudes, while attitudes reflected in the more express action commitments will be labeled Type 2.

The content and usefulness of this distinction will become more apparent as specific hypotheses are tested against the data presented in chapters 3 and 4.

The following propositional statements represent the hypotheses around which most of the data analysis will revolve.

1. Government officials who are involved with international organization activities, either as delegates to meetings or as members of interested governmental units, will develop generally favorable attitudes toward such activities, although increased sophistication will militate against uncritical acceptance.
2. Such involvement will increase the willingness of government officials to have their government take steps toward further international cooperation.
3. Such involvement will foster a greater willingness to have portions of the national sovereignty transferred to international organizations.
4. Officials who prior to their current assignments held a position in which they were involved with international organization activities will hold attitudes more favorable to such activities than those with no prior experience.
5. The more extensive a governmental unit's dealings with international organization activities, the more likely will officials in such a unit be to regard the organization as their 'client' and develop an attitude of favorable responsiveness.
6. Present incumbents in governmental units dealing with international organization activities will have more favorable and supportive attitudes toward these activities than will former incumbents.
7. National legislators serving as delegates to international organizations will develop generally favorable attitudes toward such organizations, although increased sophistication will militate against uncritical acceptance.
8. Experience with international organizations will also promote legislators' willingness to have their government take steps toward further international cooperation.
9. Such experience will also breed willingness to transfer portions of the national sovereignty to international organizations.

Hypotheses 1-3 and 7-9 are framed to probe ascending degrees of commitment to international cooperation, ranging from general evaluation of the UN to assenting in principle to a partial transfer of sovereignty. If the data support all nine hypotheses, a strong case would be made for the functionalist premise. If a more complex empirical picture appears, some portions supporting and others contradicting the hypotheses, we may be required to rethink relevant aspects of functionalism in light of those findings. Let us turn now to the data.

# III. Functional Cooperation and Attitude Change: Norway

In this chapter the hypotheses outlined above will be examined with reference to the attitudes of Norwegian public officials. The first six hypotheses deal with the attitudes of civil servants; the last three relate to parliamentarians. They will be considered in that order.

## Civil Servants' Attitudes Toward the UN

*Sample description*

Mailed questionnaires were sent to all professional level officials of the Commerce, Foreign Aid, and Foreign Affairs Departments who were stationed in Oslo at the time of the mailing (December, 1974). Our sample is thus a sample of government departments rather than a sample of government officials. Officials in the Foreign Affairs Department serving as members of the Permanent Mission of Norway to the UN were also included, and a number of these officials were personally interviewed as well during the Fall of 1974.

The three executive departments were selected because they are involved with international organization, but at the same time differ significantly in the extent of their involvement. The Commerce Department, for instance, devotes much of its time to domestic trade matters. In contrast the Foreign Affairs Department is almost exclusively concerned with international relations. These differences assured that officials in the survey would represent varying degrees of experience with international organization activities, which is a requisite for the study.

Because of the relatively small number of officials in each department, there was no need to use a sampling process. A total of 285 questionnaires were mailed, based on personnel lists provided by the Personnel Offices of the respective government departments. After one follow-up mailing a total return rate of 81.8 % was achieved. As shown in Table 1, the return rates for the individual departments vary somewhat, but on the whole may be characterized as high. The lower return rate for Foreign Affairs personnel is in part due to greater mobility of officials in the department. Some of the Foreign Affairs employees listed as stationed in Oslo at the time of the mailing had been assigned to diplomatic posts abroad by the time the questionnaire reached their home desk. The majority of these officials apparently never received the mailing.

*Table 1.* Distribution of respondents and percent questionnaire returns by government department

| Department | Number of Respondents | Percent of Respondents | Percent Questionnaire Returns |
|---|---|---|---|
| Commerce | 70 | 30.1 | 88.1 |
| Foreign Aid | 66 | 28.3 | 91.1 |
| Foreign Affairs | 97 | 41.6 | 71.4 |

*Table 2.* Number of international organization meetings attended by government officials

| Number of Meetings | Number of Respondents | Percent of Respondents |
|---|---|---|
| No Meetings | 53 | 22.7 |
| 1-10 | 86 | 36.9 |
| More than 10 | 94 | 40.4 |

*Table 3.* Percentage work time officials devote to international organization activities

| Percent of Meetings | Number of Respondents | Percent of Respondents |
|---|---|---|
| No Time | 27 | 12.0 |
| Less than 50% | 142 | 62.8 |
| 50% or more | 57 | 25.2 |

Tables 2 and 3 give the distribution of respondents by extent of interna-

41

tional organization experience. Information on other survey group characteristics is also available. All the respondents are civilian, almost all have college or university degrees, all are career officials, and none are politically appointed. The average age is 43; 13 % of the respondents are women.

The questionnaires sent to the civil servants are reproduced in appendix A. Each questionnaire contains 12 statements about the United Nations or about values and policy positions that have been at issue in the World Organization.

### General evaluation of the UN

Our first hypothesis postulates that government officials who are involved with international organization activities will develop attitudes generally favorable to those activities. The following three questionnaire items bear directly on this hypothesis:

Item 1. The UN, and what the organization in principle stands for, represents the most important 'cornerstone' in Norwegian foreign policy.

Item 2. The UN helps to promote a more peaceful, cooperative world.

Item 3. Anything that strengthens the UN is likely to be good for Norway.

These three statements are designed to probe what we have previously denominated 'Type 1' attitudes. They involve general evaluations of the UN, but do not necessarily imply any commitments to further action.[1] Respondents were asked to choose from a five point scale (strongly agree, agree, undecided, disagree, strongly disagree) the response closest to their own attitudes on each item. For purposes of our analysis, responses are scored ordinally from 1 for 'strongly agree' to 5 for 'strongly disagree' when rank order measures are used. When a single percentage agreement figure is given, it includes all respondents who marked either 'strongly agree' or 'agree' for a given item.[2] The scores are calculated for groups of respondents with different amounts of international organization experience, the experience variables being the number of international meetings attended and percentage work time devoted to international organization activities.[3]

If hypothesis 1 is to gain support, civil servants having experience with international organizations should have a higher agreement score than civil servants lacking such experience. In fact, our findings tend to be in the predicted direction, although the group differences are small.

42

Table 4 shows percentage agreement scores for three pairs of respondent groups. The first pairing divides all respondents into those who have attended one or more meetings of any international organization and those who have not. The second pairing distinguishes all respondents by whether or not their present official duties relate to international organization activities in any way. The third pairing is drawn only from the group of Foreign Affairs Department respondents and separates those who at any time have been delegates to the United Nations and those who have not. The more experienced group in each pairing shows higher agreement scores in 7 of the 9 cases, which suggests a relationship in the hypothesized direction.[4]

*Table 4.* Percent agreement of paired groups with questionnaire items involving general evaluation of the UN

| Item | Attended an IO Meeting | | Work Involves IO | | Experience with UN | |
|---|---|---|---|---|---|---|
| | *Yes* | *No* | *Yes* | *No* | *Yes* | *No* |
| 1 UN is cornerstone for Norway | 70.0 | 69.8 | *71.5* | 55.0 | *85.7* | 60.0 |
| 2 UN promotes peace | *84.4* | 77.0 | *81.0* | 76.9 | *94.7* | 83.1 |
| 3 Strengthening UN is good for Norway | 69.2 | *71.7* | 70.0 | *70.3* | *73.7* | 64.1 |
| | N=180 | N=53 | N=199 | N=27 | N=19 | N=78 |

Note: Italics have been used for emphasis to show the higher score of each pair.

It might be argued that the group differences could be explained by a self-selection factor.[5] People engaged in international organization affairs or international meetings may have sought such appointments due to a prior favorable outlook toward multilateral cooperation. The argument is a plausible one, since personal placement preferences are given some consideration in all three government departments. As a rule, however, professional expertise represents the crucial basis for selecting international conference participants and assigning international organization work.

Furthermore, the self-selection argument loses its force when respondents are grouped by varying amounts of international organization experience.[6] If we discover that respondents with the greatest

*Table 5.* Attendance at international organization meetings and work time devoted to international organization affairs as related to general evaluation of the UN

| Questionnaire Item | Number of Meetings Attended | | | | Percentage Work time | | | |
|---|---|---|---|---|---|---|---|---|
| | No Meetings | 1-10 | More than 10 | | No time | Less than 50% | 50% or more | |
| | %Agreement | | | Tau B | % Agreement | | | Tau B |
| 1. UN is cornerstone for Norway | 69.8 | 68.6 | 70.2 | .023 | 55.0 | 71.7 | 71.9 | .060 |
| 2. UN promotes peace | 77.0 | 73.3 | 90.4 | .099* | 76.9 | 78.9 | 85.9 | .075 |
| 3. Strengthening UN is good for Norway | 71.7 | 64.7 | 73.4 | .058 | 70.3 | 63.3 | 75.5 | .060 |
| | N=53 | N=86 | N=94 | | N=27 | N=142 | N=57 | |

*Significant at .05

exposure to international activities are most supportive of international cooperation, we may conclude that exposure rather than self-selection exerts the positive attitude effect. Table 5 shows that exposure, operationalized as meetings and work time, is positively related to questionnaire Items 1-3. Although most of the relationships as measured by rank order correlation (Kendall tau beta) are not statistically significant, they show consistency in the predicted direction.

Hypothesis 1 gains further support when the returns are grouped by government department. The predicted association is most clearly pronounced for responses from the Foreign Affairs Department, the one department in our survey most heavily involved in international organization activities.The association is stronger for work time than for meeting attendance (see Table 6).

Work time, in fact, is generally a better predictor than meeting attendance across all three departmental groups. A possible explanation is that the former reflects more continuous and thorough contact with multilateral cooperation activities, so that the impact on attitudes is less likely to be attenuated by intervening experiences.

With three executive departments, three questionnaire items, and two measures of experience, it is possible to calculate a measure of association (Kendall tau B) for a total of eighteen relationships. Of these, fifteen are in the predicted direction,[7] while three relationships show negative coefficients. Combined with data in Tables 4-6, these computations provide modest support for the first hypothesis.

*Table 6.* Work time and meeting attendance as related to general evaluation of the UN for respondents from the Foreign Affairs Department

| Questionnaire Item | Meeting Attendance | Percentage of Work Time |
|---|---|---|
| | Tau B | Tau B |
| 1. UN is cornerstone for Norway | .007 | .092 |
| 2. UN promotes peace | .083 | .125 |
| 3. Strengthening UN is good for Norway | .118 | .123 |
| | N=96 | N=92 |

## Action commitment attitudes

Hypothesis 2 asserts that involvement with international organizations will increase the officials' willingness to have their nation take steps toward further international cooperation. The inquiry moves from general evaluation of the UN (using Type 1 statements), to more explicit evaluative statements that entail some kind of action commitment (Type 2). Here we look for the effect of experience upon the respondents' willingness to commit their government to extended international cooperation, implying increased transfers of financial and human resources. Six questionnaire items are employed to tap attitudes of this kind.

Item 4. Norway ought to be generally more involved in the work of the UN.

Item 5. The UN ought to have greater financial resources available.

Item 6. Norway ought to channel a greater percentage share of its foreign aid through the UN's multilateral programs.

Item 7. Norway ought to grant greater trade preferences to the developing countries.

Item 8. Norway ought to increase its overall foreign aid package.

Item 9. Norway ought to give increased humanitarian aid to the Palestinians.

Presentation of our findings will follow the same format used in our discussion of the general evaluative questionnaire items. Table 7 shows agreement percentages of the three paired groups on questionnaire Items 4-9, drawn from the general survey of three government departments. The findings support the hypothesis in that the more experienced group in each pairing shows higher scores of agreement in 16 of the 18 cases.

The findings in Table 8 also point in the predicted direction, and five of the twelve positive relationships are strong enough to meet the .05 significance test or better. Worth noting also is the fact that the statistically strongest relationships appear on Items 4-6, all involving some measure of commitment to increased use or support of the United Nations.

The same directional tendency appears when rank order measures of association are applied to the 36 possible relationships resulting from six questionnaire items, three executive department groups, and two measures of international organization experience. Twenty-seven of the 36 show the predicted positive association between experience and favorable attitudes toward international cooperation. Eight of the 27 are statistically significant. The departmental breakdown reveals two

46

Table 7. Percent agreement of paired groups with questionnaire items probing the 'action commitment' dimension of official attitudes

| Item | Attended an IO Meeting | | Work Involves IO | | Experience with UN | |
|---|---|---|---|---|---|---|
| | Yes | No | Yes | No | Yes | No |
| 4. Norway should be more involved in UN | 73.0 | 67.9 | 73.9 | 59.3 | 79.0 | 68.8 |
| 5. Increase UN financial resources | 81.0 | 62.2 | 75.8 | 81.5 | 89.5 | 80.5 |
| 6. Channel more foreign aid through UN | 30.8 | 30.7 | 29.9 | 29.6 | 57.9 | 28.6 |
| 7. Grant trade preferences | 73.9 | 73.6 | 73.4 | 70.3 | 73.7 | 64.1 |
| 8. Norway should increase its overall foreign aid package | 67.4 | 57.7 | 66.8 | 48.1 | 52.6 | 66.3 |
| 9. Norway should increase Palestinian aid | 45.2 | 43.2 | 44.3 | 40.7 | 55.6 | 50.0 |
| | N=180 | N=53 | N=199 | N=27 | N=19 | N=78 |

Note: Italics have been used for emphasis to show the higher score for each pair.

Table 8. Attendance at international organization meetings and work time devoted to international organization affairs as related to the action-commitment dimension of official attitudes

| Questionnaire Item | Number of Meetings Attended | | | | Percentage Work Time Devoted to International Organization Matters | | | |
|---|---|---|---|---|---|---|---|---|
| | %Agreement | | | Tau B | %Agreement | | | Tau B |
| | None | 1-10 | More than 10 | | No Time | Less than 50% | 50%or More | |
| 4. Norway should be more involved in UN | 67.9 | 73.0 | 72.8 | .037 | 59.3 | 70.7 | 82.2 | .137* |
| 5. Increase UN financial resources | 62.2 | 76.7 | 84.9 | .219* | 81.5 | 72.3 | 84.2 | .119* |
| 6. Channel more foreign aid through UN | 30.7 | 32.6 | 29.1 | .093** | 29.6 | 26.4 | 38.6 | .124* |
| 7. Grant trade preferences | 73.6 | 74.4 | 73.4 | .054 | 70.3 | 69.1 | 84.2 | .080 |
| 8. Norway should increase overall foreign aid package | 57.7 | 70.9 | 64.1 | .016 | 48.1 | 66.2 | 68.5 | .042 |
| 9. Norway should increase Palestinian aid | 43.2 | 47.1 | 43.5 | .024 | 40.7 | 43.1 | 47.3 | .073 |
| | N=53 | N=86 | N=94 | | N=27 | N=142 | N=57 | |

*Significant at .01
**Significant at .05

*Table 9.* Work time and meeting attendance as related to 'action-commitment' attitudes for respondents from the Foreign Affairs Department

| Questionnaire Item | Meeting Attendance | Percentage of Work Time |
| --- | --- | --- |
| | Tau B | Tau B |
| 4. Norway should be more involved in UN | .129 | .329* |
| 5. Increase UN financial resources | .231* | .254* |
| 6. Channel more foreign aid through UN | .158** | .203* |
| 7. Grant trade preferences | .130 | .344* |
| 8. Norway should increase its overall foreign aid package | .073 | .259* |
| 9. Norway should increase Palestinian aid | .084 | .118 |
| | N=96 | N=92 |

*Significant at .01
**Significant at .05

other patterns in the data similar to those discovered in previous tables. Work time generally is a better predictor than meeting attendance, and responses from the Foreign Affairs Department (Table 9) have the best fit with the hypothesized relationship. As noted earlier, these officials represent the survey group having the most extensive dealings with international organization.

Looking more closely at the data in Table 8, we see greater willingness among all respondents to increase Norway's overall foreign aid package than to channel a larger percentage share of the aid through UN. If viewed in isolation from the responses to Items 4-5, this finding might indicate a relative reluctance to be involved in the UN. As already observed, however, this is probably not the case because the other responses show a general willingness to strengthen the World Organization. The lack of enthusiasm for channelling more foreign aid through the UN would rather seem to articulate a feeling of, aid to poor nations yes, but (at this time at least) it may be dispensed more effectively outside the UN framework.

A departmental breakdown of the data shows interesting differences on the question of allocating aid to poor nations through the United Nations. In contrast to the other departments, increased international organization experience apparently makes foreign aid officials somewhat less supportive of channelling more aid through the UN. Yet this group is most favorable toward increased Norwegian aid generally. A likely reason is that they work for an agency whose primary responsibility is to administer Norway's bilateral aid programs. The Foreign Aid Department's client network has been built up largely through bilateral channels. Allocating a larger proportion of foreign aid to UN projects would mean a reduced share for the Department's primary client activities. One additional explanation may simply be that members of the Foreign Aid Department know more about the relative effectiveness and efficiency of bilateral vs. multilateral aid programs. Officials in the Department with the most international organization experience may have found that bilateral forms of aid are to be preferred – perhaps combined with a feeling that 'we can do it better than they . . .'

The latter interpretation seems reasonable in view of comments accompanying some of the questionnaire returns. Typical in this respect is the following remark from a foreign aid official, 'My reservation against more aid through the UN does not mean I'm opposed to the Organization. On the contrary, I'm a strong supporter. However, I happen to believe the UN aid apparatus is less efficient relatively speaking than our own foreign aid program.'[8]

Breaking down our findings by departments depicts another attitudinal dimension not otherwise apparent. With respect to Item 7 (trade preferences) attitudes of respondents from the Commerce Department, in contrast to the other departments, are negatively related to the experience dimension. This runs contrary to our hypothesis and is of special interest because Commerce Department officials are more involved with trade matters than their colleagues in the other two government departments. The explanation may lie in the conflict of interest between two sets of client activities, foreign and domestic.[9] For a number of commodities, such as textiles, liberalizing trade conditions for foreign producers will adversely affect the ability of some competing Norwegian firms to remain on the consumers' market. Officials in the Commerce Department with international organization experience may be in the best position to assess the domestic economic impact of extensive trade concessions to developing countries. Commerce officials may thus be more perceptive of and responsive to the interests of their domestic clients.

Such anomalies in the data underscore the fact that our findings do not give unconditional support to functionalist assumptions. By way of summary, nevertheless, the findings reported in Tables 7-9 appear to reflect real differences in attitudes across groups with differential amounts of exposure to international organization activities. The directional consistency in the correlation coefficients is sufficiently persuasive for us to conclude that the relationships did not occur by chance. But the differences are rather small, and the observed associations show the process of functional learning to be subject to conditions and limitations. The limitations of the functionalist premise will become more obvious as we move to the third functionalist hypothesis, bearing on the question of sovereignty transfers.

## Sovereignty transfers

Hypothesis 3 states that involvement with international organizations will foster a greater willingness among the participants to have slices of the national sovereignty transferred to international organizations. Item 10 pertains directly to this proposition and reads as follows:

Item 10. The UN should have more authority to enforce its rules upon member states.

Our findings flatly contradict the hypothesis. Referring to the paired groups previously utilized, the percentage agreement of the experienced group in each pair is lower. Those who have attended no international meetings score 74 % while those who have attended one or more average 67 % agreement. Officials who devote some portion of their work time to international organization matters show an agreement score of 68 %; officials with no such dealings score 70 %. Officials with UN experience score 50 %; those lacking such experience score 62 %.

Findings reported in Table 10 suggest that the negative association grows stronger with experience. In other words, we find decreasing willingness to support more UN authority associated with increasing international organization experience.

Responses to Item 10 clearly suggest that those most familiar with the UN, though appreciative of the importance of multilateral cooperation and Norway's need to be part of it, are the ones least ready to grant the UN more authority. This scepticism is not grounded in general misgivings about the value of joint cooperative ventures on the international scene, but seems rather to result from a perception of possible negative effects from increased UN authority. In particular, there is the practice – more pronounced in recent years – of the developing nations using their numerical strength in the UN to 'grind through' resolutions, not always with due consideration to the limitations of the UN. Many

51

*Table 10.* Attendance at international organization meetings and work time devoted to international organization affairs as related to the 'sovereignty transfer' dimension of official attitudes

| Questionnaire Item | Number of Meetings Attended | | | | Percentage Work Time | | | |
|---|---|---|---|---|---|---|---|---|
| | No Meetings | 1-10 | More than 10 | Tau B | No Time | Less Than 50% | 50% or More | Tau B |
| | | %Agreement | | | | %Agreement | | |
| 10. Give UN more authority to enforce rules | 73.6 | 69.0 | 65.6 | -.057 | 70.3 | 70.0 | 66.1 | -.072 |
| | N=53 | N=86 | N=94 | | N=27 | N=142 | N=57 | |

Western member nations, Norway being one of them, often oppose such action in the belief that it does not serve the long-term interests of maintaining the UN as a respectable and useful forum for international diplomacy.

In fact, our findings suggest that awareness of the negative effects of majority rule in the UN is associated with increased international organization experience. This conclusion derives from responses to Item 11, which states: 'The UN is dominated by small countries whose collective influence is out of proportion to their size and resources.' Officials who spend no portion of their work time on international organization activities have an agreement score of 41 %; those who spend less than half their work time score 48 %; finally, officials who spend more than 50 % work time on such activities have an agreement score of 70 %.[10] Although less pronounced, the same data trend is apparent for our other experience dimension (attendance at international meetings.)

### The Effect of Previous Experience

In hypothesis 4 we predict that officials who, prior to their current assignments, held a position where they gained international organization experience, will be more in favor of international cooperation than those lacking such prior experience. With the exception of Item 6 (foreign aid through UN) the data presented in Table 11 follow the pattern observed above.

Further detail on the positive association between past experience and the respondents' agreement scores is presented in Table 12. In this table we have established four categories of respondents, ranked in ascending order of experience: (1) no previous and no current experience, (2) previous but no current experience, (3) current but no previous experience and (4) both current and previous experience. 'Current experience' is operationalized to include only those devoting 50 % or more of their work time to international organization activities. Thus, persons having some involvement in international organization matters, but less than 50 % of their work time, are not included in any of the four categories of respondents. Although the N is reduced, this procedure was chosen in order to highlight the differential attitudinal effects of past and current experience.

Findings reported in Table 12 show consistent if modest support for our hypotheses: nine of ten associations are in the predicted direction. The one exception is Item 10, dealing with increased UN authority, where a contrary pattern has already been noted. Overall these findings tend to follow the data pattern previously observed: weak associations

*Table 11.* Percentage agreement with questionnaire items 1-10 for officials classified on the basis of previous experience with international organizations

| Questionnaire Item | Previous IO Experience | No Previous IO Experience |
|---|---|---|
| 1. UN is cornerstone for Norway | *72.7* | 67.7 |
| 2. UN promotes peace | *85.5* | 76.7 |
| 3. Strengthening UN is good for Norway | *70.9* | 69.4 |
| 4. Norway should be more involved in UN | *72.7* | 70.2 |
| 5. Increase UN financial resources | *78.2* | 76.6 |
| 6. Channel more foreign aid through UN | 28.2 | *31.5* |
| 7. Grant trade preferences | *75.5* | 71.8 |
| 8. Norway should increase overall foreign aid package | *70.9* | 58.1 |
| 9. Norway should increase Palestinian aid | *46.4* | 41.1 |
| 10. Give UN more authority | 61.8 | *72.6* |
| | N=110 | N=124 |

Note: Italics have been used for emphasis to show the higher score of the pair.

of experience and favorable attitudes on general UN evaluation, somewhat stronger associations with regard to specific action commitment, and negative association in the case of sovereignty transfer.

*The domestic organizational context*

According to Hypothesis 5, the more extensive a governmental unit's dealings with international organization activities, the more likely will officials assigned to that unit develop favorable attitudes toward multilateral cooperation. Officials so assigned may on the average be expected to have wider international organization contact than others, which, according to previous hypotheses, should make their international outlook more positive. Furthermore, officials in the unit who themselves have no dealings with international organizations may have their attitudes influenced by colleagues who do have such contact. A final rationale for the hypothesis is that the context provided by the

Table 12. Previous and current experience with international organization activities as related to responses to questionnaire items 1-10

| Questionnaire Item | Nature of IO Experience | | | | |
|---|---|---|---|---|---|
| | No Previous or Current | Previous Only | Current Only | Both Previous and Current | Tau B |
| | %Agreement | | | | |
| 1. UN is cornerstone | 52.3 | 66.7 | 70.3 | 73.4 | .090 |
| 2. UN promotes peace | 75.0 | 83.3 | 88.9 | 83.3 | .089 |
| 3. Strengthening UN | 81.0 | 33.4 | 77.8 | 73.3 | .032 |
| 4. More involved in UN | 61.9 | 50.0 | 80.9 | 83.3 | .210* |
| 5. Increase UN resources | 85.7 | 66.7 | 88.9 | 80.0 | .171** |
| 6. More aid through UN | 33.4 | 16.7 | 29.6 | 46.7 | .158** |
| 7. Trade preferences | 76.2 | 50.0 | 81.5 | 86.7 | .085 |
| 8. Increase foreign aid | 47.6 | 50.0 | 59.2 | 76.6 | .138** |
| 9. More Palestinian aid | 38.1 | 50.0 | 48.1 | 46.6 | .088 |
| 10. More UN authority | 76.2 | 50.0 | 74.1 | 58.6 | -.121 |
| | N=21 | N=6 | N=27 | N=30 | |

*Significant at .01
**Significant at .05

governmental unit may encourage its members to regard the international organization as a valued client.

The hypothesis may be viewed both from a static and a dynamic perspective. The former simply suggests that the frequency of favorable attitudes will be highest in governmental units having the most extensive dealings with international organizations. The latter presumes a dynamic interaction in which the impact of experience on attitudes is heightened by the governmental context. If such interaction in fact occurs, officials with similar amounts of international organization experience might differ in their degree of support for multilateral cooperation because they belong to governmental units with varying amounts of international organization contact. Presumably, the contextual 'booster' effect on attitude change will be strongest in units with the greatest international organization involvement.

Hypothesis 5 may be tested both in terms of the static and the dynamic conception by comparing attitudes of officials from the Foreign Affairs and Commerce Departments. The former have more contact with international organizations than the latter. More specifically, 33 % of respondents from the Foreign Affairs Department devote more than half of their work time to international organization activities as compared with 28 % for Commerce. Fifty percent of Foreign Affairs Department respondents have attended ten or more international organization meetings, while only 37 % of their Commerce Department colleagues have had as much experience.[11]

Given these figures the Foreign Affairs respondents may be expected to have developed the more favorable attitudes toward international cooperation. Data reported in Table 13, showing percentage agreement for the two groups on ten questionnaire items, provide at best only partial support for the hypothesis when interpreted from its static aspect. Although the Foreign Affairs respondents have higher agreement scores on five of six action commitment items, the Commerce respondents have higher percentage agreement on two of three general evaluation items as well as on Item 10 concerning increased UN authority.[12]

Concerning the latter item it is interesting to note that Commerce respondents are significantly more in favor of increased UN authority than Foreign Affairs respondents. This is clearly contrary to our hypothesis, since the Commerce Department has less of a client relationship with the UN and may thus be expected to be less interested in favoring a strengthening of the Organization's authority. The Commerce respondents' higher scores on this item can therefore hardly be explained by greater familiarity and extended contact with the United Nations.

56

*Table 13.* Percentage agreement on questionnaire items 1-10 for respondents from Commerce Department as compared with respondents from Foreign Affairs Department

| Questionnaire Item | Commerce Department | Foreign Affairs Dep. |
|---|---|---|
| 1. UN is cornerstone | *73.5* | 69.9 |
| 2. UN promotes peace | 82.4 | *84.7* |
| 3. Strengthening UN | *72.1* | 65.6 |
| 4. More involved in UN | 66.7 | *71.8* |
| 5. Increase UN resources | 67.6 | *81.5* |
| 6. More aid through UN | 30.9 | *34.9* |
| 7. Trade preferences | *69.1* | 65.6 |
| 8. Increase foreign aid | 51.5 | *63.0* |
| 9. More Palestinian aid | 26.5 | *51.1* |
| 10. More UN authority | *80.9* | 59.3 |
| | N=68 | N=93 |

Note: Italics have been used for emphasis to show the higher score of each pair.

It seems more fruitful to explain this finding in terms of the Foreign Affairs respondents' generally greater sophistication on UN matters. Increased sophistication may raise doubt about the desirability of increased multilateral cooperation in some areas and encourage a more critical assessment of the political consequences increased UN authority may have for Norway. Interviews with officials stationed at Norway's Permanent Mission to the United Nations suggest the validity of this line of reasoning. In response to a direct question concerning situations in which Norway's 'national interest' is at stake, each official responded along the following line, 'If I conceive the resolution of an important political issue as clearly not being in my country's best interest, I see it as my obligation to oppose such a resolution. After all, my primary duty is to watch out for what serves Norway's foreign policy interests the best.'

In any event the response pattern on Item 10 is not too surprising because it corresponds to that witnessed in previous tables. However, responses to two of the general evaluation items not only contradict our hypothesis – they also run counter to the positive relationships previously witnessed on these items. Table 14 presents a further break-down of the data which helps to account for this unexpected finding, and which enables us to test the dynamic aspect of the hypothesis. Among respondents who spend no work-time on international organization activities, those in Foreign Affairs score considerably lower than their counterparts in Commerce – with the exception only of Item 5 (increased UN finances) and Item 9 (increased Palestinian aid). This suggests that favorable attitudes among experienced officials are not necessarily transmitted to officials in the same government unit who lack international organization experience. Furthermore, the governmental context provided by a unit heavily involved in international organization activities does not *by itself* seem to promote the predicted professional/client relationship.

Almost the reverse data pattern emerges when agreement scores for the two groups of officials having experience with international organizations are compared. Foreign Affairs respondents score higher on all items, except on Item 3 (strengthening the UN) and Item 10 (increased UN authority).[13] From this comparison one may conclude that working in a unit with broad international organization contact tends to sharpen the attitudinal effect of experience, but has little or no effect unless accompanied by experience with international organizations. Further support for this conclusion is provided by the Tau beta coefficients which show the levels of association between increasing experience and agreement with the ten questionnaire items. For the Foreign Affairs respondents the Tau is higher for every item (in the case of Item 10 less negative).

The negative Tau B for Commerce respondents on six of the ten items suggests a still more complex relationship between experience, attitudes, and governmental context. Apparently the impact of experience filtered through the screen of Commerce Department norms tends to produce more negative attitudes toward some aspects of multilateral cooperation. The attitudinal effects of bureaucratic context undoubtedly merits further exploration.


*Past and present incumbents*
The sixth hypothesis asserts that present incumbents in governmental units dealing with international organizations will have more supportive attitudes toward multilateral cooperation than will former incumbents. This hypothesis may be tested by comparing attitudes of former and present members of the Permanent Mission of Norway to the UN. There is reason to believe the two groups' levels of sophistication about the UN and UN-related matters are roughly similar. Differences in attitudes should thus result from the relative immediacy of their UN experience. As a rationale for the hypothesized relationship we assume that officials currently working at the UN are more intimately involved in the subject matter presented in our questionnaire. They have a

*Table 14.* The relationship of work time to questionnaire responses by officials from Commerce Department and Foreign Affairs Department

| Questionnaire Item | Work Time Devoted to International Organization | | | | | |
| --- | --- | --- | --- | --- | --- | --- |
| | Respondents from Commerce Department | | | Respondents from Foreign Affairs Department | | |
| | No Work Time | Some Work Time | | No Work Time | Some Work Time | |
| | %Agreement | | Tau B | %Agreement | | Tau B |
| 1. UN is cornerstone | 90.0 | 70.7 | -.132 | 30.0 | 74.7 | .202* |
| 2. UN promotes peace | 80.0 | 82.8 | .028 | 77.8 | 85.6 | .120 |
| 3. Strengthening UN | 80.0 | 70.7 | -.063 | 60.0 | 66.3 | .027 |
| 4. More involved in UN | 80.0 | 64.3 | -.107 | 30.0 | 76.8 | .294* |
| 5. Increase UN resources | 70.0 | 67.2 | -.041 | 80.0 | 81.7 | .124 |
| 6. More aid through UN | 30.0 | 31.1 | .123 | 20.0 | 36.6 | .116 |
| 7. Trade preferences | 90.0 | 65.5 | -.152 | 30.0 | 69.9 | .247* |
| 8. Increase foreign aid | 40.0 | 53.4 | .064 | 20.0 | 68.3 | .242* |
| 9. More Palestinian aid | 30.0 | 26.8 | .071 | 40.0 | 52.5 | .089 |
| 10. More UN authority | 90.0 | 79.3 | -.135 | 60.0 | 59.2 | -.084 |
| | N=10 | N=58 | | N=10 | N=83 | |

* Significant at .01

59

*Table 15.* Percentage agreement scores on questionnaire items 1-10 for current UN respondents as compared with former UN respondents

| Questionnaire Item | Current UN Personnel | Former UN Personnel |
|---|---|---|
| | %Agreement | |
| 1. UN is cornerstone | 85.7 | 75.0 |
| 2. UN promotes peace | 100.0 | 91.7 |
| 3. Strengthening UN | 85.8 | 66.7 |
| 4. More involved in UN | 100.0 | 66.7 |
| 5. Increase UN resources | 85.7 | 91.7 |
| 6. More aid through UN | 85.7 | 41.7 |
| 7. Trade preferences | 85.7 | 66.7 |
| 8. Increase foreign aid | 85.7 | 41.7 |
| 9. More Palestinian aid | 85.7 | 36.4 |
| 10. More UN authority | 66.7** | 54.5* |
| | N=7 | N=12 |

*N = 11
**N = 6

Note: Italics have been used for emphasis to show the higher score of each pair.

greater personal stake in making the Mission function within the UN framework. The perceived importance and value of their UN job task is likely to exert a stronger influence on their responses than in the case of former members of the Mission, the latter group having a less personal and generally more removed relationship to ongoing issues in the UN context. We therefore expect higher agreement scores for current Mission members than for former Mission members on the questionnaire items.

With such small Ns it would not seem fruitful to single out specific subsets of responses for analysis, but data reported in Table 15 by and large fit the predicted relationship.

*Correlates of officials' attitudes*

Besides amount and kind of international organization experience three other respondent attributes have been examined as possible correlates of attitudes toward the United Nations. They are education, age, and residence in a developing country. Table 16 reports these additional findings. By and large formal education appears to have a supportive effect on attitudes toward the World Organization. There is very little difference in agreement on the general evaluation statements (Items

60

*Table 16.* Percentage agreement with questionnaire items 1-10 for respondent groups classified by respondent attributes

| Questionnaire Item | Education | | Age | | Third World Visited | |
|---|---|---|---|---|---|---|
| | Advanced Degree | No Advanced Degree | Under 43 | 43 and Over | Has Visited | Has Not Visited |
| 1. UN is cornerstone | 69.8 | 68.3 | 67.2 | 71.7 | 76.3 | 66.2 |
| 2. UN promotes peace | 80.7 | 82.5 | 74.3 | 87.4 | 86.7 | 78.3 |
| 3. Strengthening UN | 69.6 | 70.7 | 62.5 | 76.7 | 76.3 | 66.7 |
| 4. More involved in UN | 72.0 | 70.7 | 77.5 | 66.4 | 82.7 | 66.5 |
| 5. Increase UN resources | 80.1 | 61.0 | 78.6 | 75.0 | 86.7 | 72.0 |
| 6. More aid through UN | 32.6 | 22.0 | 29.4 | 32.1 | 36.5 | 29.3 |
| 7. Trade preferences | 73.4 | 75.6 | 81.4 | 66.7 | 77.6 | 72.0 |
| 8. Increase foreign aid | 68.3 | 51.2 | 76.8 | 54.2 | 73.0 | 61.5 |
| 9. More Palestinian aid | 48.1 | 28.2 | 55.0 | 35.0 | 48.6 | 42.9 |
| 10. More UN authority | 69.3 | 65.9 | 60.9 | 75.8 | 68.0 | 69.0 |
| | N=191 | N=41 | N=112 | N=120 | N=76 | N=156 |

Note: Italics have been used for emphasis to show the higher score of the pair.

61

1-3), but respondents with advanced degrees (any degree above the B.A. level) score considerably higher on most of the action commitment statements.

To determine possible attitudinal effects from the age factor the respondents were divided at the average age of 43. The results are mixed. The older group agrees most strongly with the three general evaluation statements. The younger group is more supportive of action commitment to the UN. The fact that the older respondents have higher agreement scores for only half of the questionnaire items shows that their generally longer experience does not exert a uniform effect on their international cooperation outlook. Generally the youth factor seems to promote favorable attitudes toward international action commitment, particularly as regards assistance to the developing countries. This support is, however, linked to a somewhat greater reservation against extensive reliance on the UN apparatus. The most consistent differences appear when the respondents who have visited a developing country are compared with those who have not. Except on Item 10 (increased UN authority) officials with Third World experience show the highest agreement scores on all statements. Civil servants who have been directly exposed to the problems of development thus seem to feel most strongly the need for increased international cooperation.[14]

In addition to this simple grouping of respondents in terms of their level of education, age, and visit to a developing country, rank order correlations of attitudes and experience were carried out, controlling for each of the three attributes.[15] Briefly summarized these findings show that the attitude-experience relationship grows more positive for respondents with Third World experience, except on Item 10 (increased UN authority). The attitude-experience relationship grows somewhat more positive for the group of young respondents, more so when work time rather than meeting attendance is the experience variable. With respect to education no general intervening impact on the attitude-experience relationship is discovered, although the relationship grows slightly more positive for the better educated group on some of the general evaluation statements.

This examination of correlates of officials' attitudes supports a conclusion that the attitudinal effects of experience with international organizations may occur independently of respondent attributes. Youth and high level of education seem to spur support for international cooperation on a number of points, but the impact is neither consistent nor substantial. Direct exposure to the problems of development also has a small but consistent booster effect; yet such exposure is not a requisite for the attitude-experience relationship to be positive. The effects of experience may thus be modified by, but are not wholly dependent upon, those respondent attributes.

*Civil servants' attitudes: a summation*

The survey shows quite clearly that Norwegian civil servants' outlook on a broad range of issues concerning multilateral cooperation is affected by their experience with international organizations. This conclusion derives from the totality of our findings across a variety of respondent groupings. Although generally weak, the various statistical associations show overall consistency in the predicted direction.

The empirical substance of our survey does not, however, give unconditional support to the functionalist premise. The picture that has emerged strongly suggests that the hypothesized attitude-experience relationship cannot usefully be conceptualized in terms of a simple evolutionary process. Put differently, increased experience with international organization does not necessarily lead to increased willingness to engage in multilateral cooperation. Indeed the reverse attitudinal process may occur.

Our design for research was constructed to permit examination of increasing degrees of commitment to multilateral cooperation. The ten questionnaire items were intended to tap three dimensions of cooperation: favorable general evaluation, action-commitment to further cooperative ventures, and willingness to transfer sovereignty. While the first two dimensions proved to be positively related to increasing international organization experience, the third dimension shows a negative relationship – thus contradicting the functionalist notion of a simple positive one-to-one linkage between experience and attitude.

Closer examination of the data suggests that the action-commitment dimension may usefully be expressed as two 'sub-dimensions', one pertaining directly to the UN (Items 4-6) and one pertaining to development assistance to poor countries (Items 7-9). The latter sub-dimension may be labelled 'international cooperation' while the label 'action-commitment to the UN' may be retained for the former. Using as a crude indicator the average of coefficients attained by rank order correlation of our two measures of experience with the questionnaire items in each category, we arrive at four separate dimensions. These dimensions may be arrayed in relation to the experience variables, as shown in Figure 1.

FIGURE 1

| Action Commitment to UN | General Evaluation of UN | International Cooperation | Transfer of Sovereignty |
|---|---|---|---|
| ++ | + | + | − |

By viewing these four dimensions along a continuum of multilateral cooperation, experience with international organization correlates most positively with attitudes toward more extended commitment to and use of the UN, less positively with general evaluation of the UN and with extended cooperation with poor countries, and negatively with transfer of sovereignty. Even though this array is based on rank order correlations of questionnaire responses with work time and meeting attendance, we find a generally similar empirical pattern when testing for hypotheses 4-6. The array is particularly pronounced in Table 12, which shows the attitudinal effect of experience with international organization in a previous job assignment.[16]

Viewed as a whole, the Norwegian data suggest that experience with international organizations generally promotes increased willingness to cooperate multilaterally, but that the reverse occurs on the highly sensitive political question of surrendering slices of sovereignty. Thus a person may become more convinced of the virtue of transferring economic resources and, at the same time, become less convinced of the virtue of transferring political resources to international organization. By implication there is reason to question the functionalist assumption that the system of separate states will ever give way to a functionally ordered world through the willing relinquishment of national sovereignty.

## Parliamentary Attitudes Toward the UN

Thus far our analysis has focussed on the attitudes of civil servants. Civil servants come closer to the model of a functional actor than legislators, since they tend to be subject matter specialists involved in relatively non-controversial activities. In contrast, legislators typically fill highly politicized roles, more often than not as subject matter generalists. Although role politicization may be a potential hindrance to the learning of positive attitudes toward international organizations,[17] there is no good theoretical reason not to include legislators in our study, and a very good practical reason for doing so. Legislators represent an important policy linkage between their government and international organizations. Legislators' attitudes toward such organizations are important if the functionalist dynamic is to exert a substantial impact on national policy.

In analyzing parliamentary attitudes toward the United Nations we shall differentiate between parliamentarians who have been delegates to the UN General Assembly and those who have not. We will also compare delegates and non-delegates to international organizations other than the UN. From its inception the UN General Assembly has been attended by Norwegian parliamentarians, illustrating the high degree of importance which the *Storting* (Parliament) attributes to the Organization. At first limited to half a dozen parliamentarians with high seniority and prestige, frequently reassigned to the UN over several years, the number of delegates per General Assembly session underwent a steady increase until it leveled off at approximately 13 delegates per session in the mid 1960s. Also at that time the length of the assignments was shortened from 12 weeks to 6 weeks. There are now two groups of parliamentarians during a 12-week long session, each group consisting of 6 or 7 members.[18] The sheer magnitude of the parliamentary participation is impressive: during the course of one 4-year Storting period about one third of the legislators will have been assigned to the UN.[19]

The Storting members' contact with international organizations is not limited to the United Nations General Assembly. More than half of all the members have at one time or another been named delegates to such organizations as the North-Atlantic Union, the Council of Europe, the Nordic Council, and the Inter-Parliamentary Union, as well as various UN specialized agencies and special international conferences. Typically such representational tasks occupy the parliamentarians for very short periods of time, often not more than a couple of days at each meeting. Thus such assignments normally mean less extensive and intensive contact with international organization activities than assignments to the United Nations General Assembly.

To further examine the functionalist premise the parliamentarians' attitudes toward multilateral cooperation will be analyzed in the light of their differential experience with the UN and with other international organizations. Our analysis will be based on data derived from a questionnaire mailed to all members of the Storting, supplemented by interviews with some of the UN delegates.

### The survey research design

In 1974 all 155 Storting members received the questionnaire. The survey instrument contained ten questionnaire items identical with those forwarded to the civil servants. Parliamentarians who had served as UN delegates were in addition asked to respond to three substantive items directly related to their experience at the UN. After a second mailing we attained a final response rate of 73 %.

The respondent group is quite representative for the Storting at large, both in terms of party distribution and sex distribution:

5 – Beyond Functionalism

| | Respondent group | All Storting members |
|---|---|---|
| Socialist | 45% | 51% |
| Non-Socialist | 55% | 49% |
| Females | 14% | 15% |

The fact that non-socialist parliamentarians are slightly overrepresented in the respondent group does not present problems of methodology or substantive analysis, since we are primarily interested in comparing attitudes across groups of delegates and non-delegates to international organizations.

Our parliamentary data analysis will be concerned with the same attitudinal effects predicted for civil servants. More specifically, we postulate that parliamentary delegates will generally have more supportive attitudes toward multilateral cooperation than non-delegates (hypothesis 7), be more favorable toward further international cooperation (hypothesis 8), and be more willing to let portions of the national sovereignty be transferred to international organizations by way of increased UN authority (hypothesis 9). As with hypotheses 1-3 in the case of civil servants' attitudes, hypotheses 7-9 have been framed to probe ascending degrees of commitment to international cooperation.[20]

*The recruitment factor*

Before the data are examined one important aspect of the research design should be clarified. This concerns the possibility that attitudinal differences between the test groups (delegates) and the control groups (non-delegates) are due to self-selection by members of the test groups. We have previously asserted that the self-recruitment factor is not a serious design problem for the Norway group of UN delegates.[21] That assertion is based on our understanding of the way in which Storting members are assigned to the General Assembly.

First of all, the assignments are generally filled on the basis of quotas in accordance with the political parties' numerical strength in the Storting. The parties tend to select their delegates with a view toward achieving a broad representation of their members. A second consideration is the work load of the members: those most heavily involved with legislative responsibilities and/or internal party responsibilities are least likely to be asked to accept international organization assignments lasting for a period of 6 weeks.

The meeting of 'knowledge needs' represents a third consideration in the selection of UN delegates. For instance, freshman members of a Storting committee dealing with foreign policy issues will often be thought in need of some practical 'schooling' in foreign affairs. Appropriate international organization assignments are considered opportunities for such schooling.

Finally, to the extent that adjustments can be made in keeping with these considerations, the parliamentarians' personal preferences are taken into account. In the event that a member expresses a desire to receive an assignment to the General Assembly, his or her party caucus will try to accommodate such a wish. Judging by our interviews with UN delegates, however, such explicit preferences are not common. Although self-recruitment plays a part, it is not a dominating factor in the overall process of selecting delegates.

Self-selection may play a somewhat greater role in the recruitment of parliamentary delegates to international organizations other than the UN.[22] Probably the most important reason is that these assignments are much shorter and thus more attractive for a number of parliamentarians. If so, greater caution will be required when interpreting the data relating to this experience dimension.


*Testing the hypotheses: group comparisons*
General evaluation of the UN

Hypothesis 7 predicts that national legislators serving as delegates to international organizations will develop generally favorable attitudes toward multilateral cooperation. This is qualified by the proviso that increased sophistication will militate against uncritical acceptance. To test this hypothesis we solicited the parliamentarians' responses to the same three general evaluation statements (previously denominated 'Type 1') presented to civil servants:

Item 1. The UN, and what the organization in principle stands for, represents the most important 'cornerstone' in Norwegian policy.

Item 2. The UN helps to promote a more peaceful, cooperative world.

Item 3. Anything that strengthens the UN is likely to be good for Norway.


Agreement scores for the two pairs of respondent groups give general but not consistent support to the hypothesis. As reported in Table 17,

*Table 17.* Agreement with questionnaire items as related to experience with international organizations

| Questionnaire Item | Delegate to UN General Assembly | | Attended Other International Meeting | |
|---|---|---|---|---|
| | Yes | No | Yes | No |
| | %Agreement | | %Agreement | |
| 1. UN is cornerstone | 74.5 | 88.7 | 78.2 | 86.6 |
| 2. UN promotes peace | 87.5 | 83.8 | 87.5 | 82.7 |
| 3. Strengthening UN | 85.4 | 82.3 | 85.7 | 80.8 |
| 4. More involved in UN | 93.7 | 91.9 | 92.9 | 92.3 |
| 5. Increase UN resources | 89.6 | 83.3 | 89.2 | 82.0 |
| 6. More aid through UN | 36.9 | 38.7 | 37.0 | 36.5 |
| 7. Trade preferences | 87.5 | 85.5 | 78.5 | 94.2 |
| 8. Increase foreign aid | 85.5 | 82.3 | 82.1 | 86.6 |
| 9. More Palestinian aid | 55.4. | 35.5 | 41.8 | 44.2 |
| 10. More UN authority | 70.9 | 75.8 | 69.6 | 77.0 |
| | N=48 | N=62 | N=56 | N=52 |

Note: Italics have been used for emphasis to show the higher score of each pair.

the more experienced parliamentary group in each pairing shows higher percentage agreement in 4 of the 6 cases.

It is not entirely clear why the responses to Item 1 (UN as cornerstone) do not fall in the predicted direction. The lower agreement scores among experienced parliamentarians are perhaps due to increased sophistication on their part. While the cornerstone-notion has been treated almost like a truism in Storting circles during most of the post-war period, the delegating of greater numbers of legislators to international organizations may in recent years have led to a sharper and more critical assessment of the UN's importance for Norway. It may therefore be appropriate to interpret the responses to Item 1 as representing an increasingly critical appraisal of the cornerstone-notion rather than decreased support for the UN – especially since responses to Items 2-3 point in the direction of increased support.

### Action commitment attitudes

Hypothesis 8 asserts that participants in the work of international organizations will become more willing to commit their government to further international cooperation. Responses to the following state-

68

ments – once more identical with those appearing in the civil servants' questionnaire, have been used to test this hypothesis.

Item 4. Norway ought to be generally more involved in the work of the UN.

Item 5. The UN ought to have greater financial resources available.

Item 6. Norway ought to channel a greater percentage share of its foreign aid through the UN's multilateral programs.

Item 7. Norway ought to grant greater trade preferences to the developing countries.

Item 8. Norway ought to increase its overall foreign aid package.

Item 9. Norway ought to give increased humanitarian aid to the Palestinians.

Comparison of agreement scores for UN-delegates and non-delegates (Table 17) shows overall support for the hypothesis. Only on Item 6 (more aid through the UN) is the data pattern the reverse of that predicted. The following remark by a delegated parliamentarian to the UN seems to illustrate a common sentiment among the delegates on this point: 'This enormous [UN]bureaucracy may simply be too costly and inefficient for our aid to have the intended effect.' The fact that Norway in 1974 for the first time gave more bilateral than multilateral aid may perhaps be seen in light of the parliamentarians' experience at the UN.

Referring back to Table 7 we find on two of the three comparisons that there is virtually no difference between delegated and non-delegated civil servants' attitudes on Item 6, thus underscoring what appears to be a general hesitancy to make extended use of the UN aid apparatus. Comparing the overall response pattern in Table 17 and Table 7, it may be noted that the legislators are generally more supportive of extended multinational cooperation than the civil servants.

The data in Table 17 give less support to the hypothesis when responses are compared for delegates and non-delegates to international organizations other than the UN. On the three UN-related action commitment statements (Items 4-6) the experienced parliamentarians score the highest; on the three statements concerning aid questions not directly related to the UN, the inexperienced legislators show the highest agreement. Apparently, experience with international organizations other than the UN brings greater willingness to cooperate with the UN, but less willingness to channel aid to poor nations outside the UN framework. The responses to Item 7 (trade preferences) show a particularly great attitudinal difference between the two groups.

The inconsistent responses to Items 7-9, as between UN delegates and delegates to other international meetings, suggest the existence of a differential milieu impact. The nature of the UN milieu is such that the delegates are directly confronted with the problems and demands of the poor countries. Such contact may win the Third world countries support and sympathy, as illustrated by the following remark made by one of the parliamentary delegates, 'You know, this is the first time in my life that I have had direct personal contact with representatives from the recipient countries. The contacts have made me more convinced that our aid is needed.'

Delegates to international organizations other than the UN are not ordinarily faced with the same sort of 'global-aid-issues' milieu. As a rule, such regional organizations as the European Parliament and the Nordic Council do not have North-South relations on their meeting agenda and there are no Third World representatives present to lobby for increased aid and more favorable trade regulations.[24] These organizations are first and foremost meant to serve the mutual interests of the member nations, and the organizational milieu may not always be favorable to increased aid transfers to poor non-member nations.

Viewed as a whole the findings reported in Table 17 give directional support to the hypothesis; the most experienced parliamentary groups in the two pairings show higher agreement scores in 8 of the 12 cases. If only the substantive items pertaining to multilateral cooperation within the UN are considered, the case is somewhat stronger. Even though the group differences tend to be small, the fact that attitudinal differences exist at all is in a sense remarkable. Here we are speaking of politically experienced 'generalists' (as opposed to 'functionalist specialists') who have spent only six weeks of their lives at the UN, or perhaps a few days at other international organization meetings. From a functionalist perspective, the likelihood of discovering *any* attitude change under these circumstances may have been judged to be very small.[25]

Sovereignty transfers

Hypothesis 9 postulates that legislators assigned to international organizations will become more willing to support the transfer of slices of the national sovereignty to the United Nations. Questionnaire Item 10 bears on this dimension.

Item 10. The UN should have more authority to enforce its rules upon member states.

The attitudinal pattern observed on several previous occasions appears again in Table 17: diminished willingness to support more UN authority flows from increased international organization experience. This applies to both comparison groups. The hypothesis unquestionably is not confirmed by the data.

Viewed collectively the findings presented in Table 17 suggest that legislators assigned to international organizations tend to develop more favorable attitudes on matters concerning general evaluation of and action commitment toward the UN. This increased support is countered, however, by decreased willingness to have the national sovereignty abridged by more UN authority.

## *Self-assessment of the UN experience*

The preceding section has discussed the impact of international organization experience on legislators' attitudes as determined by responses to questionnaire items evaluating the UN and various aspects of multilateral cooperation. To obtain the legislators' own assessment of their experience three additional questionnaire items were included in the mailed questionnaire. Specifically, former UN delegates were asked to respond to three statements concerning their assignments to the World Organization. The wording of the three items (A, B and C) is given in Table 18. Item A and B tap the cognitive feedback from the delegates' experience. Item C is designed to tap the affective feedback.

Findings reported in Table 18 strongly attest the parliamentarians' belief that their experience has made them more familiar with and interested in the UN. Our data is in full accord with Bonham's and Kerr's findings of cognitive learning among parliamentary delegates to international organizations.[26] Responses to Item B (more actively concerned with UN matters) are also worth noting in view of the fact that legislators represent an important policy linkage between their government and the UN.[27]

More important to our general inquiry is the fact that over 80 % of the respondents believe their delegation experience made them take a more positive view of the UN. The agreement score seems very high in comparison with Bonham's findings on Scandinavian parliamentary delegates to the European Consultative Assembly. According to his study, 'only 11 per cent of these delegates said that it [their participation] made them more favorable toward Europe [i.e., European integration].'[28] Bonham attributes this relatively low percentage to the strong pro-European outlook of many of the delegates prior to their actual Assembly participation. Presumably, if the Norwegian UN-delegates were more favorably disposed toward the UN prior to their assignment than their non-assigned colleagues,[29] we should not expect such a high agreement score on Item C. Responses to this item, which

71

*Table 18.* Parliamentary UN delegates' agreement with three questionnaire items concerning self-assessment of their delegation experience

| Questionnaire Item | % Agreement | N |
|---|---|---|
| A. My stay at the UN increased my understanding of the Organization | 100.0 | (48) |
| B. The UN-stay has led me to become more actively concerned with the UN and UN-related matters | 93.7 | (48) |
| C. I have developed a more positive attitude toward the UN and UN-related matters | 83.4 | (48) |

essentially taps affect, may therefore be interpreted as giving further support to the functionalist premise.

Interviews with several parliamentary UN delegates provide additional evidence that positive affect generally flows from the delegation experience. Although mixed with a certain amount of scepticism about various facets of the UN machinery, most of the delegates' comments expressed tangles of hope and appreciation for the performance of the Organization. Typical in this respect is one delegate's remark, 'My stay at the UN has led me to question many aspects of the Organization, but not enough to make me want to abandon it. After all, where would the world be without the UN apparatus?'

### Correlates of legislators' attitudes

The preceding discussion of hypothesized relationships generally suggests that legislators' participation in international organization activities promotes their willingness to support multilateral cooperation. In order to determine whether any of these two-variable relationships are conditional, we shall introduce a number of stratified test factors. By stratifying on a test factor we will be able to compare the relationships in the contingent associations with the original relationship. This will enable us to judge whether these factors strengthen or weaken the observed impact of international organization experience on the legislators' attitudes toward the UN. Besides examining whether the observed relationships are of a conditional nature, we wish to assess which of these factors predict to legislators' propensity to favor multilateral cooperation.

Six factors will be introduced, four pertaining to the legislators' personal background (age, education, white collar vs. blue collar background, and rural vs. urban background), one pertaining to political party affiliation (socialist/non-socialist party bloc), and one pertaining to previous residence/non-residence in a less developed country. Studies which have examined the attitudinal effect of personal background characteristics suggest that youth, high education, high income, and urban residence are associated with high knowledge of, and interest in, foreign policy issues.[30] Political party affiliation has not been found to be a generally good predictor of a person's stand on multilateral cooperation. This is further evidenced by the substantial inter-party consensus in Storting foreign policy debates. A difference of 'internationalist ideology' does, however, exist between the socialist and non-socialist parties, the most important element being that the former give high priority to promoting international solidarity with the underprivileged working classes in the world.[31] Implicit in this ideology is the notion that a restructuring of the international class system of rich and poor nations is necessary if a more just and peaceful international order is to be achieved. While the non-socialist parties are less inclined to project this sort of analysis, they are nevertheless equally strong supporters of the need for increased multilateral cooperation. For our purposes the line of division between the two party blocs, one of degree rather than kind, is that the non-socialist parties tend to focus more exclusively on cooperation through the UN than the socialist parties do. The forces of change in the UN are in certain instances thought to be too slow from the socialist parties' viewpoint, and other means of multilateral cooperation need therefore be pursued.

The sixth test-factor, previous residence/non-residence in a less developed country, is included because of our assumption that direct observation of development problems will create empathy and support for programs designed to deal with those problems. As such it is an assumption intimately in line with functionalist reasoning.

Bivariate analyses, associating each of the six attributes with questionnaire responses from UN-delegates and non-delegates respectively, were carried out. The results of the analysis associating the attributes with the 62 non-delegated Storting members' responses are summarized in Table 19 in the form of Tau B coefficients. Generally the Tau B's are of modest strength. The strongest correlations result from the use of LDC-visit as a test factor while they are less prominent concerning age and party affiliation, and show no clear pattern whatsoever on education and professional and residential background. That

73

Table 19. Personal and background attributes of parliamentarians as related to questionnaire responses (Kendall tau beta)

| Questionnaire Item | Party Bloc | Education | Previous Occupation | Urban Background | Age | Visit to Third World |
|---|---|---|---|---|---|---|
| 1. UN is cornerstone for Norway | .187 | -.148 | -.243* | -.143 | .155 | .343* |
| 2. UN promotes peace | .092 | -.032 | .018 | -.143 | .239* | .245* |
| 3. Strengthening UN is good for Norway | .186 | -.111 | -.185 | .015 | -.031 | .309* |
| 4. Norway should be more involved in UN | .273* | .086 | -.070 | -.099 | .150 | .118 |
| 5. Increase UN financial resources | .150 | .013 | -.028 | -.036 | .149 | .072 |
| 6. Channel more foreign aid through UN | .382* | .047 | .129 | .088 | .233* | -.121 |
| 7. Grant trade preferences | .120 | -.095 | -.016 | .027 | .050 | .230* |
| 8. Norway should increase foreign aid package | -.023 | .070 | .251* | .064 | .064 | .209* |
| 9. Norway should increase Palestinian aid | .168 | -.030 | .021 | .175 | .160 | .266* |
| 10. Give UN more authority | .236* | -.166 | -.235* | -.171 | .033 | .202* |

*Significant at .05

N=62

is, favorable responses are more pronounced among legislators with LDC-experience (than those without such experience), more pronounced among young legislators, and more pronounced among non-socialist legislators. Regarding education and previous (white collar) occupational and residential background, the associations are small and erratic, mixed across issue dimensions, and thus not indicating a directional pattern affecting attitudes one way or the other. Our expectations have therefore only been met – and only partially at that – concerning the attitudinal impact of age, party affiliation, and visit to a Third World nation. Incidentally, our findings on the effect of LDC-visit and age converge to a great extent with our observations of civil servants' attitudes.

When rank order correlations were run separately for the 48 Storting members who have served as delegates to a session of the UN General Assembly, the following picture emerged: For questionnaire Items 1-6, all pertaining directly to multilateral cooperation within the UN, the relationships between attributes and questionnaire responses remained about the same as for non-delegates' responses.[32]

However, for Items 6-8 (previously denominated the international cooperation dimension), the relationships between four of the attributes (education, age, previous occupation and previous residence) proved substantially stronger, showing generally high levels of statistical significance. These four test factors are in fact highly intercorrelated. Jointly they seem to represent a 'collective attribute' having a material booster effect on favorable attitudes toward multilateral cooperation with less developed countries – provided that it is linked with experience at the UN.[33] Apparently, legislators having what Galtung calls a 'topdog' profile more readily give their support to multilateral action commitment toward the Third World than legislators with a less typical topdog profile – even though both groups of legislators have the same UN experience.[34]

*Legislators' attitudes: a summation*

Our analysis of legislators' attitudes suggests that the functionalist dynamic is not limited to civil servants or technical experts. Even though the observed attitude change among experienced legislators is found to be less than among civil servants with international organization experience – an observation that accords with functionalist thought – the politicization of roles clearly does not preclude the occurrence of functionalist learning. Indeed, in terms of their absolute agreement scores on the various dimensions of multilateral cooperation, the legislators come out higher than the civil servants. This finding does

75

not pertain directly to the question of attitude change, but it would certainly seem to have relevance for prospects of increased functional cooperation.[35]

In harmony with our findings on civil servants' attitudes, the delegation experience reduces the legislators' support for sovereignty transfers to the UN. This provides further attestation to our observation that there is no simple one-to-one relationship between participation and positive affect.

For legislators the type of international organization experience appears to be a significant variable. Participation at the UN is on the average a better predictor of favorable attitudes than participation at other international meetings. This is particularly true of legislators' views on cooperation with Third World countries.

With respect to the personal and background correlates of attitude change, there are for the most part only modest and erratic associations. Youth, visit to a less developed country, and belonging to the non-socialist party bloc show positive, yet generally weak, associations with internationalist sentiments. The 'collective factor' of youth, high education, white collar, and urban background does, however, materially sharpen the impact of UN participation on attitudes toward the developing countries.

# IV. Functional Cooperation and Attitude Change: The United States

## Civil Servants' Attitudes Toward the UN

Surveying attitudes of governmental officials in the United States presents a problem of scale quite different from that of the Norwegian survey. All professional level officials of the Commerce, Foreign Aid, and Foreign Affairs Departments of the Norwegian government stationed in Oslo could be contacted with a modest mailing of less than 300 questionnaires. In the U.S. government, the analogous agencies (Departments of State and Commerce, and the Agency for International Development) employ several thousand persons in the professional grades, in addition to many thousands more in clerical, technical and service capacities. Given these numbers, resort to a sampling procedure was inevitable.

But what populations should be sampled and how should the sample be drawn? United States involvement with international organizations is not limited to the Departements of State and Commerce. Every major department of the federal government is in some important way concerned with the activities of international organizations. Because of this widespread involvement with multilateral cooperation, a decision was made to sample a broad cross-section of government officials, and ultimately the Departments of Agriculture, Commerce, HEW, Housing and Urban Development, Interior, Labor, State, Transportation and the Treasury were included in the survey.

The purpose of the study required that the respondents have varying amounts of experience with international organizations, preferably ranging from officials concerned full time with international organizations to those having no experience at all. To assure an adequate number of respondents with international experience, employee rosters for international affairs sub-units of several departments were obtained. Where these were not available, officials contacted personally in each of the departments were generally cooperative in supplying lists of persons having some responsibility for U.S. representation in multilateral activities. These lists were supplemented by several hundred additional names drawn randomly from departmental telephone directories.[1] None of these sampling methods was calculated to produce a genuinely random sample of government employees. In fact, efforts were made to exclude from the sample clerical and technical employees whose interest in policy issues was likely to be incidental. The success of this exclusionary policy is suggested by the fact that 98 % of the returns were at the level of GS 9 or higher and 91 % were GS 12 or above. A return rate of 56 % produced 454 completed questionnaires.[2]

The sampling process was successful in obtaining the desired range of international organization experience. Table 1 gives a breakdown of respondents by number of international organization meetings attended, and Table 2 distributes respondents in terms of their estimated present job time concerned with the activities of international organizations. One remarkable aspect of Table 2 is the high proportion of respondents whose work is a least tangentially related to international

*Table 1.* Number of international organization meetings attended

| Number of Meetings | Number of Respondents | Percent of Respondents |
|---|---|---|
| None | 181 | 39.9 |
| 1 only | 37 | 8.1 |
| 2-5 | 92 | 20.3 |
| 6-10 | 54 | 11.9 |
| 11-20 | 33 | 7.3 |
| More than 20 | 55 | 12.1 |
| No Response | 2 | .4 |

*Table 2.* Percentage of work time concerned with activities of international organizations

| Percent of Work Time | Number of Respondents | Percent of Respondents |
|---|---|---|
| None | 88 | 19.4 |
| Less than 10% | 167 | 36.8 |
| 10-24% | 95 | 20.9 |
| 25-49% | 39 | 8.6 |
| 50-74% | 25 | 5.5 |
| 75% or more | 36 | 7.9 |
| No Response | 4 | .9 |

organizations. Only 88 persons, less than 20 % of all respondents, replied that no portion of their time-in-present-job was concerned with international organizations. We would expect most of the people on the special lists to have some involvement with international organization activities. But 385 of the questionnaire recipients were drawn randomly from agency telephone directories. If their response was proportionate to the overall response of 56 %, some 215 questionnaires may have been received from that group. Even if all 88 respondents who indicated no experience with international organizations came from the randomly selected group, there still remain 59 % who claimed that part of their official duties related to international organizations. Taking into account a possible questionnaire response bias, the 59 % is probably an inflated figure. Persons drawn from the international sub-unit rosters and the special lists may have replied in greater proportions than the telephone directory group, and those having experience with international organizations may have been more prone to respond than those without. Yet, even with a discount for this bias, the figures still suggest that a surprisingly large proportion of government officials (that is, officials whose status or position entitled them to an organizational listing in an executive department telephone directory) have duties related to international organization matters. This represents very extensive interpenetration of the U.S. government and multilateral agencies.

Other characteristics of the sample may be of interest. All are civilian respondents except for nineteen members of the U.S. Coast Guard within the Department of Transportation. Men are overwhelmingly represented – 90.7 % of the total. The average respondent is 47 years of age, has 17 years of service with the federal government, and holds a GS grade (or corresponding foreign service grade) of 14 or 15.

In addition to the general survey of nine executive departments, two smaller groups of government officials were selected for special analysis. One group consisted of current professional grade personnel of the Department of State Bureau of International Organization Affairs (IO Bureau) and the U.S. Mission to the United Nations in New York (USUN). An attempt was made to identify all personnel not engaged in clerical or technical services for inclusion in the survey. Ultimately, 77 completed questionnaires were received, for a return rate of 51 %.[3] A second group consisted of persons who formerly had served in other than administrative or technical support capacity with the IO Bureau, the U.S. Mission to the UN, or the U.S. Mission to the UN European Office at Geneva. Names for this group were obtained from IO Bureau records, but current addresses had to be gleaned from the Foreign Service List. Because of the difficulty of finding addresses, the number of questionnaires mailed was 128, far fewer than the 479 persons on the IO Bureau list. Of these, 13 were returned undelivered and 62 completed, for a 54 % return of the deliverable questionnaires.

The respondents in these two groups have all had extensive experience with international organizations, but otherwise their characteristics do not differ much from the general survey group. Average age of current IO employees is identical with the general group – 47. Sex distribution is 89.5 % male, compared with 90.7 % for the general survey. Grade is about the same, averaging between GS 14 and 15 (or the FS equivalent), and years of government service are slightly greater – an average of 20 for the IO group as compared with 17 for the general group. The former IO officials, as one might expect, are slightly older on the average – 49 years, with 22 years of government service and an average GS equivalent of 15. As might also be expected, the proportion of women is smaller – 6.5 %.

The questionnaires sent to each of the three groups are reproduced in Appendix B. In addition to questions soliciting biographical information, each contains statements about the United Nations or about values and policy positions that have been at issue in the United Nations. A number of the questions are identical with those used in the Norway survey, although a few have been altered somewhat to fit the American context. Additional items are included to probe other dimensions of official attitudes toward international cooperation.

Considered as a test of the hypotheses set forth in Chapter 2, the results of the survey suggest that the functionalist approach has some validity but needs to be carefully hedged and qualified. The hypotheses, briefly summarized, postulate that government officials having dealings with international organization activities will develop attitudes generally favorable to those activities (hypothesis 1). They will be more willing to approve further international cooperation (hypothesis 2), and willing even to have portions of national sovereignty transferred to international organizations (hypothesis 3). We also posit that government officials having past (as distinguished from current) dealings with international organizations will be more favorable to multilateral cooperation than officials without such prior experience (hypothesis 4); that officials in governmental units having extensive dealings with international organization activities will develop more favorable attitudes than officials in other agencies (hypothesis 5); and that present role incumbents in such governmental units will be more supportive than former role incumbents (hypothesis 6). Each of these propositions will be examined in the light of the survey findings.

*General evaluation of the UN*

Four items in the survey bear directly on the first hypothesis, i.e., that contact breeds generally favorable attitudes toward international organizations. The items as presented in the questionnaire read as follows:

Item 1. The UN helps to promote a more peaceful, cooperative world.
Item 2. The UN is important to the United States as a means of carrying out our foreign policies.
Item 3. Anything that strengthens the UN is likely to be good for the United States.
Item 4. International organizations such as the UN and its specialized agencies are a necessity in today's complex world.

Respondents were asked to choose from a five-point scale (strongly agree, agree, undecided, disagree, strongly disagree) the response closest to their own attitudes on each item. All four statements are intended to probe what has previously been denominated 'Type 1' attitudes, that is, those involving general evaluations of the UN and UN-related matters but not necessarily implying any evaluative commitments to further action.[3] For purposes of the analysis, responses are scored ordinally from 1 for 'strongly agree' to 5 for 'strongly disagree' when rank order measures are used. When a single percentage agreement figure is given, it includes all respondents who marked either 'agree' or 'strongly agree' for a particular item.

If hypothesis 1 is to be confirmed, respondents having experience with international organizations should have a higher agreement score than respondents without such experience. Data from the general survey of nine executive departments in fact tends in this direction, but the group differences are small. Table 3 presents percentage agreement scores for three pairs of groups drawn from the general survey data. The first pairing divides respondents into those who have attended one or more meetings of any international organization and those who have not. The second pairing classifies respondents by whether or not their present official duties relate to international organization activities in any way. The third pairing distinguishes those who at any time have had experience with the United Nations from those who have not.[4] The more experienced group in each pairing has higher agreement scores in 10 of the 12 cases, which suggests a relationship in the predicted direction, but in only two cases (both on item 2) are the differences large enough to be statistically significant.[5]

It might be contended that even these small differences could be explained by a self-selection factor.[6] People who work with international organization affairs or attend international meetings may have sought such appointments because of a prior favorable orientation toward multilateral cooperation. The facts in this case argue otherwise, however. Our data show that most of the respondents who spend more than 10 % of their job time in international organization activities are administratively located within an international affairs sub-unit of one of the executive departments, such as the Office of the Assistant Secretary for International Affairs (Treasury), Office of International Marketing (Commerce), or Office of International Labor Affairs (Labor). Those who attend international meetings are ordinarily drawn from international affairs sub-units, or else they are selected because of their professional expertise in a field that is the subject of an international conference, such as health, maritime safety, education, housing, or agricultural economics. Conference participants drawn from the latter group are likely to be subject matter specialists from a wide

*Table 3.* Percent agreement of paired groups with questionnaire items involving general evaluation of the UN

| Item | Attended an IO Meeting | | Work Involves IO | | Experience with UN | |
|---|---|---|---|---|---|---|
| | *Yes* | *No* | *Yes* | *No* | *Yes* | *No* |
| 1. UN promotes peace | *88.1* | 86.0 | *87.5* | 87.4 | 87.0 | *87.1* |
| 2. UN important | *64.6* | 48.6 | *59.1* | 56.8 | *69.5* | 53.4 |
| 3. Strengthening UN is good for U.S. | 36.0 | *39.1* | *40.2* | 37.2 | *46.2* | 36.8 |
| 4. UN a necessity | *90.7* | 87.8 | *90.2* | 88.6 | *91.6* | 88.7 |
| | N=271 | N=181 | N=362 | N=88 | N=131 | N=321 |

Note: Italics have been used for emphasis to show the higher score of each pair.

variety of fields having, as a group, no particular biases for or against international organizations. Participants selected from the international affairs sub-units might well be subject to some bias of self-selection, at least as it relates to their choice of assignment to their present position in the sub-unit. Whatever the bias may be, however, it does not include significant pro-UN leanings. A comparison of agreement percentages for respondents from international sub-units with agreement

Table 4. Attendance at international organization meetings and work time devoted to international organization affairs as related to general evaluation of the UN

| Questionnaire Item | Number of Meetings Attended | | | | Percentage Work Time | | | |
|---|---|---|---|---|---|---|---|---|
| | No Meetings | 1-10 | More than 10 | Tau B | No Time | Less than 50% | 50% or More | Tau B |
| | %Agreement | | | | %Agreement | | | |
| 1. UN promotes peaceful, cooperative world | 86.1 | 87.3 | 89.7 | .052 | 87.3 | 86.6 | 91.8 | .043 |
| 2. UN important to U.S. | 48.6 | 59.8 | 74.4 | .151* | 56.9 | 55.2 | 78.4 | .101* |
| 3. Strengthening UN is good for the U.S. | 39.1 | 35.4 | 48.8 | .020 | 37.2 | 38.6 | 48.3 | .009 |
| 4. International Organizations are a necessity | 87.8 | 89.0 | 94.3 | .051 | 88.7 | 89.2 | 95.1 | .080** |
| | N=181 | N=183 | N=88 | | N=88 | N=301 | N=61 | |

N=61
*Significant at .01
**Significant at .05

83

percentages for all other respondents shows the latter group to have a higher score than the former on three of the four items. The difference on Item 3 (strengthening the UN is good for the U.S.) is significant at .05 (chi square). If there is any pre-existing bias, for this group it runs in the opposite direction.

A better test of the hypothesis, and one which obviates the self-selection problem, is to take account of the duration or magnitude of exposure to the international organization experience. This can be done by reference to the same variables used in the Norwegian survey to establish the comparison groups – that is, the number of international meetings attended and percentage of work time devoted to international organization activities. Table 4 presents data on meetings and work time, respectively, as they relate to questionnaire Items 1-4. The relationships as measured by rank order correlation (Kendall tau beta) all point in the predicted direction, and three are statistically significant to a fair degree of confidence. When the same tests are applied to various subgroups within the sample, the results tend in the same direction.

When returns are grouped by executive department the results are mixed, but the data overall give further support to the proposition that increased experience with international organizations tends to bring more favorable general evaluation of multilateral cooperation. None of the departmental samples is large enough to create great confidence in any generalizations about individual departments, but considered collectively they provide another indicator of general tendencies within the sample as a whole. Kendall tau B correlation coefficients were calculated with two measures of experience (work time and meeting attendance) on four questionnaire items for each of the nine departments, for a total of 72 relationships. Of these, seventeen are sufficiently strong to be significant at the .05 level. Three of the 17 are on Item 1, seven on Item 2, four on Item 3, and three on Item 4. All seventeen are in the predicted direction; no negative association is strong enough to be significant. If we ignore strength of association and look only to direction, the results are more ambiguous. The 72 cases show 49 in a positive direction and 23 negative. The figures give some support to the functionalist thesis, although they do not attest to a strong and pervasive relationship.

For the two specialized groups surveyed, the present and former officials of the IO Bureau and USUN, one supplementary questionnaire item pertains directly to the question of attitude change. For those assigned to IO or USUN (as of 1974), the statement reads, 'I have gained a more favorable opinion of the UN as a result of my present assignment.' For the group of former IO, USUN, or Geneva Mission officials, the statement is, 'I gained a more favorable opinion of the UN as a result of my experience with IO (or USUN, or Geneva).' Of the present IO and USUN officials, 58.3 % agreed, 26.4 % disagreed, and 15.3 % were undecided, indicating a tendency toward change in a favorable direction.[7] On the other hand, only 35.5 % of the former IO, USUN and Geneva officials agreed with the statement, while an even 50 % disagreed, and 14.5 % were undecided.[8]

Perhaps one more comparison should be offered to underscore the complexity of the attitude-experience relationship as it applies to international organizations. If experience with the UN promotes favorable attitudes, surely this should appear in the responses of current employees of the IO Bureau and USUN as compared with respondents from the general survey who indicate that no part of their present job assignment is concerned with international organizations. Theoretically, the former group should register greater agreement with all items than the latter. In fact, their agreement scores are as follows:

*Table 5.* IO/USUN compared with respondents having no work time devoted to international organization activities

| Item | IO/U.S.U.N. | No Work Time |
|------|-------------|--------------|
| 1. UN promotes peace | 84.4 | 87.4 |
| 2. UN important to U.S. | 67.1 | 56.8 |
| 3. Strengthening U.N. | 38.2 | 37.2 |
| 4. IO a necessity | 96.1 | 88.6 |
| | N=77 | N=88 |

The IO/USUN group does score higher on three of the four items, but the difference on Item 3 is only a single percentage point. The vastly greater experience does not produce vastly greater approval of the UN along all dimensions.

For officials thus widely experienced in UN affairs, the picture is anything but black and white. Many respondents falling in this category obviously found the questionnaire difficult to answer because their experience could not be adequately expressed along an agree-disagree continuum addressed to these questionnaire items. Their impatience with the strictures imposed by such a coarse-grained screen is evident from written notes modifying questionnaire items, commenting (sometimes adversely) on the items, and commenting on their own responses. Three comments illustrate the point. In response to the item, 'I gained a more favorable opinion of the UN as a result of my assignment with

IO . . .,' one former IO official states, thoughtfully: '[I] came to know its limitations and possibilities better.' Another former IO Bureau official, responding to the same item says, 'I went in favorable – came out with more awareness of problems.' And one current member of the IO Bureau comments at the end of the questionnaire, with great poignancy and some frustration (presumably both with the UN and the questionnaire): 'Note: It is difficult to answer some questions because some words and expressions could mean various things. I am a basic friend of the UN and believe in the importance of international organization. I would be more positive in my responses if the UN system worked. I wish it did but am afraid it does not ....'

*Action-commitment attitudes*
Despite the provisos and qualifications, our evidence tends to support the hypothesis that experience with international organizations is modestly associated with favorable general evaluation of multilateral cooperation. We must now ask whether this relationship persists when we move from general evaluation (Type 1 statements) to the more explicit evaluative statements (Type 2) involving some kind of 'action commitment' to increased transfers of financial and human resources. Our second hypothesis postulates that experience with international organizations will tend to promote people's willingness to have their nation take steps toward further international cooperation. Five items in the questionnaire bear on attitudes of this kind.

Item 5. In its own self-interest, the United States should be more willing than at present to make use of the UN.
Item 6. The UN should have greater financial resources to carry out its programs.
Item 7. The United States should channel more of its foreign aid through UN programs for economic development.
Item 8. The United States should grant trade preferences to developing countries.
Item 9. It is in the United States' interest to promote economic development of poorer countries, even at some present sacrifice to ourselves.

In presenting our findings, we will follow the same format used in the preceding discussion of questionnaire items relating to the general evaluative dimension of official attitudes. Table 6 gives agreement percentages of three paired groups on questionnaire Items 5-9, drawn from the general survey of nine executive departments.

Table 6. Percent agreement of paired groups with questionnaire items probing the 'action-commitment' dimension of official attitudes

| Experience with UN | Attended an IO Meeting | | Work Involves IO | | Experience with UN | |
|---|---|---|---|---|---|---|
| Item | Yes | No | Yes | No | Yes | No |
| 5. U.S. should use UN more | 49.6 | *53.3* | 50.4 | *55.7* | *58.3* | 48.4 |
| 6. Increase UN financial resources | 61.0 | *70.6* | 63.9 | *69.3* | 61.2 | *66.3* |
| 7. Channel aid through UN | 42.5 | *47.8* | 44.3 | *47.7* | *46.5* | 43.9 |
| 8. Grant trade preferences | 62.9 | *63.9* | *63.8* | 59.8 | *68.5* | 60.8 |
| 9. Promote development of poorer countries | *80.2* | 80.1 | *83.0* | 70.5 | *90.0* | 76.3 |
| | N=271 | N=181 | N=362 | N=88 | N=131 | N=321 |

Note: Italics have been used for emphasis to show the higher score of each pair.

Table 7. Attendance at international organization meetings and work time devoted to international organization affairs as related to the action-commitment dimension of official attitudes

| Questionnaire Item | Number of Meetings Attended | | | | Percentage Work Time Devoted to International Organization Matters | | | |
|---|---|---|---|---|---|---|---|---|
| | None | 1-10 | More than 10 | Tau B | No Time | Less than 50% | 50% or More | Tau B |
| | %Agreement | | | | %Agreement | | | |
| 5. U.S. should use UN more | 53.3 | 48.3 | 52.3 | -.044 | 55.7 | 50.0 | 53.3 | -.003 |
| 6. Increase UN financial resources | 70.5 | 65.6 | 51.7 | -.110* | 69.4 | 65.2 | 57.4 | -.062 |
| 7. Channel foreign aid through UN | 47.7 | 46.4 | 34.5 | -.088* | 47.7 | 43.6 | 47.6 | -.019 |
| 8. Grant trade preferences | 63.9 | 61.0 | 67.0 | .017 | 59.8 | 63.4 | 65.6 | .121* |
| 9. Promote development of poorer countries | 80.2 | 78.0 | 84.9 | .071** | 70.5 | 81.9 | 88.4 | .178* |
| | N=181 | N=183 | N=88 | | N=88 | N=301 | N=61 | |

*Significant at .01
**Significant at .05

The results depict an interesting dichotomy. On the first three items, all involving some degree of commitment to greater use or support of the United Nations, the higher agreement scores tend to be found in the groups having the least experience with international organizations. The two exceptions are found on Items 5 and 7 where the group with UN experience is more willing to use the UN and channel aid through it (but *not* to increase its financial resources) than the group without such experience. On the other hand, for the two questions implying a commitment to assist poorer countries, without any reference to the organizational framework of cooperation, the more experienced group scores higher in all but one instance. Apparently, experience with international organizations brings greater willingness to cooperate with other countries, but less willingness to support increased cooperation within the United Nations framework.

The problem of a pro-UN self-selection bias obviously is not an issue here, since the findings negate the existence of any pro-UN bias. For the trade and aid items the differences are consistent with the possibility of a pro-international cooperation bias. But a more detailed analysis of responses from the entire general survey (Table 7) supports the conclusion that differential experience with international organizations, rather than pre-existing attitudes, is the better explanation of group differences.

For the first three items – those implying greater use or support of the United Nations – the relationship between exposure to international organizations and UN support is negative. The relationships are weak – only two of the six are strong enough to meet the .05 significance test, but the direction seems clear. Experience with international organizations has, on the average, a tendency to make respondents slightly less willing to commit greater resources to the United Nations or to endorse generally greater use of it. On the other hand, the willingness to support trade preferences and development aid for poorer countries has a consistent and, in three of four cases, statistically significant relationship with magnitude of experience with international organizations.[9]

Data from respondents grouped by executive department confirm the same tendency – a negative relationship with experience for the UN support items and a positive relationship for aid and trade.[10] A comparison of the IO/USUN group with the respondents having no work time allotted to international organization activities reflects generally the same pattern (Table 7a).

There is another pattern in the data not readily apparent from tables previously presented, which depicts what we may call a 'disillusionment factor'. It is expressed in a tendency for those having a little experience with international organizations to be less supportive than

*Table 7a.* IO/USUN compared with respondents having no work time devoted to international organization activities

| Item | IO/US-UN | No Work Time |
|---|---|---|
| 5. Use UN more | 52.6% | 55.7% |
| 6. More UN resources | 59.7 | 69.3 |
| 7. More aid through UN | 46.8 | 47.7 |
| 8. Trade preferences | 59.7 | 59.8 |
| 9. Development aid | 85.5 | 70.5 |

those with none at all. On all questionnaire items heretofore considered, with one exception, officials who had attended a single meeting of an international organization score lower than officials who had not attended any. The one exception is item 4, dealing with UN importance, on which the former group scores higher. A similar though less pronounced trend is apparent on the work time variable. Officials having nothing to do with international organizations in their job assignments have a higher agreement score than the 'some-but-less-than-10-percent' group on all but items 1 (UN promotes peace), 3 (strengthening the UN), and 9 (promoting development). As initial contacts are broadened and expanded, through attending additional meetings or devoting more work time, the agreement curve tends to rise again on the general evaluation and international cooperation items. With increased experience, disillusionment apparently gives way to a realistic but more balanced view that recognizes both strengths and weaknesses of international organization.

The responses on questionnaire items 5-9 do not unconditionally support the proposition that exposure to international organization activities makes government officials more willing to support increased international cooperation. To the extent that trade preferences and aid to poorer countries may be equated with international cooperation in general, the hypothesis finds support in the data. But this is not translated into greater willingness to use the United Nations – the arch-symbol of postwar hopes for organized multilateral cooperation. Within the whole survey group, more respondents agree than disagree with all of these statements. Nevertheless, the more experienced the respondents, the less likely they are to perceive a broad U.S. interest in using the UN more, providing it with greater resources, or channeling more U.S. aid through the UN. One former IO Bureau official (with some 21 years experience in that capacity) who was basically very favorable both to the United Nations and to the whole system of multilateral cooperation disagreed with item 7 (more aid through the UN) and commented, 'I doubt that the UN can administer more U.S. funds than we are already contributing – I favor all possible contribution, but experience shows there are limits to capacity.' The functionalist premise assumes that participants in international organization activities will see the manifest advantages of cooperation and be led to further action commitments along the same line. For this group of officials, at least, the advantages of supplying greater resources to the United Nations are outweighed by a perception of problems and limitations sharpened by experience.[11]

*Sovereignty transfers*

If responses to questionnaire items probing the action commitment attitudinal dimension evoke mixed conclusions, the evidence bearing on the third hypothesis – dealing with sovereignty transfer – is less ambiguous. Only one questionnaire item relates directly to the proposition that increased experience with international organizations will bring greater willingness to countenance transfers of national sovereignty to them. This is item 10, which reads: 'The UN should have more authority to enforce its rules upon member states.' Responses to that item show a clear and unmistakable trend: officials with the most experience are the least likely to agree with the statement. This contradicts our hypothesis, but the conclusion is unavoidable. With all of the paired groups previously utilized, the percentage agreement of the experienced group in each pair is lower: those who have attended no international meetings score 53 % while those who have attended one or more average 45 % agreement. Officials with UN experience score 47 %; those without score 54 %. Those with some portion of their work time devoted to international organization activities have an agreement score of 60 %; officials with none at all score 64 %. Even more telling is the agreement score of the group having the most current experience with the UN, the officials from the IO Bureau and the US Mission to the UN. Their agreement score is 26 %, much lower than any of the other groups, and 59 % flatly disagree with the statement.

Furthermore, the relationship tends to grow stronger with experience. Table 8 shows an association between increasing experience and decreasing willingness to support more authority for the UN. Data for departmental groupings point in the same direction. The implications of these data are obvious. Those who are most familiar with the functioning of the UN and other international organizations may be somewhat more inclined than others to recognize the usefulness of multilateral cooperation. But they are considerably more aware of the prospect that

*Table 8.* Attendance at international organization meetings and work time devoted to international organization affairs as related to the 'sovereignty transfer' dimension of official attitudes

| Questionnaire Item | Number of Meetings Attended | | | | Percentage Work Time | | | |
|---|---|---|---|---|---|---|---|---|
| | No Meetings | 1-10 | More than 10 | Tau B | No time | Less than 50% | 50% or More | Tau B |
| | %Agreement | | | | %Agreement | | | |
| 10. More UN authority to enforce rules | 61.4 | 51.4 | 34.2 | -.149* | 72.8 | 48.4 | 41.0 | -.114* |
| | N=181 | N=183 | N=88 | | N=88 | N=301 | N=61 | |

* Significant at .001

UN majorities hostile to, or at least with interests different from, the United States may gain control of the decision-making machinery. Their reaction is cooperation 'yes' but enforcement of majority rule 'no'.[12]

This conclusion is further supported by responses to questionnaire item 11 dealing with mini-state domination of the United Nations. The item states: 'The UN is dominated by small countries whose collective influence is far out of proportion to their resources or real interests.' In each case, the experienced groups score lower on item 10 (UN authority) and higher on item 11 (mini-state domination). By rank order measures, responses to questionnaire items 1-10 are all positively correlated with one another, many at high levels of association. But all are negatively associated with responses to item 11. That means, other things being equal, that the more the respondent is convinced of mini-state domination of the United Nations, the less likely he is to agree with any of the statements involving general approval of the UN, commitment of resources, or increased UN authority. Awareness of mini-state domination is more closely associated with attendance at international meetings than with percentage of work time devoted to international activities. This accords with common sense expectations as well, since those who attend the meetings are much more likely to have first-hand experience with the operation of the majority coalition system. This dichotomy is strongly evident within the IO/USUN group, where the agreement with item 11 is 65 % for the IO Bureau group and 100 % for the respondents from the U.S. Mission. The USUN group is also somewhat less inclined to favor increased authority for the United Nations.

*The effect of previous experience*

Data bearing on Hypothesis 4, that experience with international organizations in a previous job assignment will create more supportive attitudes, follow much the same pattern witnessed above. Here we are referring to officials who, prior to their present post, held a governmental position that involved them in some way with the activities of international organizations. Associations with past experience tend to be positive on the general evaluative dimensions, positive on the action-commitment items relating to trade and development, negative on the action commitments relating specifically to the United Nations, and very negative on sovereignty transfer. This is shown in Table 9 comparing percentage agreement scores for respondents classified in terms of previous international organization experience.

More detail is presented in Table 10 where previous and current experience are combined to create four categories of respondents

*Table 9.* Percentage agreement with questionnaire items 1-10 for officials classified on the basis of previous experience with international organizations

| Questionnaire Item | Previous IO Experience | No Previous IO Experience |
|---|---|---|
| 1. UN promotes peace | *90.8%* | 85.2% |
| 2. UN important to U.S. | *67.7* | 52.5 |
| 3. Strengthening the UN | *46.7* | 34.9 |
| 4. IO a necessity | *93.0* | 87.5 |
| 5. Use UN more | *56.8* | 48.4 |
| 6. More UN resources | 64.1 | *66.0* |
| 7. More aid through UN | 45.2 | *45.7* |
| 8. Trade preferences | *65.8* | 61.1 |
| 9. Promote development | *85.4* | 77.4 |
| 10. More UN authority | 49.2 | *54.5* |
| | N=190 | N=261 |

Note: Italics have been used for emphasis to show the higher score of the pair.

ranked in ascending order of experience: (1) no previous and no current experience; (2) previous but no current experience; (3) current but no previous experience; and (4) both current and previous experience. Current experience is operationalized to include only those whose work assignments are concerned 50 % or more with international organization activities. This configuration produces positive associations between increasing experience and agreement on all of the general evaluative items, and on the trade and development items. For other items the correlations are negative or insignificant.

## The domestic organizational context

The fifth hypothesis predicts that officials in governmental units having extensive dealings with international organization activities will develop attitudes more favorable to multilateral cooperation than officials in other agencies. The assumptions underlying this hypothesis were examined in chapter 3 but for convenience of reference will be restated here. If contact breeds favorable attitudes, this proposition should hold true simply because officials in governmental units with special international organization responsibilities are more likely than others to have extensive contact with international organizations. Moreover, officials who themselves have no experience with international organi-

*Table 10.* Previous and current experience with international organization activities as related to responses to questionnaire items 1-10

| Questionnaire Item | Nature of IO Experience | | | | |
| --- | --- | --- | --- | --- | --- |
| | No Previous or Current | Previous Only | Current Only | Both Previous and Current | Kendall Tau B |
| | %Agreement | | | | |
| 1. UN Promotes Peace | 84.6 | 95.2 | 91.6 | 91.7 | .110 |
| 2. UN Important to U.S. | 53.0 | 71.4 | 70.9 | 83.4 | .208* |
| 3. Strengthening UN | 34.4 | 47.6 | 45.8 | 51.4 | .098 |
| 4. IO a Necessity | 89.4 | 86.7 | 91.7 | 97.2 | .133** |
| 5. Use UN More | 53.0 | 66.7 | 45.8 | 60.0 | .040 |
| 6. More UN Resources | 66.7 | 80.9 | 70.8 | 50.0 | -.100 |
| 7. More Aid Through UN | 46.9 | 52.3 | 45.8 | 50.0 | -.022 |
| 8. Trade Preferences | 60.6 | 60.0 | 66.7 | 63.9 | .128** |
| 9. Promote Development | 68.2 | 80.9 | 79.2 | 94.3 | .286* |
| 10. More UN Authority | 69.7 | 85.7 | 45.8 | 38.9 | -.185* |
| | N=61 | N=21 | N=24 | N=36 | |

*Significant at .01
**Significant at .05

zations may be influenced in their views by other officials in the unit who do. A further rationale for the hypothesis is the possibility that governmental units will develop a professional-client relationship with international organizations, accompanied by a widely shared feeling that the unit must in some sense look out for the interests of its clients.

As observed in chapter 3, the hypothesis can be interpreted as having both a static and a dynamic aspect. As a static conception, it postulates that officials in one governmental unit will have, on the average, more favorable attitudes toward international organization than officials in some other unit. We might also assume, however, a dynamic process at work in which the characteristics of the governmental unit interact with experience to strengthen the positive impact of experience upon attitudes. If increasing experience is accompanied by a heightened appreciation of the client relationship with the international agency, for example, this could have a 'booster' effect upon attitude change. Such an effect would not occur in a governmental unit that does not regard international organizations as its clients.

*Table 11.* Percentage agreement on questionnaire items 1-10 for respondents from international sub-units as compared with other respondents

| Questionnaire Item | International Sub-Units | Other |
|---|---|---|
| 1. UN promotes peace | *87.2* | 86.9 |
| 2. UN is important to U.S. | 57.5 | *58.6* |
| 3. Strengthening UN is good for U.S. | 32.4 | *44.6* |
| 4. International organizations a necessity | 88.3 | *90.3* |
| 5. U.S. should use UN more | *54.7* | 49.2 |
| 6. Increase UN resources | 65.9 | 64.2 |
| 7. Channel more aid through UN | *46.1* | 44.0 |
| 8. Grant trade preferences | *72.8* | 56.6 |
| 9. Promote development | *86.2* | 76.5 |
| 10. Give UN more authority to enforce its rules | 45.6 | *56.6* |
| | N=183 | N=271 |

Note: Italics have been used for emphasis to show the higher score of each pair.

The most appropriate way to test this hypothesis with available data is to group the respondents in the general survey according to their assignment to an international affairs sub-unit within their respective

*Table 12.* The relationship of work time to questionnaire responses by officials from international affairs sub-units as compared with other respondents

| | Work Time Devoted to International Organization Matters | | | | | |
| Questionnaire Item | Respondents from International Sub-units | | | Other Respondents | | |
| | No Work Time %Agreement | Some Work Time %Agreement | Tau B | No Work Time %Agreement | Some Work Time %Agreement | Tau B |
|---|---|---|---|---|---|---|
| 1. UN promotes peace | 80.0 | 88.3 | .071 | 88.7 | 86.7 | -.013 |
| 2. UN is important to U.S. | 53.4 | 58.5 | .124** | 58.3 | 59.3 | .093* |
| 3. Strengthening UN is good for U.S. | 6.7 | 35.2 | .065 | 44.2 | 44.6 | .020 |
| 4. International organizations a necessity | 80.0 | 89.6 | .206* | 90.3 | 90.7 | -.030 |
| 5. U.S. should use UN more | 53.3 | 55.2 | .051 | 56.9 | 46.9 | -.064 |
| 6. Increase UN resources | 66.7 | 66.0 | -.028 | 70.8 | 61.9 | -.126* |
| 7. Channel more aid through UN | 40.0 | 47.0 | .031 | 50.0 | 42.3 | -.091** |
| 8. Grant trade preferences | 66.7 | 73.2 | .169* | 59.2 | 55.7 | -.027 |
| 9. Promote development | 80.0 | 87.8 | .170* | 69.5 | 78.9 | .112* |
| 10. Give UN more authority to enforce its rules | 66.7 | 43.6 | -.026 | 75.0 | 49.7 | -.161* |
| | N=15 | N=164 | | N=72 | N=195 | |

*Significant at .01
**Significant at .05

7 – Beyond Functionalsim

executive departments. We may assume, and questionnaire responses in fact show, that the international sub-units have more extensive dealings with international organizations than the organizational units to which other officials are assigned. The data in Table 11, giving percentage agreement for the two groups on ten questionnaire items, indicate that the hypothesis as a static proposition is at best only partially supported. Differences on most items are small and not all as predicted. On three of four general evaluation items the 'others' score higher than the international sub-unit respondents. This is also true of item 10, relating to increased UN authority, a relationship to which by now we have become accustomed. On the other hand, the international sub-unit group has a higher percentage agreement for all five action commitment items, and the difference is great enough to be statistically significant for the two international cooperation items (trade preferences and development aid).[14]

The response to the general evaluation items and the three UN-related action-commitment items presents a different pattern from data previously examined. Generally, we have seen a positive relationship between experience and favorable general evaluation of the UN, and a somewhat negative association between experience and agreement with the three UN action commitment items. With respect to the latter one might conclude that the client relationship and other features of the international sub-unit context had made the difference; but this can scarcely account for the lower scores on three of the first four general evaluation items.

A further break-down of the responses sheds some light on this anomaly. Table 12 indicates that among respondents who spend no work-time on international organization, those within international sub-units score noticeably lower than their counterparts in other organizational units. Indeed, the former score lower on all items except trade preferences and development aid, which are not specifically related to international organization. This suggests that the more favorable attitudes of experienced officials are not necessarily passed on to other officials in the same sub-unit, and that the sub-unit context affects attitudes only selectively. The relatively lower scores of the no-work-time group in the international sub-units even suggest negative attitudinal effects, deriving perhaps from a feeling that their own area of international activity is more significant than that occupied by international organizations.

Data in Table 12 do indicate, however, that hypothesis 5 is more viable in its dynamic aspect. We have just observed that the no-work-time respondents from international sub-units score lower on most items than no-work-time respondents from other organizational units.

Among respondents having experience with international organizations, however, the international sub-unit group scores higher on all five action-commitment items and within two percentage points of the other respondents on three of four general evaluation items. From this comparison of experienced and non-experienced groups, we conclude that job assignment in a unit having extensive dealings with international organization does not necessarily give rise to favorable attitudes. But being located in such a unit appears to have a booster effect upon attitude change for those whose work assignment does include experience with international agencies. This conclusion is further supported by the Tau beta coefficients showing the extent of association between increasing experience and agreement with the questionnaire items. For every item the Tau is higher for the international sub-unit group, indicating a stronger positive (or in two cases less negative) association of experience with favorable attitudes than is the case with respondents from organizational units having less extensive dealings with international organization activities.

*Past and present incumbents*

Our sixth hypothesis asserts that present incumbents in governmental units dealing with international organizations will have more favorable attitudes toward their activities than will former incumbents. Here a comparison of responses from current and former officials of the State Department IO Bureau and the U.S. Mission to the UN can provide a direct test of this proposition. Assuming that both groups are similarly sophisticated and knowledgeable with respect to the workings of the United Nations and related agencies, differences in response (other than those attributable to the sampling process) should flow from differences in the immediacy of the experience. Former officials presumably have a more detached perspective; present officials have current personal and career interests bound up in the fate of U.S. policies in the United Nations. This difference in perspective suggests that the current officials should have a higher agreement score than the former officials on the eight questionnaire items dealing with the United Nations, except perhaps for item 10 which calls for more UN authority to enforce its rules. With respect to that item, the domination of the smaller states in the UN has become more pronounced in recent years, and officials presently involved in UN processes should be more keenly aware of the problems posed by enforcement of UN decisions on reluctant minorities.

The data in Table 13 on the whole conform to these expectations. The group of former officials registers substantially greater support of more

*Table 13.* Percentage agreement scores on questionnaire items 1-10 for current IO/USUN respondents as compared with former IO/USUN respondents

| Questionnaire Item | Current IO/USUN | Former IO/USUN |
|---|---|---|
| 1. UN promotes peace | *84.4* | 80.3 |
| 2. UN is important to U.S. | *67.1* | 58.1 |
| 3. Strengthening UN is good for U.S. | 38.2 | *40.3* |
| 4. International organizations a necessity | *96.1* | 95.2 |
| 5. U.S. should use UN more | *52.6* | 36.7 |
| 6. Increase UN rescources | 59.7 | 59.7 |
| 7. Channel more aid through UN | *46.8* | 38.7 |
| 8. Grant trade preferences | 59.7 | *62.9* |
| 9. Promote development | 85.5 | *93.5* |
| 10. Give UN more authority to enforce its rules | 26.2 | *40.7* |
| | N=77 | N=62 |

Note: Italics have been used for emphasis to show the higher score of each pair.

authority for the UN and slightly higher agreement with strengthening the UN. The percentage agreement on increasing UN resources is identical for both groups, although a further breakdown of responses indicates a larger proportion of the current officials in 'strong agreement' with the statement. On the other UN items the current officials respond more favorably to international organizations. Of some interest is the higher score of former officials on the two items not specifically relating to the UN – trade preferences and development assistance. Perhaps their impressions stemmed from an earlier period of the UN when developing countries were collectively less organized and demanding, and therefore evoked more sympathetic consideration of their needs.

*Political versus functional activities*

The preceding discussion of United States officials' attitudes toward international organization has called into question – or at least raised questions about – a number of the propositions that we derived from functionalist theory. In fairness to the theory, however, we should point out that the very basic functionalist distinction between 'political' and 'functional' activities has been largely ignored. Critics of functionalism, as noted in an earlier chapter,[15] have challenged this distinction by insisting that politics cannot be banished from international decision-making, whatever the subject matter of the decisions. This argument, while true almost by definition, does not wholly dispose of the distinction. Functionalists may still argue that functional activities are less 'political', less controversial, less highly-charged, and therefore more subject to fruitful international cooperation than issues of power, prestige, and national security. In any event, anyone seeking to evaluate functionalism empirically ought not to gloss over important functionalist tenets.

Yet, this, to some extent, we have done. Both the Norwegian and the United States surveys are designed to probe official attitudes toward the United Nations rather than more strictly functional international organizations. This was done because of our assumption that government officials and legislators responding to the questionnaire would be much more likely to have knowledge and opinions about the United Nations than about any particular functional organization. This decision carried with it the risk that attitudinal change presumed by functionalist theory to be associated with functional cooperation might not be so pronounced with respect to the United Nations. The United Nations, manifestly, is concerned with political and security problems as well as more strictly 'functional' economic and social activities. Given the varied background of the American respondents, the data is capable of testing only whether experience with international organizations in general has a carry-over in more favorable attitudes toward the United Nations. Thus far, therefore, we have largely ignored the distinction between 'political' and 'functional' activities which was so important to Mitrany.

Three additional questionnaire items were included in the United States survey to take account of this distinction and see if functional activities and organizations elicited more approval than the UN and its security activities. These items are the following:

Item 12. The UN is more effective in dealing with economic and social problems than with political and security problems.

Item 13. The specialized agencies of the UN perform their tasks more effectively than does the UN itself.

Item 14. The specialized agencies of the UN are more useful to the United States than is the UN itself.

Table 14 shows substantial agreement among all groups that the UN is more effective in economic and social matters than in dealing with

Table 14. Percentage agreement of selected respondent groups on three questionnaire items dealing with political versus functional activities

| Item | Attended an IO Meeting | | Work Involves IO | | Experience With UN | | IO/USUN Officials | |
|---|---|---|---|---|---|---|---|---|
| | Yes | No | Yes | No | Yes | No | Current | Former |
| 12. UN more effective in economic and social matters | 69.4 | 67.2 | 69.0 | 65.9 | 66.2 | 69.4 | 59.2 | 67.2 |
| 13. Specialized agencies more effective than UN | 76.4 | 66.4 | 74.4 | 64.8 | 75.4 | 71.4 | 61.0 | 70.0 |
| 14. Specialized agencies more useful than UN | 43.4 | 35.4 | 41.6 | 31.8 | 39.1 | 40.4 | 28.6 | 31.7 |
| | N=271 | N=181 | N=362 | N=88 | N=131 | N=321 | N=77 | N=60 |

political and security problems, and that the specialized agencies are more effective than the United Nations. There is less agreement that the specialized agencies are more 'useful'. On item 12 there is surprising uniformity of response among all groups drawn from the general survey, regardless of experience with international organizations. However, the group most directly involved with the United Nations, current IO/USUN officials, has a noticeably lower agreement score. It is not clear whether this represents a higher opinion of UN performance in the security sphere or a lower opinion of the economic and social activities. The substantial agreement on items 12 and 13 is consistent with the functionalist position that bonds of mutually reinforcing international cooperation will grow faster and stronger in economic and social areas than in forums where the daily grist is international disputes and threats to peace. The much lower agreement scores on item 14, where 'usefulness' rather than 'effectiveness' is at issue, suggest a note of caution in interpreting this data as a clear-cut victory for the functionalist position. Apparently many officials regard political and security problems as so salient to the national interest that they refuse to categorize the specialized agencies as more useful, even though more effective in performing their respective tasks.

On items 13 and 14, dealing with effectiveness and usefulness, there is a tendency for strength of agreement to increase as meeting attendance and work time increase. Rank order correlations with both meeting attendance and work time are significant at .05 or better. This also is consistent with the functionalist rationale. There is a further caveat, however. In the general survey of executive departments from which the data were taken, only 28 % of the respondents had any contact with the United Nations, while 60 % had some dealings with one or more intergovernmental functional organizations. Experience with international organizations as reflected in work time and meeting attendance must therefore be interpreted as contact mainly with functional agencies rather than with the United Nations. The respondents, apparently, came increasingly to favor the kind of organizations with which they had the most contact. This could help explain why the current IO/USUN officials were less prone than other groups to agree that the specialized agencies were more effective or useful than the UN. Nevertheless, partiality to client organizations cannot be a complete explanation of the preference for specialized agencies, since the IO/USUN group is well above 50% in recognizing the effectiveness of the specialized agencies and the functional side of the UN. Overall the responses to these three items give support to the distinction between functional and political activities. In this survey the former clearly elicit the more favorable evaluation, even when discount is made for the

Table 15. Mean scores on questionnaire items for respondent groups classified by selected respondent attributes

| Questionnaire Item | Military Status | | Education | | Age | |
|---|---|---|---|---|---|---|
| | All Respondents | Military Only | Advanced Degree | No Advanced Degree | Under 47 | 47 and Over |
| 1. UN promotes peace | 87.1 | 78.9 | 86.6 | 87.9 | 86.8 | 88.5 |
| 2. UN important to U.S. | 58.1 | 63.2 | 61.1 | 54.0 | 53.2 | 63.7 |
| 3. Strengthening UN | 39.5 | 36.8 | 40.4 | 38.2 | 28.7 | 50.7 |
| 4. IO a necessity | 89.6 | 100.0 | 88.5 | 90.8 | 86.9 | 92.0 |
| 5. Use UN more | 51.2 | 36.8 | 52.5 | 48.3 | 49.3 | 53.8 |
| 6. More UN resources | 64.8 | 63.2 | 68.1 | 59.5 | 67.5 | 62.7 |
| 7. More aid through UN | 44.7 | 26.3 | 48.9 | 39.8 | 48.6 | 41.9 |
| 8. Trade preferences | 63.0 | 31.6 | 69.4 | 54.4 | 64.9 | 62.4 |
| 9. Promote development | 80.3 | 63.2 | 88.0 | 68.3 | 82.7 | 78.3 |
| 10. More UN authority | 52.1 | 47.4 | 48.1 | 57.6 | 54.2 | 49.8 |
| | N=454 | N=19 | N=270 | N=175 | N=216 | N=230 |

* The higher score in each pair is italicized for emphasis.

tendency of respondents to favor the organizations with which they are most familiar.

*Correlates of officials' attitudes*

In addition to magnitude and kind of experience with international organizations, a number of other respondent attributes were examined as possible correlates of attitudes toward the United Nations. Some of these findings are set forth in Table 15.

Non-military status and education are consistent indicators of support for the United Nations and international cooperation. The sample of military personnel is very small, and consists entirely of respondents from the U.S. Coast Guard in the Department of Transportation. This obviously limits any attempt to extend generalization to all military personnel. Nevertheless, we note with interest that the military group scores lower than other respondents on most questionnaire items. The military group does score a bit higher on item 2 and substantially higher on item 4, which posits the necessity of 'international organizations such as the UN and its specialized agencies . . . in today's complex world.' A number of the Coast Guard respondents had experience with the Intergovernmental Maritime Consultative Organization (IMCO), and the high agreement score on item 4 may indicate a generally favorable experience with that organization. On the question of the specialized agencies effectiveness and usefulness, the Coast Guard group has higher agreement scores than any other sub-group we tested, 84 % and 58 %, respectively. For all other respondents agreement on these two items is 72 % and 39 %.

Formal education also appears to have an effect on attitudes, and the larger N's give us somewhat greater confidence in the reliability of the findings. In Table 15 the basis of classification is whether or not the respondent has an advanced academic degree (M.A., Ph.D., J.D., M.D., etc.). On every statement involving an action commitment, either to the UN or to helping less developed countries, the group with more formal educational training scores higher. The better educated respondents also agree more consistently with the statements that the UN is important and that strengthening the UN is likely to be good for the United States. They score slightly lower than the less educated respondents in agreement with the notions that the UN promotes a more peaceful, cooperative world and that international organizations are a necessity.

For purposes of age comparisons, respondents are divided at the median age of 47. The results are not easy to explain. The older group agrees most strongly with the four general evaluative statements and with the proposition that the United States ought to be more willing to use the United Nations. On the other five statements the younger group has the higher agreement score. If the older group had also scored higher on trade preferences and promoting development, we might assume differential experience with international organizations was a contributing factor. Although distribution of both groups according to percentage of work time with international organization activities is almost identical, the older group has had much more opportunity to attend international organization meetings. The older group is also more likely to have had experience with international organization in a previous government assignment. In view of our findings about the effects of experience, these differences could account for the higher scores of the older group on the first four items and lower scores on items 6 (more UN resources), 7 (more aid through the UN), and 10 (more UN authority). It could scarcely account, however, for the large difference in response to the proposition that anything strengthening the UN is likely to be good for the United States. Furthermore, if experience were determinative the older group should also support trade preferences and assistance to poorer countries more enthusiastically than the younger respondents. There must, then, be something in the youth factor or some unidentified variable associated with it that causes the younger respondents to show more empathy for the developing countries but greater skepticism about indiscriminate strengthening of the United Nations.

Certain other respondent attributes were examined, in most instances with no very strong or consistent relationships appearing. Respondents were asked to indicate their religious preference, which most did. One consistent relationship is an obvious and understandable anti-UN bias among the Jewish respondents. These respondents are much less likely to agree that the UN promotes a more peaceful world, that it is important, should be used more, should have more resources, or should have more authority to enforce its rules on member states. This bias is quite specific to the UN, since the Jewish group does not score lowest on the trade preference and development items, or even the item on channeling more US aid through the UN. Further, on item 4 (international organizations a necessity) the Jewish group scores 91 %, higher than either Catholics or Protestants. An explanation of the Jewish response to the questionnaire is perhaps best given in the words of one respondent who appended this comment to his returned questionnaire:

I am Jewish and pro-Israel. My attitudes towards the UN *are* affected by the actions of that body towards Israel.

The numerical dominance of the new nations, have-not nations and 'third world' nations has resulted in UN actions which are mischievous and frequently anti-U.S.

It goes almost without saying that the Jewish respondents register by far the greatest agreement with the proposition that 'The UN is dominated by small countries whose collective influence is far out of proportion to their resources or real interests.' The average agreement score for this group is 71.8 %. For the next highest (Protestant) group it is 55 %.

Region of birth was considered as a possible correlate of officials' attitudes, but no strong or consistent relationships emerged. Respondents were also grouped on the basis of past residence of a year or more in a developing country. Generally the results parallel those earlier obtained when experience with international organizations was used as the basis of group comparisons. The persons who have lived in a developing country tend to respond more favorably on general evaluation (items 1-4) and on helping poorer countries (items 8 and 9) than those without such experience. But the former group scores lower on action commitment to the UN (items 5-7) and giving the UN more authority to enforce its rules (item 10).

Numerous differences appear when respondents are grouped by executive department, but generally the Ns for individual departments are too small to give great credence to the findings. Despite this cautionary note, a few trends may be worth noting. On seven of the 10 items we have used as the indicators of UN support, the Treasury Department (N=61) has a lower agreement score than any other Department. The three exceptions are items 7, 8 and 9, dealing respectively with aid through the UN, trade preferences, and economic development; and Treasury respondents score lower than average on 7 and 8. If these respondents are a representative sample, Treasury officials have a relatively low opinion of the United Nations. This is also reflected in Treasury responses to the statements on the greater effectiveness and usefulness of the specialized agencies. On both of these items, the Treasury has a higher agreement score than any other department. On the other hand, the UN generally receives the most favorable rating from the Departments of State and Commerce. One or the other is highest on eight of ten items.[16] Interior, whose respondents had the least extensive experience with international organizations of all executive departments, is high on the other two: enforcement of UN rules, and agreement that anything strengthening the UN is likely to be good for the United States.

From the standpoint of functionalist theory, identifying respondent

107

attributes that affect attitudes toward international organization is less important than determining whether those attributes alter in any significant way the relationships between attitudes and experience with international organization. Our data suggest that the attitude-experience relationships are largely independent of the attributes we have examined, except for differences among government departments. The variation from one department to another[17] may reflect differences in departmental goals, different degrees of contact with international organizations, and dealings with different international organizations, among other things. This is an area in which conclusions must await further investigation, because the number of respondents from each department is too small to admit great confidence that they reflect real departmental differences.[18]

None of the other attributes we examined show consistent and substantial impact upon the attitude-experience relationship. When respondents are grouped by age the over-all tendency on the action-commitment items to grow more negative with experience is somewhat exaggerated in the older group. And, for the younger respondents, the association between experience and positive attitudes toward trade preferences, assistance to poorer countries and the need for international organizations generally becomes more pronounced. A similar accentuation of the positive relationship for these same three items occurs for the respondents who have lived a year or more in a developing country. In both of the latter instances, the accentuation is more evident when meeting attendance rather than work time is the experience variable.[19] The failure to discover more consistent and dramatic intervening variables is, of course, no threat to functionalist theories. It merely suggests that the attitudinal effects of exposure to international organizations occur for the most part independently of the personal attributes we have examined. Departmental variations suggest that the nature of the experience, including the particular international activity involved, may be a very important determinant of attitudinal change. But that, as we have noted, is a subject for further investigation.

The findings from our study leave little doubt that experience with international organizations does affect the way in which U.S. governmental officials evaluate the United Nations. The generally low correlation coefficients indicate that sheer magnitude of experience explains only a small part of the variation in attitudes. But tests of statistical significance and the consistency with which the same variations are found across different groupings suggest that the relationships, if weak, are nevertheless real.

The evidence gives support to some elements of functionalist theory, while strongly negating the idea of a direct linear relationship between working with international organizations and the development of favorable attitudes toward them. In formulating specific hypotheses about attitude change, we attempted to draft statements that would probe increasing degrees of commitment to multilateral cooperation. The questionnaire items were framed to fit three categories or dimensions of cooperation: favorable general evaluation, action commitment to further acts of cooperation, and willingness to transfer sovereignty. We originally assumed that increasing experience with international organization would be positively associated with these three dimensions. In examining questionnaire responses, however, we found the attitude-experience relationship to be expressed in four rather than three dimensions and not all of them positive. The fourth category was obtained by grouping the three UN-related action-commitment items separately from the two items dealing with aid to developing countries. The category was labelled 'international cooperation'. Using as a rough measure the average of coefficients obtained by rank order correlation of meeting attendance and work time with the questionnaire items in each category, the four dimensions can be arrayed in relation to the experience variables, as follows:

FIGURE 1

| International Cooperation | General Eval- uation of UN | Action Commit- ment to UN | Transfer of Sovereignty |
|---|---|---|---|
| + + | + | – | – – |

As Figure 1 shows, experience with international organizations is positively associated with favorable attitudes toward international cooperation, less positively related to favorable evaluation of the UN, negatively associated with commitment to greater use of or increased resources for the UN, and still more negatively related to transfer of sovereignty.[20]

Although the array in Figure 1 is based on rank order correlation of questionnaire responses with work time and meeting attendance, the other measures of experience considered in hypotheses 4-7 follow a generally similar pattern. Thus, exposure to international organization in a previous job assignment, and a present assignment in a governmental unit that is itself heavily involved with international organization activities, are associated with higher than average agreement scores on the international cooperation and general evaluation dimensions, and lower than average scores on items involving action commitment to the UN and transfer of sovereignty.

Considered as a whole, these findings should raise a serious question about the ultimate reach of the functionalist evolutionary process. The evidence of attitude change is consistent with the prognosis of a gradual growth of multilateral cooperation, but not with the notion that a system of inter-locking global functional units will eventually replace the state through the piece-by-piece transfer of little slices of sovereignty.

## Congressional Attitudes Toward the UN

National legislators are important links in the chain of policy that connects governments to the workings of international organizations. Relations with international agencies are maintained by means of resources the legislature appropriates and within the framework of laws prescribed by the legislature. If the functionalist dynamic is to have its maximum impact, it must reach these key policy-makers in national political systems.

There are, in fact, numerous opportunities for members of Congress to attend international meetings in some official capacity. Two members of the U.S. House or Senate are regularly appointed to serve as United States delegates to the annual session of the UN General Assembly. Members of Congress were part of the United States delegation to the San Francisco Conference in 1945 and also served on delegations to the 1946 and 1947 sessions of the Assembly. Beginning in 1950, President Truman established a policy of appointing two members of Congress, one Democrat and one Republican, to serve during each regular Assembly session. Senators not standing for re-election are appointed in even years, House members in odd years. As the policy has evolved, members of Congress are selected in rotation from the respective House Committee on International Relations (formerly Foreign Affairs Committee) and the Senate Foreign Relations Committee, omitting, of course, any Congressman not willing to serve.[21] From 1950 through 1973, some 49 members of the House and Senate had served as UN delegates, and of these 26 were still serving in Congress in early 1974.

In addition to the UN Assembly assignments, members of Congress are often invited to serve on U.S. delegations to other international agencies, such as the International Labor Organization, UNESCO, and the Food and Agriculture Organization, or special UN meetings like the Law of the Sea conferences or the Stockholm UN Conference on the Human Environment. Congress also selects its own delegates to meetings of various interparliamentary groups, most notably the Interparliamentary Union (in which well over 100 national legislatures are now represented), the North Atlantic Assembly (established in 1955 to

110

parallel the military and governmental structure of NATO), the Canada-United States Interparliamentary Group, and the Mexico-United States Interparliamentary Group. During the period 1949-1970 more than 400 Senators and Representatives attended at least one interparliamentary group meeting.[22]

Most of the interparliamentary meetings do not occupy the Congressman more than a week, and of this time only two or three days may be devoted to business sessions. The UN General Assembly assignment, by contrast, includes a full three months in New York, from September to December of each year. Even here, some Congressional delegates choose to spend only a few days at Assembly business, perhaps the first and last week of the session, and continue to devote the bulk of their time to activities in Washington or in their constituencies. Others, however, move their families to New York and become heavily involved in the work of the United Nations. On the average, certainly, the UN assignment brings longer and more intensive contact with international organizations than other opportunities available to members of Congress.

This pool of sitting congressmen who have, if but briefly, attended meetings of international organizations provide the basis for further examination of functionalist assumptions about attitude change. In this portion of the study two sources of data are used to measure attitudes. One is a questionnaire circulated to a sample of Representatives and Senators in 1974, supplemented by a number of personal interviews. The other is a content analysis of speeches of Congressmen who served as U.S. delegates to the UN General Assembly from 1950 to 1971. The two bodies of information will be developed separately, beginning with the survey data, but conclusions about congressional attitude change will be based on both data sources.

*The survey research design*

The survey instrument was mailed to each of 26 delegates to the General Assembly who then (1974) held seats in Congress. In addition, questionnaires were sent to a larger, systematically selected sample of both Houses, including 50 Senators and 217 Representatives. For most of the sample, the mailed questionnaire was supplemented by subsequent personal contact with the legislator or a member of his staff. Despite these efforts, the return was 11 of 26 for the delegate questionnaire (42 %), 88 of 217 for the House (41 %), and 15 of 50 Senators (30 %). The following comparison of party and regional distribution will give some basis for estimating the representativeness of the sample:

## Party Distribution

| | Respondent Sample | All Members of Congress |
|---|---|---|
| Democrat | 70% | 57% |
| Republican | 30% | 43% |

## Regional Distribution

| | Respondent Sample | All Members of Congress |
|---|---|---|
| Northeast | 19% | 23% |
| North Central | 23% | 27% |
| South | 30% | 31% |
| West | 27% | 19% |

A high degree of representativeness, fortunately, is not critical to the study, since the analysis is concerned primarily with comparison of subgroups within the sample rather than drawing inferences about the behavior or characteristics of the Congress as a whole.

The questionnaire sent to Congressmen is an abbreviated version of the instrument to which officials of the executive departments responded. There are eight substantive items, all identical with corresponding questions in the executive department questionnaire. The research purpose also is the same – to determine if members of Congress with experience as delegates to international organizations have attitudes more favorable to multilateral cooperation than Congressmen without such experience. Specifically, it is postulated that the delegates, as compared with non-delegates, will have attitudes generally more favorable to the United Nations (hypothesis 7), more supportive of further international cooperation (hypothesis 8), and more sympathetic to the transfer of small slices of national sovereignty to the United Nations through increasing UN authority (hypothesis 9). For convenience of reference the questionnaire items will be repeated at appropriate points in the analysis.

### Testing the hypotheses: group comparisons

Two questionnaire items relate to the proposition (hypothesis 7) that national legislators who have been delegates to international organizations will be more favorable to multilateral cooperation than those who have not. These are the Type 1 or general evaluation statements previ-

*Table 16.* Agreement with questionnaire items as related to experience with international organizations

| Questionnaire Item | Delegate to UN General Assembly | | Attended Other International Meeting | |
|---|---|---|---|---|
| | Yes | No | Yes | No |
| | %Agreement | | %Agreement | |
| 1. UN promotes peace | *100.0* | 80.4 | *90.3* | 76.1 |
| 2. UN is important to U.S. | *100.0* | 74.8 | *80.7* | 72.2 |
| 3. U.S. should use UN more | *81.8* | 65.7 | *74.2* | 62.0 |
| 4. UN should have more resources | 63.6 | *72.7* | *83.8* | 67.6 |
| 5. Channel more aid through UN | *54.5* | 45.6 | *58.1* | 40.3 |
| 6. Grant trade preferences | *80.0* | 57.8 | *71.0* | 52.1 |
| 7. Comply with UN sanctions against Rhodesia | *66.7* | 50.0 | *58.1* | 46.5 |
| 8. Give UN more authority | 54.5 | *60.4* | *67.8* | 57.1 |
| | N=11 | N=103 | N=31 | N=72 |

Note: Italics have been used for emphasis to show the higher score of each pair.

ously identified. The statements, with which the legislator was asked to register his agreement or disagreement on a five-point scale, read as follows:

1. The UN helps to promote a more peaceful, cooperative world.
2. The UN is important to the United Staes as a means of carrying out our foreign policies.

The responses as presented in Table 16 fall in the predicted direction. Former UN delegates are in greater agreement with both statements than are non-delegates. Indeed, all eleven delegates who responded were affirmative. Furthermore, members of Congress who had attended one or more meetings of some international organization other than the UN General Assembly score higher than those who had not attended a meeting. All cases, therefore, support the functionalist hypothesis.

There is a very real possibility, however, that such a result could reflect pre-existing attitudes rather than attitude change brought about by experience with international organizations. Service at the UN or attending any other international meeting is voluntary, and desire to serve is an important element in determining who goes. UN delegates are generally selected in rotation from the membership of the foreign relations committees of the two Houses of Congress, but any unwilling candidate may decline the honor, and a few have done so. Delegations to inter-parliamentary meetings are also filled on a voluntary basis: a Congressman invited to attend any international meeting is free to reject the invitation. It is reasonable to suppose, therefore, that most of those who participate have positive attitudes toward international cooperation to begin with. We do not have data that would enable us to make comparisons based on the amount or extent of international organization experience, as was done with civil servants. Even were the data available, the comparisons might not be very meaningful. Because a Congressman may freely decline a second invitation if the initial experience is not satisfying, a classification based on degree of experience might serve mainly as a means of identifying which ones enjoyed the international scene enough to accept repeated invitations rather than indicating the effect of repeated experiences upon the legislator's attitudes. Other data bearing on the self-selection will be examined in a following section. Leaving that issue aside, responses on the first two items clearly support the hypothesis.

Five items have relevance for hypothesis 8, which postulates increased support for further international cooperation. We have labeled these Type 2 or 'action commitment' statements. The five items are as follows:

3. In its own self-interest, the United States should be more willing than at present to make use of the UN.
4. The UN should have greater financial resources to carry out its programs.
5. The United States should channel more of its foreign aid through UN programs for economic development.
6. The United States should comply with UN sanctions by not importing chrome from Rhodesia.
7. The United States should grant trade preferences to developing countries.

Figures in Table 16 again lend support to the hypothesis. On four of five items the former UN delegates score higher than non-delegates, and those with other international experience score higher on all items than their colleagues who have never attended an international meeting. The one item on which the former UN delegates agree less strongly is the desirability of giving the UN greater financial resources. Their percentage is in fact lower than that of any other group in the Table. Presumably experience has indicated that the UN is receiving about as much money as it can handle effectively.

The differences between experienced and inexperienced groups in both cases is particularly pronounced for the trade preference item. This is consistent with responses to the appointed officials questionnaire. On the four UN-related items, however, there is apparent divergence from the responses of the appointed officials. For civil servants, rank order measures of association generally indicate a negative relationship between experience and agreement with the UN action-commitment items, while for members of Congress a positive relationship appears.

There is in fact no divergence with respect to the responses of the UN delegates. The comparison based on the presence or absence of *UN experience* in Table 6 shows the same response pattern for appointed officials as appears for Congressmen in Table 16. That is, on items relating to use of the UN, aid through the UN, and trade preferences, the respondents with UN experience – whether appointed officials or Congressional UN delegates – score higher; and on the item suggesting more resources for the UN, they score lower. Although appointed officials' responses to the item dealing with sanctions against Rhodesia are not included in Table 6, the UN-experienced group scores higher on that item as well, just as does the Congressional UN delegate group.

The disparity between appointed officials and U.S. Congressmen is very real, however, when experience with organizations other than the UN is the basis of comparison. On the UN-related action-commitment items, appointed officials with international organization experience are more negative than their inexperienced colleagues (Tables 6, 7), while Congressmen with experience at international meetings are more positive on every item. This difference is probably attributable to a number of circumstances, including the nature of the experience with international organization, the nature of the Congressional (as contrasted with the bureaucratic) milieu, and the participant's pre-existing attitudes.[23] With regard to the first circumstance, the prospects of a good experience abroad are probably higher for Congressmen than for most appointed officials doing duty at international meetings. The Congressman is in a better position to combine business with vacation;[24] and, while on the job, his status as a national legislator will win him more than average deference, at least within his own delegation.

The impact of milieu, the second factor, becomes particularly relevant when the Congressman returns home. He has become more expert in international affairs, which in some measure may enhance his prestige among fellow Congressmen. Constituents will also be impressed if the trip abroad is viewed as adding to his expertise rather than merely a junket at taxpayer's expense. The Congressman himself is likely to value the new insights gained and the new contacts made. Undoubtedly, he will make some rough assessment of these factors before deciding to attend. And if upon return he in fact feels better informed, and this is recognized by colleagues and constituents, the experience in retrospect will appear even more positive.

Pre-existing attitudes may also help to explain why, in contrast to appointed officials, Congressmen who attend international meetings score higher than non-attenders on these items. As previously noted, the assignment is voluntary and Congressmen who choose to attend meetings of international organizations are more likely than others to believe that international agencies are useful and worthwhile. The same might be hypothesized of appointed officials as well, but our data have suggested that self-selection is not an important element in explaining their responses. In contrast there is evidence in the Congressional data that pre-existing attitudes are an important determinant of responses to our questionnaire statements. This will be further explored below.

There is just one questionnaire item relating to hypothesis 9, which deals with the notion of sovereignty transfer:

8.  The UN should have more authority to enforce its rules upon member states.

The percentage agreement figures for UN delegates and non-delegates follow the pattern previously observed in appointed officials: the more experienced are the least willing to increase UN authority. This reflects, presumably, the recognition that increased authority may be used by UN majorities or perhaps by international bureaucracies in ways inimical to U.S. interests. The other group comparison, however, runs counter to previous findings: Congressmen who have attended meetings of international organizations other than the UN General Assembly are, on the average, more willing to see UN authority increased. We attribute this to the same factors that seemed to affect responses to the UN-related action-commitment items–pre-existing favorable attitudes, the nature of the experience, and the Congressional milieu. In addition to what was said above about the nature of the experience, it is possible that some of the Congressmen who attended meetings of international organizations did not stay long enough or become sufficiently involved to gain full awareness of ways in which international secretariats or non-Western voting majorities might use increased authority to the detriment of U.S. interests. Moreover, such tendencies are less apparent in interparliamentary meetings. It may be significant that three of four persons who had attended meetings of the

116

*Table 17.* Congressmen who would welcome an appointment to the UN delegation compared with those who would not welcome such an appointment

| Questionnaire Item | Would Welcome Appointment | Would Not Welcome Appointment | |
|---|---|---|---|
| | % Agreement | | Tau B |
| 1. UN promotes peace | *91.7* | 70.4 | .372* |
| 2. UN is important to U.S. | *81.3* | 69.1 | .286* |
| 3. U.S. should use UN more | *83.3* | 50.0 | .323* |
| 4. UN should have more resources | *85.1* | 61.5 | .333* |
| 5. Channel more aid through UN | *62.5* | 30.9 | .335* |
| 6. Grant trade preferences | *66.7* | 50.0 | .161** |
| 7. Comply with UN sanctions against Rhodesia | *60.4* | 40.7 | .178** |
| 8. Give UN more authority | *78.7* | 44.4 | .324* |
| | N=48 | N=55 | |

\* Significant at .001
\*\* Significant at .05

Note: Italics have been used for emphasis to show the higher score of each pair.

International Labour Organization, from which the United States has served notice of withdrawal, did not favor increased UN authority. Their experience apparently ran counter to the trend among Congressional participants in other international meetings.

We now face directly the question of self-selection: were those who attended international meetings already more favorable to international cooperation and, perhaps, more susceptible to being influenced positively by the experience? The question, unfortunately, cannot be answered directly because of the practical difficulty of gathering before-and-after questionnaire or interview responses from the Congressmen who attended meetings.[25] However, inferential evidence of pre-existing attitudes may be gleaned from responses to another questionnaire item which reads: 'I would welcome an appointment to serve as a U.S. delegate to a session of the UN General Assembly.' Inferences as to pre-existing attitudes are based on the assumption that persons who would welcome a UN assignment will have a better opinion of international organization that those who would not. In Table 17 questionnaire responses of Congressmen who agree with that statement are compared with who disagree or are undecided. On all eight items the 'would welcome' group scores significantly higher than

117

Table 18. Effect of meeting attendance on respondents to questionnaire items, controlling for respondents' desire to serve as a UN delegate

| Questionnaire Item | Would Welcome UN Appointment | | | Would Not Welcome UN Appointment | | |
|---|---|---|---|---|---|---|
| | Attended Meeting | Did Not Attend Meeting | Tau B | Attended Meeting | Did Not Attend Meeting | Tau B |
| | %Agreement | %Agreement | | %Agreement | %Agreement | |
| 1. UN promotes peace | 95.3 | 88.8 | .134 | *80.0* | 68.2 | .030 |
| 2. UN is important to U.S. | 85.7 | 77.7 | .125 | *70.0* | 68.9 | -.032 |
| 3. U.S. should use UN more | 85.7 | 81.4 | .152 | *50.0* | 50.0 | -.003 |
| 4. UN should have more resources | 90.5 | 80.8 | .200 | *70.0* | 59.5 | .074 |
| 5. Channel more aid through UN | 66.7 | 59.2 | .094 | *40.0* | 28.9 | .032 |
| 6. Grant trade preferences | 71.5 | 63.0 | .066 | *70.0* | 45.4 | .131 |
| 7. Comply with UN sanctions against Rhodesia | 61.9 | 59.2 | .073 | *50.0* | 38.7 | .028 |
| 8. Give UN more authority | 76.2 | *80.7* | .120 | *50.0* | 43.2 | .065 |
| | N=21 | N=27 | | N=10 | N=45 | |

Note: Italics have been used for emphasis to show the higher score of each pair.

the others. Percentage differences are substantial, and the Tau B column gives coefficients higher than we have found for most other group comparisons. All but the items relating to trade preferences and sanctions are significant at .001. Those two are significant at .05. Clearly, Congressmen who would welcome the opportunity to serve as a UN delegate have a higher opinion of the UN and of multilateral cooperation than those who would not welcome such an assignment.

Table 18 provides further evidence that pre-existing attitudes (as measured by response to the UN appointment item) are a better predictor than attendance at international meetings. On all but item 6 (trade preferences), respondents who would welcome a UN appointment, but have not attended an international meeting, score higher than the 'would not welcome' group who *have* attended such meetings. As might be expected, the 'would welcome' respondents are heavily over-represented among the international meeting attenders. Although they constitute only 47 % of all respondents, they make up 68 % of those who attended an international meeting. Of respondents who had not attended an international meeting, only 38 % would welcome an appointment to the United Nations. These findings strongly support the inference that participants in international meetings have more favorable attitudes toward international organization because of a selection process that recruits people with already favorable attitudes.

A further break-down of the data, however, indicates that experience has a positive effect that is to some extent independent of the pre-existing attitudes. Table 18 controls for the effect of pre-existing attitudes by segregating respondents who would welcome a UN appointment from those who would not, and examining the impact of experience upon each group separately. The unusually large and significant Tau B scores are gone, but responses in fourteen of the sixteen cases show a positive association with experience. And, again with two exceptions, a higher percentage of the experienced respondents in both groups agree with the eight questionnaire items.

## Correlates of legislators' attitudes

The preceding discussion of Congressional attitudes toward the United Nations strongly suggests that participation in international meetings does, on the average, condition members of Congress to view multilateral cooperation in a more favorable light. It does not explain, however, why some individuals experienced no change in the predicted direction nor does it account for differences in pre-existing attitudes. For that we may seek clues in the literature on Congressional voting behavior which, generally speaking, offers explanations based on party, constituency type, region or section, individual characteristics of Congress members, and the legislative process itself.[26] Only a few such studies focus exclusively on foreign policy questions,[27] but it is not uncommon for analysis of Congressional voting behavior to include a foreign policy or international voting dimension among the dependent variables. Generally speaking, the independent variables predict less well to foreign policy issues than to voting on other kinds of issues, and one widely cited study of constituency influence concludes that such influence is virtually non-existent with respect to foreign policy questions.[29] Nevertheless, one may glean from these studies that the Congressman who votes for international involvement is, typically, a Democrat with a non-business background from a northern, urban, higher income and relatively well educated constituency.[30] He is also likely to lean toward the liberal end of the ideological spectrum.

In pursuance of these leads, data were gathered to test the hypothesis that approval of the United Nations would respond to similar variables. This included information on constituency characteristics – the Congressman's geographical region; percentages for urban population and foreign stock; and figures on education and family income.[31] In addition we obtained information on the individual member's party affiliation, education, age, and 1973 voting performance as rated by the Americans for Democratic Action. The ADA rating was presumed to be a measure of the member's location in the liberal-conservative ideological spectrum. Chamber of Congress (House/Senate) and previous occupation were also treated as independent variables.[32]

The results of bivariate analysis, associating each of these constituency or personal characteristics with questionnaire responses, are summarized in Tables 19 and 20 in the form of Tau B coefficients. On the whole the evidence supports the findings of previous studies concerning the relationship of these variables to a Congressman's propensity to support internationalist causes. Except for ADA score the Tau B's are of modest strength. Nevertheless, they are strong enough to be significant at .05 for half or more of the questionnaire items on all but Chamber of Congress and constituency education. On all variables the association on a majority of items is in the predicted direction. That is, favorable responses are more pronounced among Senators (than Representatives), Democrats (than Republicans), younger members, the better educated, those with higher ADA ratings, and members from non-business backgrounds.[33] In Table 20 the data show favorable responses to be clearly associated with urban, higher income constituencies having a relatively high proportion of first and second generation immigrants, and located outside the South.[34] The relationship with constituency education is less pronounced. In most previous

120

*Table 19.* Personal and background attributes of congressmen as related to questionnaire responses (Kendall tau beta)

| Questionnaire Item | House of Congress | Party | Year of Birth | Education | Previous Occupation | 1973 ADA Rating |
|---|---|---|---|---|---|---|
| 1. UN promotes peace | .074 | .101 | .101 | .099 | .263* | .433* |
| 2. UN is important to U.S. | .014 | .052 | .083 | .081 | .147 | .409* |
| 3. U.S. should use UN more | .073 | .203* | .137* | .218* | .220* | .499* |
| 4. UN should have more resources | .060 | .104 | .090 | .161* | .195* | .451* |
| 5. Channel more aid through UN | .141 | .158* | .191* | .179* | .205* | .534* |
| 6. Grant trade preferences | .139 | .198* | .178* | .087 | .248* | .373* |
| 7. Comply with UN sanctions against Rhodesia | .075 | .325* | .183* | .150* | .124 | .582* |
| 8. Give UN more authority | .045 | .153* | .153* | .114 | .138 | .438* |

* Significant at .05
N=103

121

Table 20. Congressional constituency characteristics as related to questionnaire responses (Kendall tau beta)

| Questionnaire Item | Geographic Region | Urban Population | Foreign Stock | Education | Family Income |
|---|---|---|---|---|---|
| 1. UN promotes peace | .161* | .111 | .082 | -.055 | .007 |
| 2. UN is important to U.S. | .145 | .132* | .148* | .017 | .096 |
| 3. U.S. should use UN more | .283* | .192* | .193* | .021 | .168* |
| 4. UN should have more resources | .285* | .190* | .192* | .007 | .087 |
| 5. Channel more aid through UN | .248* | .170* | .263* | .109 | .214* |
| 6. Grant trade preferences | .054 | .201* | .130* | -.019 | .037 |
| 7. Comply with UN sanctions against Rhodesia | .234* | .187* | .185* | .036 | .204* |
| 8. Give UN more authority | .216* | .264* | .276* | -.031 | .140* |

* Significant at .05

N=103

studies, Congressional and constituency characteristics have been used to explain voting behavior. Our findings show they are also modestly useful in explaining Congressional attitudes toward multilateral cooperation as expressed through questionnaire responses.

The information in Tables 19 and 20 relates only to the 103 members of the House and Senate who had not served as delegates to a session of the UN General Assembly. Rank order correlations were run separately for the eleven former delegates, but relationships between attributes and questionnaire responses were neither as consistent nor as statistically significant. This is in part because of the smaller N which reduces reliability and requires higher Tau Bs for statistical significance. It may also mean, however, that the effect of personal and constituency characteristics is muted by the greater impact of the participation experience. As noted earlier, most delegates to a session of the General Assembly are heavily immersed in international organization activity over a three-month period, as compared with just a few days for Congressmen attending most other international meetings. To

*Table 21.* Differing international organization experience as related to questionnaire responses, controlling for political party

| Questionnaire Item | Experience as UN Delegate | | Other IO Experience | |
|---|---|---|---|---|
| | Republican | Democrat | Republican | Democrat |
| | Tau B | | Tau B | |
| 1. UN promotes peace | .000 | .042 | .098 | .203* |
| 2. UN is important to U.S. | .020 | .091 | -.012 | .176 |
| 3. U.S. should use UN more | .149 | -.042 | .114 | .165 |
| 4. UN should have more resources | .024 | -.166 | .150 | .237* |
| 5. Channel more aid through UN | .112 | .078 | -.050 | .218* |
| 6. Grant trade preferences | .295* | .068 | .106 | .206* |
| 7. Comply with UN sanctions against Rhodesia | .211 | .064 | .033 | .172 |
| 8. Give UN more authority | .028 | -.065 | -.092 | .269* |
| * Significant at .05 | N=33 | N=79 | N=29 | N=72 |

the extent that their views are changed by the experience of participation, the other variables that might predict attitudes become less relevant. This may help explain why the associations between those variables and the questionnaire responses are weaker and more erratic for the former UN delegates.

Another indication that the more prolonged and intensive experience produces the greater attitude change may be inferred from ADA ratings. In Table 19 it is strikingly evident that the Congressman's liberal-conservative orientation as measured by ADA ratings is the best predictor of his questionnaire responses. It is, indeed, a much better predictor than experience or lack of experience with international organizations. We have shown that Congressmen who have attended an international meeting score higher on the questionnaire items than other Congressmen, but they also score significantly higher on the ADA scale – an average of 60 on a 0-100 scale, compared with 48 for the others. On the other hand, the former UN delegates also score higher on the questionnaire than non-delegates, but their average ADA rating is lower than that of the non-delegates, 42 to 52. This suggests that the more intensive UN experience may have had sufficient impact to modify substantially the influence of ideological orientation.

That the *kind* of participation experience makes a difference becomes clearly evident when the effect of experience upon attitudes is measured while controlling for various background and constituency variables. In this case the 'control' is applied by dichotomizing respondents on each of eight variables (all those in Tables 19 and 20 except constituency education and familiy income), then testing for the effect of experience within each group. This is done by running a rank order correlation of questionnaire responses with each of the two experience variables (UN delegate/non-delegate, and participant/non-participant in other international meetings) across each of the control variables. With one partial exception, a strikingly similar pattern appears. When experience as a *UN General Assembly delegate* is tested, the group on the control variable having the *least favorable* attitudes toward international organization shows the most positive 'change'. Conversely, when participation in *other international meetings* is the test variable, the group on the control variable *most favorable* to multilateral cooperation shows the most positive change.[35] This is illustrated in Table 21 which gives Tau B coefficients as a measure of the association between experience and favorable attitudes, controlling for political party and treating experience as a UN delegate separately from other international organization experience. With just two exceptions (items 1 and 2) the Republican UN delegates show more positive change than the Democrats; but among Congressmen who had attended some other international meeting, Democrats show much more positive change than Republicans. This same pattern appears virtually without exception for each of the eight control variables.

124

If these figures reflect genuine differences, as we believe they do, they must surely mean that the shorter and more casual experience with international organizations tends to reinforce whatever points of reference the Congressman already has – his party, his occupation, his ideological orientation, his educational background, his constituency. Thus, a Congressman with a non-business background and an advanced academic degree who is young, Democratic, liberal, and speaks for a relatively high income, educated, urban constituency outside the South that has a high proportion of foreign stock, is likely to return from his international meeting with a somewhat more internationalist viewpoint. Members of Congress with points of reference less favorably disposed to multilateral cooperation, e.g., Republican, conservative, Southern – will be influenced less in an internationalist direction and may even become more negative toward international organization as a result of their experience.

On the other hand, the figures in Table 21 also indicate that the more extensive and intimate contact with multilateral diplomacy provided by the UN General Assembly provokes significant re-evaluation among most participants, regardless of their partisan, ideological, and constituency characteristics. The result is a partial convergence of viewpoints. The participants who are at first less favorably disposed (as judged by personal and constituency characteristics) achieve a greater appreciation of the UN; while those more favorable at the outset become only minimally more positive, and in some respects less positive, as UN limitations become apparent. Percentage agreement figures for both groups do not reach perfect convergence. On most control variables, the group more positive at first is still somewhat more favorable to multilateral cooperation after the period of UN service, That is, e.g., Democrats still appear a bit more internationalist across the range of questionnaire items than the Republicans; and members with high ADA ratings are consistently more internationalist than their more conservative brethren, notwithstanding their common experience at the United Nations.

*Content analysis and congressional attitudes: the research design\**

In addition to the survey data just analyzed, an attempt was made to transcend the limitations of the static group comparison by gathering attitudinal data on Congressmen at two points in time, before and after participation in international meetings. The vehicle chosen was content

\* This portion of the study is a revised version of an article by one of the authors, 'One Small Step for Functionalism: UN Participation and Congressional Attitude Change,' *International Organization,* Vol. 31, No. 3(Summer 1977), pp. 515-539.

analysis of speeches appearing in the *Congressional Record* before and after the Congressman's period of service as a UN delegate. The analysis includes 22 House members and 21 Senators who served as delegates from 1950 to 1971.[36]

This portion of the study pertains to the same central question that has guided the earlier research: does participation in an international agency induce attitudinal change in the individual participant? It is, however, designed to distinguish the cognitive from the affective dimension of participant attitudes and to explore each dimension separately.

A brief recapitulation of assumptions may be helpful. The hypothesis of attitudinal change, implicit in functionalist theory, is based on the assumption that participation brings greater understanding of the institution and its activities, and that this understanding leads to greater interest in the organization. Using the Kerr definition of cognitive change, the participant comes to know more about international organization, he views it in a different light, and it becomes more central to his beliefs.[37] Positive affect for the United Nations is also a likely outcome of participation.[38] More often than not, we assume, the participant will begin to adopt non-national viewpoints – or at least develop a broader concept of the national interest which takes into account the needs of other countries. To the extent that the participant finds the experience personally rewarding, he will tend to identify himself in some way with the work of the organization and, overall, gain a more positive impression of the United Nations and the work it is doing. These assumptions may not hold true for all participants; some delegates may have a positive experience, others negative. The data in fact show that all do not return with more favorable attitudes toward the United Nations. But if functionalist theory is to hold, such a change should commonly occur.[39] As previously observed, the United Nations General Assembly may be one of the less favorable forums in which to test functionalist theory. Political non-controversiality is supposed to be part of the setting in which the functionalist dynamic works best. Although the General Assembly deals with many issues, some of which are relatively non-controversial, all too often controversiality is its hallmark. If positive affect follows from experience as a General Assembly delegate, it should follow in a more typical functional setting.

The data used, unlike most previous studies, do not depend on responses to personal interview or mailed questionnaire. Instead they are derived from the analysis of speeches relating to the United Nations appearing in the *Congressional Record*. The Congressman is not required to assess his own attitudes; this is done by the analyst from an examination of the written materials. Examining the *Record* a year

126

before and a year after the time of UN assignment provides data for a pre and post test. A matched control group is provided by analyzing speeches in the *Congressional Record* during the third year preceding the time of service, for the same members of Congress. If significant differences appear in comparing the year after with the year before, but not in comparing the two prior years, a strong case is made that differences are due to the General Assembly experience.

Initially, two simple propositions were framed: 1) Members of Congress will tend to pay more attention to the United Nations after serving as delegates than before. 2) Members of Congress will tend to have more favorable attitudes toward the United Nations after serving as delegates than before. The first proposition relates to the cognitive attitudinal dimension, the second proposition to the affective.

The first proposition was operationalized by identifying 'attention' with frequency of reference to the United Nations. Thus, the measure is a simple count of the number of speeches in the *Congressional Record*. Each speech delivered in Congress (or at least represented as being delivered) by the Congressman was counted as a single item, regardless of length.

The second proposition, dealing with affective change, was operationalized by making judgments whether or not a statement in the *Record* is favorable to the United Nations. Research assistants were asked to read every speech in which a United Nations reference appeared, coding each paragraph bearing a reference to the UN, and also coding the speech as a whole, on a three-point scale: favorable, neutral, and unfavorable. The first rule was to 'use common sense' but additional detailed rules were provided in case of doubt. A reliability check was obtained by having four coders read a number of test paragraphs, which produced a paired agreement score of 83 %. In only 3 % of the cases were the paired ratings diametrically opposed, that is, one coder rating a paragraph 'favorable' while another rated it 'unfavorable'.[40]


*Findings on attitude change: cognition*

The evidence of attitude change following upon UN participation is very convincing. Although the evidence for cognitive change is somewhat stronger than for affective change, the comparison of before-and-after speech-making shows statistically significant differences along both dimensions.

The data do not show that all Congressmen serving as delegates to the UN General Assembly experienced the predicted change, only that the majority did. And no more was expected, for a number of reasons.

Table 22. Number of speeches about the UN by 43 congressmen before and after participation as UN delegates

| | Third Year Before UN Participation | First Year Before UN Participation | First Year After UN Participation |
|---|---|---|---|
| Number of Congressmen mentioning the UN in 0-1 speeches | 19 | 17 | 9 |
| Number of Congressmen mentioning the UN in 2 or more speeches | 24 | 26 | 34 |

In the first place, the method does not exclude the possibility of error in the process of gathering and coding the data. Some relevant items in the *Congressional Record* may have been missed, and the coding of speeches and other materials undoubtedly fell somewhat short of 100 % validity and reliability. Apart from the method used, both the number and the character of speeches about the United Nations are heavily affected by extrinsic events.[41] Crisis in the Middle East, for example, is likely to increase the volume of speech-making over a year in which there is no such crisis, and evaluations of the UN will undoubtedly be influenced by the special characteristics of the event. On the other hand, a relatively quiet year might bring a reduced level of speech-making.[42]

There is another equally basic reason for supposing that not all delegates would experience change in the predicted direction. The UN experience will not be uniform from year to year, and all individuals will not react to their experience in the same way. If functionalist theory is to hold, such change must be the dominant pattern. But this need not preclude the possibility that some persons will have a negative reaction, or be largely unaffected. Indeed, the dimensions of the experience vary substantially from one Congressman or Senator to another. As previously noted, some have moved their families to New York for the full session and attended meetings nearly every day, while others have shown up only for the first and last week of the session. To some extent, moreover, the attitude of the Permanent Representative who heads the U.S. Mission to the UN will determine how much Congressional delegates are encouraged to participate. Congressional delegates who share the President's political party affiliation may also receive more encouragement to participate than those who do not. Thus a variety of intervening conditions virtually guarantee differences in individual responses.

With this comment on the method and its underlying assumptions, we may now present the data bearing on attitude change. Table 22 classifies the 43 members of Congress with respect to number of speeches mentioning the UN in each of the three years for which data were gathered. The number of Congressmen making reference to the UN in two or more speeches is approximately the same for each of the years prior to service as a General Assembly delegate, 24 and 26 respectively; but the figure is substantially higher, 34, during the year after the UN experience. The average number of UN speeches for all 43 Congressmen increased from 3.7 during the third year before to 4.1 the first year before, and 6.0 the year after the UN experience. This indicates an increase in the average number of speeches for each two-year interval, but with a much larger increase occurring after the

9 – Beyond Functionalsim

*Table 23.* Speeches about the UN as a percentage of all speeches by 43 congressmen before and after participation as UN delegates

|  | Third Year Before UN Participation | First Year Before UN Participation | First Year After UN Partication |
|---|---|---|---|
| Number of Congressmen mentioning the UN in 0-5% of all speeches | 32 | 29 | 16 |
| Number of Congressmen mentioning the UN in over 5% of all speeches | 11 | 14 | 27 |

first-hand exposure to the United Nations. The small increase from the third to the first year before may be no more than a random variation, although it could also be interpreted as a propensity for members of the House and Senate to make remarks for the *Record* more frequently as they gained seniority in Congress.[43]

Attention measured by absolute numbers of speeches may be less revealing than the relative amount of attention paid to the UN by the Congressman. Table 23 illustrates this dimension by presenting speeches about the UN as a percentage of all speeches by each Congressman appearing in the *Congressional Record*.[44]

Again, the difference for the two 'before' years is small, but that between the years immediately before and after is substantial. Only 33% of the members of Congress mentioned the UN in more than 5 % of their speeches during the year before UN participation; in the year after, 63 % did so.[45] These data give strong support to the hypothesis that the UN experience significantly increased the attention paid by Congressmen to the United Nations. Table 24 provides a third measure of difference. The preceding table (Table 23) presents data on the number of Congressmen whose UN speeches were more or less than 5 % of all their speeches appearing in the *Record* during each of the three

*Table 24.* Change in number of UN speeches as a percentage of all speeches by 43 congressmen before and after participation as UN delegates

|  | Time Periods Compared | |
| --- | --- | --- |
|  | Third Year Before, First Year Before UN Participation | First Year Before, First Year After UN Participation |
| Number of Congressmen with higher % UN speeches in subsequent year | 20 | 31 |
| Number of Congressmen with no change in subsequent year | 3 | 3 |
| Number of Congressmen with lower % UN speeches in subsequent year | 20 | 9 |

Table 25. Ratings of speeches by congressmen as favorable, neutral, or unfavorable toward the United Nations

|  | Third Year Before UN Participation | First Year Before UN Participation | First Year After UN Participation |
|---|---|---|---|
| Number of Congressmen with speeches favorable to the UN | 19 | 19 | 34 |
| Number of Congressmen with speeches neutral to the UN | 9 | 13 | 4 |
| Number of Congressmen with speeches unfavorable to the UN | 4 | 3 | 1 |
|  | * N=32 | N=35 | N=39 |

* The N differs for each year because Congressmen who gave no speeches about the UN in a given year could not be rated on the scale.

sample years. By contrast, Table 24 gives the number of Congressmen who showed an increased, decreased, or unchanged proportion of UN speeches, without regard to the size of the percentage, in two sets of paired years. As in preceding tables, the before-and-after years are intended to show the impact of UN participation, while the two 'before' years serve as a control for comparison purposes. The comparison is striking. Increases and decreases are equal in number for the two years prior to the UN experience, but increased percentages far outnumber decreases following the UN experience.[46]

Although this portion of the study relies mainly upon content analysis, an effort was made to obtain corroborating evidence from members of Congress themselves. Of 26 former UN delegates still in Congress in 1974, ten answered our mailed survey calling for a response to the statement, 'I have paid more attention to the United Nations since serving as a UN delegate than I did before.' Possible responses ranged along a five-point scale from 'strongly agree' to 'strongly disagree.' Six of the ten respondents agreed, three strongly agreed, and one disagreed.[47] Even with discount for possible bias in response to the questionnaire, this evidence further substantiates the fact of cognitive change.

*Attitude change: affect*

In addition to the numerical count of speeches, each reference to the United Nations was also scored on a three-point scale for positive or negative evaluation of the United Nations. A score of 300 was assigned for a favorable reference, 200 for a neutral statement, and 100 for an unfavorable comment. Scores for each member of Congress were aggregated to obtain an average for all speeches and for speech paragraphs. This score is hereafter designated as a 'favorable-unfavorable' or 'F-U' score. Results of this content analysis for affect are presented in Tables 25 and 26.

Table 25 indicates that a majority of Congressmen who served as UN delegates had a favorable impression of the United Nations even before their UN experience. The number expressing favorable opinions sharply increased during the year after, however. Translating the figures to percentages, 59 % and 54 %, respectively, had average speech scores higher than 200 on the F-U scale during the two prior years as compared with 87 % during the year after.[48] On the F-U scale, the average Congressman's score was 230 for the year before UN participation and 252 for the year after. The probability that mean scores would be subject to chance variation of such magnitude is only one in a hundred.[49] These figures suggest that the United Nations experience

did, indeed, make a difference in Congressional affect toward the UN –
at least as expressed in speeches given during the year immediately
following.

Table 25 is a before-and-after comparison showing the number of
Congressmen in the sample who were favorable, neutral, or unfavorable toward the United Nations at three points in time. Table 26, by
contrast, shows the number of Congressmen who shifted from one
position on the F-U scale to another during each of the two-year
periods. For the two-year period prior to the UN participation, nearly
as many moved to a lower position (less favorable) on the scale as to a
higher position. During the two-year interval embracing the period of
UN service, the number moving upward on the scale (more favorable)

*Table 26.* Change in affect toward the UN as measured by speeches of
43 congressmen before and after participation as UN delegates

|  | Time Period Compared | |
| --- | --- | --- |
|  | Third Year Before, First Year Before UN Participation | First Year Before, First Year After UN Participation |
| Number of Congressmen more favorable to UN in sub- sequent year | 14 | 20 |
| Number of Congressmen with no change in subsequent year | 3 | 5 |
| Number of Congressmen less favorable to UN in subsequent year | 10 | 8 |
|  | N=27 | N=33 |

* The N differs for each comparison because Congressmen who gave no speeches about the
UN in a given year could not be rated and compared for that year.

exceeded those moving downward by two and a half times.[50] These data
also tend to confirm the proposition that participation leads to positive
affect.[51]

134

*Explaining the unpredicted cases*

The rationale for the functionalist hypothesis of attitude change has been examined earlier, including brief reference to some of its theoretical underpinnings in social-psychological writings. Whether or not the theory is adequate, the data derived from content analysis of Congressmen's speeches give support to the hypothesis. There nevertheless remains the question of why some participants changed in the predicted direction but others did not. A number of practical barriers to wholly accurate prediction were also canvassed in the preceding pages including possible instrument error, the impact of extrinsic events on speech-making, differing individual characteristics, and the shifting character of the UN experience. Most of these are not readily quantifiable for purposes of analysis, but a number of variables that could be quantified were employed in an attempt to explain the differences in attitudinal response to service as a UN delegate. They include constituency characteristics (education, income, degree of urbanization, and percentage of foreign stock) as well as the participant's party, chamber of Congress, age, education, geographical region, occupational background, year of service as a UN delgate, and ADA (Americans for Democratic Action) rating of Congressional voting records.

Most of these variables have modest correlations with absolute numbers of speeches and F-U scores, particularly for the year prior to UN service. A Congressman in this sample is likely to have a higher interest in the UN and a more favorable opinion of it if he is a liberal, well-educated Democrat from an urban constituency outside the South that has a relatively high percentage of first and second generation immigrants. If he had a business background prior to entering Congress, he will have a very low opinion of the UN before serving as a delegate but a relatively high one afterward.

None of the variables are very useful, however, in explaining directional differences in cognitive change – why some made more speeches about the UN after serving there but others did not. We believe that cognitive change induced by the UN experience accounts at least in part for those who spoke more; but the data offer no explanation for those who evidenced no increase in attention to the UN. This may be a defect of the rather crude measure of attention utilized, i.e., number of speeches on the UN appearing in the *Congressional Record*. Indeed, the content analysis data probably understate the extent of cognitive change. By our most favorable measure of attention – the number of speeches about the UN as a percentage of all speeches – 72 % show an increase in the year subsequent to UN service as compared with the prior year. But in response to the mailed questionnaire, nine of ten former delegates indicate that they paid more attention to the UN since

*Table 27.* Regional differences in the effects of UN participation upon congressional affect toward the United Nations *

|  | Northeast | North Central | South | West |
|---|---|---|---|---|
| Number of Congressmen more favorable to UN after participation | 4 | 9 | 5 | 2 |
| Number of Congressmen with no change after participation | 4 | 1 | 0 | 0 |
| Number of Congressmen less favorable to UN after participation | 1 | 2 | 2 | 3 |

* States are grouped in standard U.S. Census regions.

serving there; and the tenth explained that his drop in attention was simply the result of a changed committee assignment.

If the predictor variables have little to say about cognitive change, they do shed light on the question of affective change. The indicators that correlate positively with prior year F-U scores tend to have a negative association with favorable change in affect. Fewer Democrats, liberals, and Congressmen from urban centers experience positive change in attitude toward the UN than do Republicans, conservatives and Congressmen from less urban constituencies. This inverted relationship is further illustrated in Tables 27 and 28, where geographic region and former occupation are cross-tabulated with change in affect.[52] More change in the predicted direction is found among members of Congress from the South and North Central regions than from the West and Northeast. Likewise, among occupational groups, those with a business background prior to their election to Congress are more likely than other occupational groups to experience an attitudinal change favorable to the UN. Tables 29 and 30 point to the same negative relationship between favorable change and prior year F-U scores: the Congressmen most prone to change have the lowest F-U scores prior to attending the UN.

The repeated occurrence of such an associational pattern suggests that the best predictor of change is not party or ADA rating, or any of the other background or constituency variables, but rather the magnitude of the prior year F-U score. The significance of this fact is confirmed by Table 31, which shows how generalized is the relationship between direction of change and prior year F-U scores. With only a few exceptions, Congressmen with scores of 250 or below for the prior year have a higher score the year after UN service; and those with prior year scores above 250 generally have lower scores the year after. Taking as a hypothesis that scores above 250 will be lower in a subsequent year and scores under 251 will be higher, directionality of change from the year before to the year after is predicted correctly in 26 of 33 cases in Table 31, or 79 % of the time.[53]

This strong relationship between directionality of change and the magnitude of prior year F-U scores might support a theory of regression, that is, the experimentally observed 'tendency for individuals with extreme scores at one time to be less extreme at the next, independent of any causally relevant variables.'[54] This is negated, however, by the evidence presented earlier that more Congressmen regard the UN favorably after serving as delegates and that the mean difference between before-and-after scores is great enough to be statistically significant. Moreover, if the base year were determinative, one should be able to predict from a subsequent to a prior year just as readily as from prior years to subsequent years. In fact, however, when the subsequent year is taken as the base year and the regression hypothesis is used to predict changes from that year to prior years, the relationship is much weaker. The hypothesis predicts correctly in reverse only 58 % of the cases for the first year prior to UN participation (as compared with 79 % when prediction runs in the normal direction).

The most plausible interpretation of this data is to treat directionality of change as a matter of convergence toward a mean value as a result of the UN experience.[55] Bauer, Pool and Keller witnessed a similar convergence toward a common norm in their study of the effects of travel upon the attitudes of American businessmen toward protectionism and free trade. In explaining why those 'who travel extensively come to resemble each other', they saw the experience as 'forcing the traveler into a new role by orienting him to a new reference group.'

The traveler no longer confined his judgments as narrowly to the needs of local and particularized interests, rather he adopted attitudes representing the 'general interest'. That part of him which identified with the specific needs of firm X in place Y was reduced in favor of that part of him which identified with the broad needs of American business in the entire nation.[56]

*Table 28.* Occupational differences in the effects of UN participation upon congressional affect toward the United Nations

|  | Law | Business | Education | Journalism | Other |
|---|---|---|---|---|---|
| Number of Congressmen more favorable to UN after participation | 8 | 4 | 3 | 2 | 3 |
| Number of Congressmen with no change after participation | 3 | 0 | 1 | 1 | 0 |
| Number of Congressmen less favorable to UN after participation | 5 | 0 | 3 | 0 | 0 |

*Table 29.* Regional differences in speech F-U scores, before and after UN service

|  | Average F-U Scores | | | |
|---|---|---|---|---|
|  | Northeast | North Central | South | West |
| First year before | 233 | 224 | 218 | 258 |
| Year after | 253 | 257 | 237 | 254 |

Such a role concept may be applicable to the experience of Congressional delegates to the United Nations.

Convergence in the present case may also be, at least in part, a product of expectations. Congressmen who expect little of the UN as reflected in an initial low opinion of the world organization, are pleased to discover it is not as bad or useless as they thought. Those who approach the UN with a very high opinion of its potentiality see a little of the luster rubbed off as they come in touch with reality. This conforms with Alger's observation that the delegates he interviewed gained a more accurate and sophisticated, if not necessarily more favorable, view of the United Nations as a result of their experience there.[57] We can feel quite comfortable with this interpretation, since the theory of a leveling of expectations upon exposure to reality conforms not only to the evidence but to common sense as well. From the functionalist viewpoint, the fact that the leveling occurs at a higher notch on the F-U scale gives some grounds for optimism about the future of international cooperation.

It is noteworthy that Karns, who draws from the same population as the present study and also used a before-and-after measurement technique, finds rather similar kinds of attitude change. His data show a slight overall tendency toward greater internationalism, along with a much more pronounced tendency toward convergence – isolationists becoming less isolationist and internationalists becoming less internationalist. As we have noted, he explains this convergence in terms of cognitive consistency theory in which the significant element is the 'psychological tension or pressure' produced by 'involvement in new situations' which 'may be relieved by a change in attitude'.[58]

There is room for difference of opinion whether the observed convergence in the present case is best explained by theories of cognitive

*Table 30.* Occupational background differences in speech F-U scores, before and after UN service

| | Average F-U Scores | | | | |
|---|---|---|---|---|---|
| | Law | Business | Education | Journalism | Other |
| First year before | 233 | 198 | 243 | 217 | 234 |
| Year after | 246 | 270 | 242 | 243 | 277 |

consistency as elaborated in the Karns study, by the new role and new reference group orientation suggested by the study of traveling businessmen, or as a case of expectations modified by contact with reality. Modified expectations may well be regarded as the result of striving for cognitive consistency. In any event the fact of attitudinal convergence appears to be a common outcome when groups of people are exposed to similar kinds of transnational experience. Convergence undoubtedly helps account for some of the Congressmen in our study at the higher end of the scale who failed to show attitude change in the predicted direction.

Karns' success in relating attitude change to domestic legislative reference groups within the context of cognitive consistency theory[59] suggests that this avenue also might be pursued as a means of further explaining our findings. The content analysis data, however, do not permit an adequate test of the proposition that the UN experience will cause Democrats and liberals to show more positive affect (or, if highly favorable at the outset, less negative affect) than Republicans and conservatives. When the delegates are grouped by party, ADA rating, and internationalism-isolationism as determined by content analysis scores, the results are mixed. More often than not the direction and relative magnitude of change in affect are as predicted by the theory. But not all of the data fit this mold, and none of the differences are statistically significant.

This may mean that the UN experience is of such duration and impact that, at least for the first year thereafter, the attitudes acquired are resistant to psychological tensions generated by decreased cognitive consistency with domestic legislative reference groups.[60] Such a conclusion is consonant with the survey finding that UN experience is associated with a pronounced convergence effect. Logically, if the

Table 31. Directional change in F-U scores as related to magnitude of F-U scores before and after UN service

| | Magnitude of F-U Score in Prior Year | | | | |
|---|---|---|---|---|---|
| | Under 200 | 200 | 201-250 | 251-299 | 300 |
| Number of Congressmen more favorable to UN in subsequent year | 3 | 9 | 8 | 0 | 0 |
| Number of Congressmen with no change in subsequent year | 0 | 2 | 2 | 0 | 1 |
| Number of Congressmen less favorable to UN in subsequent year | 0 | 1 | 1 | 3 | 3 |

convergence is strong enough, it will mute the impact of domestic reference groups. The thrust of the convergence hypothesis is that persons at either extreme of the favorable-unfavorable continuum will become less extreme through UN participation. Conversely, the legislative reference group hypothesis supports the inference that persons at the extremes are likely to stay there. The reason is the striving for cognitive consistency with reference groups. Liberal Democrats at the positive pole, for example, or conservative Republicans at the negative, could make no substantial shift toward the center without creating dissonance with signals generated by their respective reference groups. In such a situation, a strong convergence tendency would certainly dampen the hypothesized effect of reference groups.

On the other hand, the survey findings for Congressmen who attended international meetings other than the UN General Assembly are quite consistent with the hypothesis that attitude change is related to domestic legislative reference groups. On the basis of extrapolation from static group comparisons, Democrats and liberals do tend to show more positive affect than Republicans and conservatives as a result of attending such meetings. This suggests that the demands of cognitive consistency reinforce the influence of reference groups when the international experience is relatively brief and casual. But when the participant is confronted with the more involved and compelling experience often associated with the role of UN General Assembly delegate, cognitive consistency may require reorientation of past beliefs to square with present perceptions of reality, even at the cost of dissonance with respect to existing reference groups.

*Congressional attitudes: conclusions*

The functionalist dynamic is supposed to work best with 'non-political' actors, a characterization more easily identified with the bureaucratic expert or technician than with national legislators. Yet our data on members of Congress conform more closely to functionalist premises than the data on appointed officials.

Content analysis of speeches before and after UN service offers compelling evidence of *cognitive* attitudinal change, reflected in greater attention paid to the United Nations; and there is convincing, if less overwhelming, evidence of increased positive *affect* toward the UN among a majority of Congressional participants. The Congressional survey data, more directly comparable with information on appointed officials, show Congressmen who have attended international meetings other than the UN to be more favorable to multilateral cooperation on all questions and all dimensions than their colleagues without such

142

international experience. The bureaucrats with international organization experience, we may recall, are more favorable to multilateral cooperation along the general UN evaluation and international cooperation dimensions, but less favorable than others on the action commitment items and definitely more negative with respect to sovereignty transfer. There is some evidence that the more favorable responses of Congressional participants is partially attributable to an element of self-selection by Congressmen already somewhat favorably inclined to the idea of international cooperation. But the data attest that experience has a positive impact on attitudes independent of the self-selection factor. Responses of Congressmen who have served as UN delegates tend to follow more closely the pattern of the appointed officials.

The two portions of the Congressional study – content analysis and survey research – dovetail nicely with respect to the correlates of attitude and attitude change. In both sets of data, high affect is associated with the indicators generally found in the literature to be related to internationalist attitudes among Congressmen. That is, the typical internationalist is likely to be liberal, Democratic, well-educated, urban, non-Southern, etc; and these variables are associated with support for multilateral cooperation by Congressmen in our sample.

The content analysis and survey responses also provide complementary explanations of differential attitude change. Both data sets reveal a pattern of attitudinal convergence among Congressmen who serve as General Assembly delegates. Those initially most enthusiastic have their views tempered by a touch of realism; those initially very negative acquire a greater appreciation of the United Nations. This is to be contrasted with evidence of attitude change in Congressmen who attend meetings other than the UN General Assembly, where, as we have observed, pre-existing views are reinforced and often made more extreme. Taken together, these findings suggest that a brief experience with international organizations tends to reinforce existing attitudes, while extensive experience leads to basic restructuring and moderation of extreme views.


*Attitude change and the functionalist premise*
Our findings about American public officials' attitudes toward multilateral cooperation have been set forth in great detail above, and recapitulation is not appropriate here. Although the analysis provides some support for functionalist assumptions about learning and attitude change, it leads inescapably to the conclusion that the relationship

between participation and positive affect is complex and conditional. The implications of these findings for functionalist theory will be explored in a final chapter. First, however, we must determine to what extent the Norwegian and American studies point in the same direction.

# V. Norway and the United States: A Comparison

The preceding two chapters have examined a number of functionalist hypotheses in the light of data drawn, respectively, from Norway and the United States. In this chapter we shall compare the findings of the two surveys.[1] This should provide a broader basis for assessing the validity of the hypotheses and help us to draw more general conclusions about the viability of the functionalist mode of thought.

## The Basis for Comparison

In selecting respondents for the survey, an effort was made to identify officials holding comparable positions within the governments of Norway and the United States, and having approximately the same range of experience with international organizations. On the whole this objective was achieved. Nevertheless, there are differences in the circumstances and background characteristics of the two national groups that could significantly affect attitudes. Some observations on the background characteristics of the two samples might therefore be appropriate before turning to the data analysis.

First of all, we are comparing civil servants and legislators representing quite dissimilar political settings. Besides differences attributable to political culture and domestic political structures, Norway and the United States occupy strikingly different positions internationally. Although both nations are anchored in the Western tradition of democratic politics, and have formed numerous long-standing bilateral bonds in a variety of fields, they nevertheless differ substantially in their relationship to and influence on international affairs, including activities in international organizations.

The United States is a major world power with a tradition of global influence – or even dominance – in many fields. In contrast, Norway is a small nation with a very limited ability to mark the course of international cooperation. Two such dissimilar national units necessarily will differ in their reasons for being engaged in ventures of multilateral cooperation. And, if national stakes differ substantially, one may reasonably expect that their representatives in international fora will not experience altogether the same sort of functional learning.

145

A second source of difference derives from the specific composition of the two samples. Members of the Storting and the Congress are comparable in that both represent the national legislative body of their countries. Yet they come from rather different political systems. Generally speaking Norwegian legislators' views on political issues, including questions of multilateral cooperation, are more bound to stated party positions than normally is the case for U.S. legislators. Furthermore, there are differences as to the general priority given to multilateral cooperation within legislative circles in the two nations – rather high in Norway, while only moderate in the United States.[2] The sheer difference in the number of UN-delegates from the two national legislatures is a manifestation of this.

The two groups of civil servants hold somewhat more comparable positions within their respective political systems. Yet there are significant differences in the sample compositions. The Norway group consists of employees in three government departments involved with a range of international organization activities well above the average for Norwegian departments. In contrast the United States sample is composed of officials from a broad cross-section of government agencies.[3]

A third, possibly less important, area of distinction between the two national groups relates to their personal background characteristics. This area is perhaps less important in explaining attitude differences because most background characteristics are quite comparable. With respect to the civil servants' professional rank, 91 % of the United States sample are at GS12 or above, while 89 % of the Norway respondents fall within the equivalent grade level. Both samples consist of approximately 10 % women. The average age for United States respondents is 47 compared with 43 for the Norway group. As for educational background, a little over 60 % of each group have earned degrees above the Bachelor level. In both samples about one-third of the respondents report having lived in a developing country.

Differences in the legislators' personal background are more pronounced, as the following figures indicate:

|  | Education above B.A. Level | White Collar Background | Average Age |
|---|---|---|---|
| Norway | 50% | 65% | 49 |
| United States | 68% | 99% | 51 |

146

Although age is similar, the United States legislators have more formal education and are almost exclusively from white collar business and professional backgrounds. The working class element that makes up a substantial portion of the Storting, particularly among Socialist members, is almost entirely absent from our sample of the U.S. Congress. Recruitment procedures may also result in selection of legislative delegates with somewhat different backgrounds. Members of the U.S. House and Senate are chosen almost exclusively from the House Committee on International Relations and the Senate Foreign Relations Committee. In the Storting all legislative committees are represented by the selection process.

A fourth source of difference relates to the type of international organization experience. Norwegian respondents, both civil servants and parliamentarians, are for obvious reasons more engaged in European regional organizations than their American counterparts. Much of their reaction to multilateral cooperation will be based on that experience. Even for those who attend meetings of the United Nations the nature of the experience may differ. Parliamentary delegates from Norway serve only six weeks at the UN General Assembly, but during that time devote little or no time to legislative matters in the Storting. United States delegates are assigned to a full twelve-week Assembly session, but some continue with a high level of activity in Congress or in their home constituencies. In one significant respect, at least, the UN experience also has differing implications for civil servants from the two countries. Responses from members of the Norwegian UN mission reflect a belief that a UN assignment enhances their careers within the Norwegian civil service, while a similar sentiment is much less common among officials in the United States Mission to the UN.[4]

These differences in the personal and situational characteristics of the two samples will be used as interpretive aids in the comparative analysis of Norwegian and American attitudes which follows.


## Civil Servants' Attitudes Toward the UN

Although not directly relevant to specific functionalist hypotheses, a comparison of absolute agreement scores for the two survey groups provides a useful starting point. The first pairing in Table 1, comparing attitudes for all respondents in the two national surveys, reflects a clear difference in national preferences. Norwegian officials are distinctly more favorable to multilateral cooperation than their United States colleagues. Exceptions to this pattern appear only on Items 1 and 6.

In the second and third pairings this attitudinal difference becomes even more pronounced. Indeed, the attitude scores in the third pairing

*Table 1.* Comparison of percentage agreement with questionnaire items for three paired groups of Norway and United States respondents

| Questionnaire Item | All Respondents | | Foreign Affairs Personnel | | UN Mission Personnel | |
|---|---|---|---|---|---|---|
| | Norway | U.S. | Norway | U.S. | Norway | U.S. |
| | % | % | % | % | % | % |
| 1. UN promotes peace | 81.0 | 87.2 | 85.4 | 84.4 | 94.7 | 82.6 |
| 2. UN is cornerstone for Norway/important to U.S. | 69.6 | 58.1 | 71.1 | 67.1 | 78.9 | 68.2 |
| 3. Strengthening UN is good for Norway/U.S. | 69.8 | 39.5 | 66.0 | 38.2 | 73.7 | 34.8 |
| 4. Norway should be more involved in UN/U.S. use more | 71.7 | 51.1 | 70.1 | 52.6 | 79.0 | 43.5 |
| 5. Increase UN financial resources | 76.8 | 64.8 | 82.3 | 59.7 | 89.5 | 56.5 |
| 6. Channel more foreign aid through UN | 30.8 | 44.6 | 34.4 | 46.8 | 57.9 | 34.8 |
| 7. Grant trade preferences | 73.9 | 63.3 | 65.0 | 59.7 | 73.7 | 47.8 |
| 8. Give UN more authority to enforce rules | 68.7 | 52.1 | 60.0 | 26.0 | 50.0 | 21.7 |
| | N=233 | N=449 | N=96 | N=77 | N=19 | N=23 |

NOTE: Italics have been used for emphasis to show the higher score of each pair. Only those items that were similar in the two questionnaires have been included in this comparison table.

(UN mission personnel groups) show substantially greater enthusiasm among the Norway respondents on all issue dimensions. Viewing the data in Table 1 as a whole, the clearest attitudinal differences appear on the action-commitment statements (Items 4-7). Worth noting also is the fact that the Norway respondents express much greater willingness than the United States respondents to increase the authority of the UN (Item 8). From these comparisons we conclude that Norwegian civil servants are more willing to support a great variety of multilateral ventures than their United States counterparts.

Differences in sample composition might explain the observed attitudinal differences when all respondents are compared, because the Norway sample does include a higher proportion of persons with extensive international organization experience. This is not true of the second and third pairings, however, where the attitudinal differences are still greater. A more likely explanation, therefore, would appear to be differences in the two nations' general interest in and expectations from increased international commitments. The Norway respondents may simply feel that their nation has more to gain from a stepped-up level of UN involvement – Norway being a much smaller and less influential power, with fewer options than the United States. In contrast, United States officials may see their interests best served by relatively greater reliance on multilateral and bilateral relations outside the UN framework. There is also the possibility that the generally higher popular esteem in which Norwegians hold the UN is reflected in the civil servants' attitudes toward the Organization.[5] The oft noted United States 'crisis of confidence' in the United Nations, which is related to the decline of U.S. influence in the Organization, undoubtedly has its impact among bureaucrats as well as Congress and the U.S. public. Norway, never having played the role of leader of a winning coalition in the UN, should not be as subject to feelings of disillusionment at the loss of Western control there.

## General evaluation of the UN

Questionnaire Items 1-3 in Table 2 probe what we have previously classified as 'Type 1' attitudes, that is, the respondents' general evaluation of the UN. Rank order correlations (Kendall tau beta) for both survey groups give support to hypothesis 1. Although only three of the twelve coefficients are statistically significant, they all point in the predicted direction, suggesting that increased experience with international organizations does indeed promote more favorable evaluation of the United Nations. While the attitude change is slightly greater for the Norway officials on Item 1 and 3, the change is considerably

*Table 2.* Kendall tau b for questionnaire responses associated with attendance at international meetings and work time devoted to international organization affairs in Norway and the United States

| Questionnaire Item | Attending IO Meeting | | Working with IO Affairs | |
|---|---|---|---|---|
| | Norway | United States | Norway | United States |
| 1. UN promotes peace | .099* | .052 | .075 | .043 |
| 2. UN is cornerstone for Norway / UN is important to U.S. | .023 | .151* | .060 | .101* |
| 3. Strengthening UN is good for Norway/U.S. | .058 | .020 | .060 | .009 |
| 4. Norway should be more involved in UN / U.S. should use UN more | .037 | -.044 | .137* | -.003 |
| 5. Increase UN financial resources | .219* | -.110* | .119* | -.062 |
| 6. Channel more foreign aid through UN | .093** | -.088* | .124* | -.019 |
| 7. Grant trade preferences | .054 | .017 | .080 | .121* |
| 8. Give UN more authority to enforce rules | -.057 | -.149* | -.072 | -.114* |
| | N=233 | N=449 | N=233 | N=449 |

\* Significant at .01
\*\* Significant at .05

NOTE: Italics have been used for emphasis to show the higher (or least negative) coefficient of each pair. Only those items that were similar in the two question-naires have been included in this comparison table.

greater for the United States officials on Item 2. A possible reason for the more modest change of attitude among Norway respondents on Item 2 may be differences in wording, the cornerstone notion implying a more fundamental relationship to the UN than merely 'being of importance' (the U.S. wording).

## Action-commitment attitudes

Items 4-7 (Table 2) present comparative data bearing on hypothesis 2, which postulates increased propensity to favor further multilateral cooperation as a consequence of experience with international organization. Retaining the distinction made in chapters 3 and 4, separating action-commitment attitudes into two dimensions, the data support the hypothesis with respect to the international cooperation dimension (Item 7). On the second dimension – action commitment to the UN – the Norway data support the hypothesis while the United States data contradict it. Again, the best explanation of this divergence is probably the difference in national roles. Throughout the history of the UN the United States has been the major benefactor of that Organization – projecting herself as the vanguard of a free world and promoter of peace. Norway's past political and economic input into the UN, although relatively large, has been based on less ambitious motives, thus resulting in less frustration with the turn of events inside the Manhattan skyscraper in recent years. Given these role differences, the Norway respondents may have more reason than the United States officials to perceive the UN as a useful vehicle for the promotion of further multilateral cooperation.

## Sovereignty transfers

If responses to the action-commitment items are a mixed bag, the sovereignty transfer dimension (Item 8) suffers from no such ambiguity. The more experienced the respondent, the less likely is he to support increased UN authority. This is quite contrary to the functionalist notion that experience with international organization promotes across-the-board favorable attitudes. But all of the evidence from both countries supports this conclusion and, for the U.S. respondents, the relationships with both measures of experience are significant at the .001 level.

Responses to a questionnaire item dealing with mini-state domination of the UN, not included in the tables, clearly suggest that both Norway and United States officials see the small countries' collective influence on the Organization as a major reason for not increasing its authority.

151

The survey data, supplemented by personal interviews, indicate, however, that concern about hostile majorities in the UN is more pronounced in the United States than in Norway. This again is not surprising in view of the position of influence previously enjoyed by the United States. The attitudinal difference between the two national groupings may also mean that it is 'harder' for a major world power to relinquish sovereignty to an international body than for a small power to do so.

## The effect of previous experience

Data presented in Table 3 tend to support the hypothesis that experience with international organizations in a previous job assignment will produce more favorable attitudes. Twelve of the 16 associations point in the predicted direction. The data pattern is much like that observed

*Table 3.* Kendall tau b for Norway and United States government officials' questionnaire responses related to previous and current experience with international organization activities

| Questionnaire Item | Norway | United States |
|---|---|---|
| | Tau B | Tau B |
| 1. UN promotes peace | .089 | *.110* |
| 2. UN is cornerstone for Norway UN is important to U.S. | .090 | *.208** |
| 3. Strengthening UN is good for Norway/U.S. | .032 | *.098* |
| 4. Norway should be more involved in UN U.S. should use UN more | *.210** | .040 |
| 5. Increase UN financial resources | *.171*** | -.100 |
| 6. Channel more foreign aid through UN | *.158*** | -.022 |
| 7. Grant trade preferences | .085 | *.128*** |
| 8. Give UN more authority to enforce rules | *-.121* | -.185* |
| | N=84 | N=142 |

\* Significant at .01
\*\* Significant at .05

NOTE: Italics have been used for emphasis to show the higher (or least negative) coefficient of each pair. Only those items that were similar in the two questionnaires have been included in this comparison table.

above, except that associations with past experience are consistently stronger for the United States responses on the general evaluation dimension (Items 1-3). The overall positive relationship should not, however, obscure the fact that the correlation coefficients are negative for U.S. responses on two of the three action-commitment items (Items 5-6) and, indeed, the two involving the most specific commitments.

### The domestic organizational context

Hypothesis 5 postulates that officials in governmental units having extensive dealings with international organizations will become more supportive of multilateral cooperation than officials in other agencies. To test this proposition we undertook both a static and a dynamic comparison of attitudes within each of the two sets of data, reaching virtually identical conclusions: Job assignment in a unit having a broad range of international organization contacts is by itself not likely to give rise to favorable attitudes (cf. our static comparison). However, being located in such a unit appears to exert a booster effect upon attitude change for those whose work assignment includes dealings with international organizations (cf. our dynamic comparison). To rephrase our converging findings: working in a domestic organizational unit which has extensive international organization contacts tends to heighten the positive attitudinal impact of experience but has no positive effect on the attitudes of persons within the unit whose job assignments are unrelated to international organizations.

### Past and present incumbents

Our sixth hypothesis predicts that present incumbents in governmental units having contacts with international agencies will be more prone to favor multilateral cooperation than will former incumbents. By comparing attitudes of former and present members of the respective UN missions – for the United States including former and present members of the State Department IO Bureau – we discover overall support for the prediction. Our conclusion that the relative immediacy of the experience results in attitudinal differences, rests on the assumption that the groups of past and present incumbents are equally sophisticated and knowledgeable concerning the activities of the UN and related organizations.

### Correlates of officials' attitudes

For both the Norway and the United States survey a number of respondent attributes were examined as potential correlates of attitudes toward the UN. A general common finding is that the previously identified experience-attitude relationships are largely independent of the attributes. Some attitudinal variations across the respondents' governmental unit affiliations were discovered, however. These variations are most likely due to differences in departmental goals, as well as to differences in the kind and extent of the individual's experience with international organizations.

Examining the age factor as a possible correlate of attitudes yielded a common pattern. The older respondents in both surveys agree most strongly with the general evaluation statements, while the younger respondents agree most strongly with the action-commitment statements. The youth factor thus appears to promote greater recognition of a need for extended action commitment, even though this concern does not translate into greater willingness to transfer sovereignty to the UN.[6] The reasons why the youth factor has a booster effect on action-commitment attitudes, but not on general evaluation attitudes, are not altogether obvious. Perhaps it is because their international organization experience is rooted in a more recent time context than their older colleagues'. With the reduced political standing of the UN in recent years, linked with the increased need for cooperative action around the world, the younger generation of civil servants are less impressed with the UN generally, but feel greater need to use and strengthen the Organization as a means of international cooperation. Much the same pattern emerges when formal education serves as a correlate, which is not surprising given substantial intercorrelation between youth and high levels of education.

When respondents are grouped on the basis of past residence/nonresidence in a less developed country, generally those with LDC experience have the highest agreement scores – except on the question of sovereignty transfer where the reverse relationship exists. The effect of direct exposure to development problems is particularly evident in the Norway officials' responses. Perhaps the reason is that Norway herself is a small nation with national impoverishment being a relatively recent historical fact. Officials from such a nation may find it easier to empathize with the problems of the Third World than officials from industrialized nations, such as the United States, with a past less plagued by material scarcities.

*Summary of civil servants' attitudes*

On the whole both the Norway and the United States survey data indicate that experience with international organizations does affect

154

the way in which government officials regard the United Nations. The generally low correlation coefficients discovered in both data sets show that the sheer magnitude of experience explains only a small part of the attitudinal variances. However, tests of statistical significance and directional consistency across a great number of different respondent groupings indicate that the relationships nevertheless are real.

The underlying assumption for our joint investigation was that increasing experience with international organizations would be positively associated with our three originally conceived dimensions of multilateral cooperation: favorable general evaluation, action commitment to further acts of cooperation, and willingness to transfer sovereignty. Evidence from both surveys negate the functionalist idea of a simple linear relationship between international organization experience and the development of positive attitudes along these dimensions. Rather, four dimensions emerged from our analyses, not all of them showing a positive attitude-experience relationship. By arraying the four dimensions on the basis of the average of correlation coefficients from the two sets of findings, the following comparative picture emerges:

FIGURE 1

Dimensions of Cooperation

|  | International Cooperation | General Evaluation of UN | Action Commitment to UN | Transfer of Sovereignty |
|---|---|---|---|---|
| Norway | + | + | + + | − |
| United States | + + | + | − | − − |

As shown in Figure 1, experience with international organization activities correlates with favorable attitudes toward international cooperation and toward positive general evaluation of the UN. While the correlations point in opposite directions concerning action commitment to the UN, they converge in a negative direction on the issue of transferring sovereignty. Viewed comparatively the Norway findings give stronger support to the functionalist mode of thought than the United States findings. The data viewed as a whole provide evidence of attitude change adequate to support a gradual growth of multilateral cooperation. The evidence does not, however, sustain the vision of a foreseeable future in which a global government of interlocking func-

155

Table 4. Agreement scores for Norway and United States legislators' questionnaire responses related to attendance at UN General Assembly

| Questionnaire Item | Norway | | | United States | | |
|---|---|---|---|---|---|---|
| | Delegate | Non-Delegate | Tau B | Delegate | Non-Delegate | Tau B |
| | % Agreement | | | % Agreement | | |
| 1. UN promotes peace | 87.5 | 83.8 | .072 | 100.0 | 80.4 | .020 |
| 2. UN is cornerstone for Norway<br>UN is important to U.S. | 74.5 | 88.7 | -.012 | 100.00 | 74.8 | .065 |
| 3. Norway should be more involved in UN<br>U.S. should use UN more | 93.7 | 91.9 | .015 | 81.8 | 65.7 | .007 |
| 4. Increase UN finances | 89.6 | 83.3 | .113 | 63.6 | 72.7 | -.041 |
| 5. Channel more foreign aid through UN | 36.9 | 38.7 | -.007 | 54.5 | 45.6 | .077 |
| 6. Grant trade preferences | 87.5 | 85.5 | .087 | 80.0 | 57.8 | .142 |
| 7. Give UN more authority to enforce rules | 70.9 | 75.8 | -.049 | 54.5 | 60.4 | -.038 |
| | N=48 | N=62 | | N=11 | N=103 | |

NOTE: Only those items that were similar in the two questionnaires have been included in this comparison table.

tional units will emerge through the gradual accretion of little slices of sovereignty.

## Legislators' Attitudes Toward the UN

Table 4 compares findings from the surveys of national legislators in Norway and the United States. The legislator data parallel the civil servants' in their implications for functionalist theory. On general evaluation and action-commitment items the overall tendency supports the hypotheses, but on the sovereignty transfer item the relationship of experience to favorable attitudes is negative.[7] A similar parallel is found in the higher agreement levels of the Norway legislators over their United States colleagues on most of the action–commitment statements.

A comparison of legislators' agreement scores with civil servants' agreement scores throws a somewhat disconcerting light on the functionalist proposition that 'experts' are better carriers of functionalist values than political actors. On all our dimensions of multilateral cooperation, the legislators tend to score higher than the bureaucrats. A number of explanations are possible, all of them highly speculative. There may be something in the 'factor of politics' which promotes a stronger concern for cooperative involvement internationally than is the case for the 'factor of bureaucracy'. The former viewpoint may be rooted in a notion of responsible leadership and initiative not as prevalent in the more cautious bureaucratic mold of thinking. In the case of Norway the parliamentary respondents undoubtedly reflect the generally favorable attitudes toward the United Nations held by Norwegian political parties. The higher agreement scores of legislators may also be influenced by attitudes toward mailed questionnaires and the public relations impact of responding to them. The politicians who respond, in contrast to civil servants, may simply be trying harder to be 'agreeable'.

### Content analysis and self-assessment as learning indicators

The content analysis portion of the Congressional study offers ample evidence of *cognitive* attitudinal change, reflected in sharper attention paid to the UN. It also presents convincing evidence for greater positive *affect* toward the UN. Responses to the self-assessment questionnaire items presented to both groups of legislative UN-delegates converge with the content analysis data. Reactions to Items A and B in Table 5 clearly underscore the occurrence of cognitive learning, while the reactions to Item C – if less overwhelmingly – attest the occurrence of affective feedback from the legislators' experience with the UN.

*Table 5.* UN-delegated legislators' agreement with three questionnaire items concerning self-assessment of their delegation experience

| Questionnaire Item | Norway Legislators | United States Legislators |
|---|---|---|
| | %Agreement | |
| A. My stay at the UN increased my understanding of the organization | 100.0 | 100.0 |
| B. The UN-stay has led me to become more actively concerned with the UN and UN-related matters | 93.7 | 90.9 |
| C. I have developed a more positive attitude toward the UN and UN-related matters | 83.4 | 81.8 |
| | N=48 | N=11 |

*Correlates of legislators' attitudes*

As in the case of civil servants' attitudes, a number of respondent attributes were examined as possible correlates of legislators' attitudes toward the UN. For both Norway and the United States, high affect is correlated with attributes generally found in the relevant literature to be associated with internationalist attitudes among Storting members and Congressmen, respectively. In particular, youth and higher education, and to a lesser extent urban background, are associated with positive attitudes toward the United Nations. The legislators' propensity to support multilateral cooperation was also found to be related to political party affiliation – the Democratic Party in the United States and the non-socialist bloc in Norway. On the whole the correlates are stronger and more often statistically significant in the United States data.

It may be worthy of note that the relationships between attributes and questionnaire responses are neither as consistent nor as statistically significant when rank order correlations are run for former UN delegates only, rather than for all legislator respondents. This suggests that the effect of personal and constituency attributes tends to be overridden or muted by the impact of the participation experience.

*Legislators' attitudes: conclusion*

Our findings about legislators' attitudes toward the United Nations

158

have been presented in considerable detail in this and preceding chapters and further recapitulation here would be superflous. Two brief observations of a general nature may be in order, however. First, we take some comfort from the fact that both national surveys attest the appropriateness of including legislators in an empirical study of functionalism. Although most correlations are weak, our data indicate that political actors as well as bureaucratic-expert actors are subject to the functionalist learning process. A second observation is a counterweight to the first. For legislators as for civil servants, there is no simple linear relationship between participation and positive affect. On the sovereignty transfer dimension, indeed, experience tends to have the opposite effect. The legislator data thus confirm the conclusion that the nation-state will not soon succumb to a functionalist wave of the future.

# VI. Beyond Functionalism?

This study began with a broad overview of the theory of functionalism. It will conclude with a general assessment of the theory. Although special attention will be given to the concept of 'learning', which has been the focus of our research, we will attempt to evaluate the functionalist approach as a whole. What is its contribution as *prescription*, as *explanation*, as *prediction*, or as a general *paradigm* to organize thought and give direction to research in the international field? To address these questions will carry us well beyond any specific findings relating to attitude change. It will entail heavy reliance upon the insights of other writers as well as evidence gleaned from observation of trends within the international system. The resulting conclusions will necessarily be more speculative, intuitive and subjective than the conclusions hitherto derived from the closer, more focussed analysis of questionnaire data. We hope, nevertheless, that what is lost in precision will be more than offset by the gains in understanding resulting from the broader vision.

## Functionalism as Prescription

Of the four faces of functionalism, the prescriptive aspect is perhaps easiest to defend. In its most general form the functionalist prescription amounts to an advocacy of international cooperation, which few if any people oppose in principle. At this level of generality the case is self-evident. Cooperation should be institutionalized in areas of recognized need. If the need exists, surely the necessary cooperative acts should be undertaken. This is a rather simplistic statement of the case, but something like this line of reasoning lies at the heart of functionalism's appeal.

The functionalist approach advocates something more than cooperation in general, however. Specific functional areas of activity should be identified and organized separately as the need arises, each with sufficient autonomy and authority to carry out its assigned functions. The functional agencies should not merely *discuss* problems but *do* things for the community. The creation of working agencies, rather than just talk shops, is central to the prescription. Functionalism also suggests that the most difficult and controversial areas need not be tackled first. The secret of success is to concentrate on areas where the need for cooperation is manifestly great enough, and interests harmonious enough, to keep controversy at a relatively low level. With respect to organizational forms, the prescription remains flexible. Form is to be determined by function, that is, by the technical requirements of the situation. The very notion of function suggests that each area of activity will be treated on its own terms rather than being shaped to fit some preconceived constitutional blueprint. It also implies a preference for decentralized over centralized organization of international cooperation.

The functionalist prescription is more like a compass than a road map. Though lacking detailed signs and landmarks, it points a general direction that distinguishes it from other prescriptive orientations, such as that of the nationalist, the realist, or the world governmentalist. Functionalism would not be acceptable to the confirmed nationalist whose bias is toward national autonomy and self-sufficiency. The 'realist' who conceives of international relations primarily in terms of power distributions and power balances is also unlikely to be attracted to the functionalist prescription. A policy of enhancing national power is not necessarily incompatible with the spread of institutionalized cooperation: national power, in some respects, may be increased by cooperation with other states. Yet, ultimately, the game of power has a strong zero-sum bias, where one side's gain is the other side's loss, while the functional approach explicitly contemplates enhanced rewards for everyone. Moreover the two approaches involve different sets of values with regard to the nation state. The power game places great stress upon state goals, interests and capabilities. The functionalist prescription speaks to the needs of people, regardless of the political boundaries separating them, and presumes eventual erosion of the national barriers and loyalties that differentiate one state from another.

As for the world government orientation, functionalism has a bias against constitutional approaches to international organization, particularly those with a strong centralizing tendency. The world governmentalist, the constitutional federalist who seeks to apply his model at the regional or global level, would not be comfortable with the functionalist's piecemeal, organizationally diffuse approach to institutionalization. Both might – or might not – have the same end in view, but the means peculiar to each are philosophically incompatible with the other.

*Why functionalism?*

A defense of the functionalist prescription begins with the assertion that it fits the kind of world we live in. A technologically shrinking world constantly provides new opportunities to promote welfare and new challenges to avoid problems associated with the multiplication of human contacts. The growth of functional organization in the nineteenth century was largely a response to technologically induced change, and this in turn provided the basis for early functionalist theorizing about the international system. These conditions have been magnified in the present century. Technological change has come on with increasing rapidity, and the functional organization of international cooperation has proceeded apace. Given the imperatives of growing interdependence, all common sense supports the functionalist injunction to look for situations where appropriate international arrangements can resolve problems and promote welfare.

The case for functionalism becomes even more convincing when examined in relation to competing prescriptions. Consider, first, the alternative of maximizing national autonomy and self-sufficiency through domestic measures that insulate the state and its citizens from the effects of interdependence and make welfare as little contingent upon the cooperation of other states as possible. Efforts of the United States to achieve energy self-sufficiency represent one application of this approach. The crucial importance of energy to welfare and security, as well as the high controversy surrounding questions of its production and distribution, may make such a policy for the United States prudent and rational. Pursuing a policy of autonomy across a wide spectrum of international issues, however, is likely to impose substantial costs – less welfare and probably decreased capacity to avoid conflict and environmental deterioration. For any state the costs and benefits of international cooperation must be calculated on a case by case basis, but in a period of great and increasing interdependence the functionalist bias should result in a more rational policy for most countries. The pursuit of national autonomy appears more and more as a rear-guard action with shrinking options.

The case against a policy of autonomy is perhaps nowhere more unequivocally stated than in the 1975 Murphy Report on the Conduct of U.S. Foreign Policy:

> The most pervasive characteristic of international affairs in the next decades will be the growing interaction and tightening interdependence among the nations of the world. As the linkages between them multiply in number and in importance, even the largest nations will not be able to satisfy their basic requirements for material well being

162

through independent action. By the same token they will be unable to insulate their societies from the effects of external forces.

Domestic responsibility of governments will require those governments to work collaboratively with other states. This is the practical meaning of interdependence: on economic and technical issues, unable by independent action to meet national needs, governments will require accommodation with other societies to gain their own ends.[1]

A confirmed functionalist could not state the argument more persuasively.

If a policy of autonomy does not meet the requirements of global interdependence as well as the functionalist prescription, neither does a policy oriented toward enhancement of national power. This is particularly true when power is conceived, as has traditionally been the case, in military-security terms. Such a judgment does not rule out the importance of military power in many contexts, including U.S.-Soviet relations, the Middle East, and some aspects of every country's foreign relations. Nor does it imply that the state is about to wither away, either as an engine of domestic coercion or as the principal actor on the international scene. We see no substantial decline in the significance of national loyalties and political boundaries in the foreseeable future. Rather, the preference for functionalist over 'realist' prescriptions as a broad guide to policy is based on recognition that the world's business is conducted under conditions of interdependence which the realist model does not adequately take account of. States now share the international stage with non-state actors; no single issue – including military security – clearly dominates the global agenda; and force, in many situations, is an ineffective instrument of policy.[2]

A prescription for policy aimed at maximizing national power in the traditional sense is simply inappropriate under present world conditions. Military security, though still of great importance, can best be viewed as one of several issue or functional areas with which governments must be concerned. Cooperative international arrangements are possible in this as in any other functional area, but a national policy built around maximizing military power is ill-equipped to meet the challenge of other issue-areas. Functionalism calls attention to the increasing permeability of states and the growing communities of interest forged by transnational, transgovernmental, and intergovernmental ties cutting across state boundaries. Without deprecating the continuing significance of military power in some contexts, the functionalist prescription offers a conceptual and programmatic framework far better attuned to the complexity of present global relations than the realist prescription for the pursuit of national power.[3]

The case for functionalism versus world or regional federalism rests on different premises. Both prescriptions accept the reality of inter-dependence and both recognize the desirability of modifying the existing state system. Both may even have the same ultimate goal, if the functionalist's logical end-state – the global government of interlocking functional units – is the equivalent of the world government conceived by the federalists. There is a real question whether they are in fact the same, since one calls for centralization of governing power with some devolution to constituent geographical units, while the other preserves the principle of decentralization and autonomy of functional agencies. Whatever the degree of equivalence in outcomes, the difference in approach is a full 180 degrees. Federalists would launch a frontal assault upon the state, seeking a direct transfer of sovereignty from the state to a new global government. Functionalism, on the other hand, concentrates on meeting needs that serve state interests with the resulting transfer of small slices of sovereignty being incidental to the function performed. At one level, the difference is between feasibility and unfeasibility. Functional organizations continue to materialize, while no responsible stateman seriously believes voluntary global federation to be a realistic possibility. At another level, the choice is between activities that help build a world community as opposed to the creation of institutions that assume such a community already exists. At still a third level the difference is between centralized power, with all its potential risks for human liberty (where liberty still exists), and diffused power, where the penalty for abuse is inefficiency rather than loss of liberty. This is not the place for a detailed argument against centralized world government. But surely there is a compelling case for preferring a system of functional cooperation that already has proved workable above a prescription that appears unlikely of attainment, except possibly through coercive imposition, and which carries the substantial risks associated with centralization of power.[4]

Admittedly, the functionalist prescription is not long on details. It adjures us to identify specific needs, seek low controversiality, organize functions separately, create working (not just talking) agencies, endow them with 'sufficient' authority, let form follow function. Once the broad outlines have been drawn the formula peters out rather quickly. This leaves the practicing functionalist the task of adapting his own strategies to the specifics of each situation.[6] The flexibility of the approach is entirely self-conscious, not inadvertent, and reflects the functionalist's inherent pragmatism as well as his belief that the shifting international scene is too complex and varied to be captured in a detailed formula. Functionalists, obviously, have avoided what Falk calls 'the fallacy of premature specificity'. On balance, this is probably a strength rather than a weakness of the functionalist prescription, assuming the broad outline is sufficient to make the general direction clear.[7]

In thus presenting and defending the functionalist prescription, we have briefly outlined *what* the functionalist prescribes but have not detailed 'what for?' To some extent the 'what for' is implicit in the argument. The purpose is to satisfy human needs in specific functional areas where new opportunities and challenges have been evoked by technological change. Better world health, more effective communication, safer and better coordinated transportation, more rational trading systems, more effective diffusion of agricultural and industrial technologies, more balanced development – the list could be extended almost indefinitely. In these and other areas significant service is being performed by functional international organizations. This in itself is a vindication of the functionalist prescription and undoubtedly accounts in large part for the vigorous growth of the functionalist organizational network.

But, as we have earlier observed, functionalism is also advocated as a means of promoting world peace. Indeed, in the words of a sympathetic commentator, 'The prime prescriptive concern of functionalists is to eliminate war.'[8] Here the links between practice and purpose are vastly more tenuous. Groom, for example, from a recent study of East/West economic cooperation in Europe, concludes that conflict may in fact be diminished by creation of 'a working peace system'.[9] Susan Strange, on the other hand, observes that 'The high hopes of functionalism have been sadly disappointed,' and states flatly, 'The idea that economic cooperation will improve the chances of peace by defusing the causes of war . . . has been disproven by postwar history.'[10] The truth of the matter is obviously difficult to ascertain. The notion that functional cooperation promotes peace continues to have an *a priori* appeal and, given certain premises, has some justification on logical grounds. But the empirical evidence to prove or conclusively disprove is hard to come by. This leaves the question to a large extent in the realm of faith. Yet, the link between peace and the practice of functionalism clearly is an empirical question even if available data is inconclusive. We will explore the issue further in connection with a subsequent discussion of functionalist explanations of reality.

## Functionalism as Explanation and Prediction

Functionalism as explanation and prediction will be treated under a single heading. Analytically the two operations are distinct, and Sewell

165

found in his study of World Bank agencies that functionalist propositions which accurately predicted a number of general consequences
were inadequate to explain why the predicted consequence had occurred.[11] Nevertheless, the two are intimately related. Predictions are
generally premised on some explanatory theory, and the chief test of
any explanation is its capacity to predict. The following discussion will
emphasize functionalism as explanation but with the explicit assumption that the explanation, if adequate, may serve as the basis for
successful prediction.

The discussion of Mitrany's functionalism in Chapter I of this study
identified two broad lines of theoretical development. The first was
characterized as a 'rudimentary theory of institutional growth at the
international level.' The second asserted a linkage between
functionalist practice and world peace. These two themes will be
examined in order.


## Explanation of Institutional Growth

*Initiating the process*

The explanation of institutional growth begins with the same empirical
point of reference as the prescription: the perception of need for common action in some international problem area. Functionalist writers
say little about the process of need perception or what functional areas
are the likeliest candidates for institutionalization. Economic and social areas are of course considered riper for action than problems
centering around territorial disputes, sovereign prerogatives or military
security. This distinction, however, provides only the scantiest hint of
where the next growth spasm is likely to occur.

Low controversiality is offered as one variable supposed to distinguish prospectively successful attempts at institutionalization from less
successful ones, but, as Sewell points out, this has little precise opera-
tional meaning. In his interpretation of the literature, '. . . the functional is by definition the non-political, and thus is synonymous with
"non-controversial" or "technical" in terms of procedure, and
"economic" or "social" in its substantive aspect.'[12] If 'economic' is by
definition 'non-controversial', the term loses all common sense meaning, since economic issues give rise to some of the most heated international controversies and have often been associated with the outbreak
of armed conflict. Perhaps some sense could be retained for the concept
by equating low controversiality with the absence of strongly held,
irreconcilable views among the states concerned. It then becomes
almost a tautology, however, with little utility either for prediction or

explanation. The cause of understanding is not advanced much by saying agreement among states will occur in areas where it is easiest to agree. The tautological aspects might be mitigated if economic and social issues were admitted to be least controversial; but such an issue category would first have to be defined and, as noted above, the proposition is not wholly self-evident.

### Learning as a growth accelerator

To proceed with the explanation, once the creation of functional organizations has begun, a learning process sets in. One aspect of the process centers around the 'demonstration effect' by which a successful functionalist venture provides a model for application to new areas through expanded functions or the establishment of new organizations. This may be one of the strongest elements in the functionalist explanation of institutional growth, since the evidences of borrowing and adaptation are legion. Historically, the Rhine River Commission served as a model for the Danube Commission. Organizational pioneering in the International Telegraphic Union helped pave the way for the Universal Postal Union. In recent times the example of the European Community has inspired a host of less successful attempts at common markets in other parts of the world. There is probably no international organization created in the past century that is not in some way a product of its predecessors. The demonstration effect unquestionably has been an important dynamic element in the growth of international organization.

A second aspect of the learning process consists of individual attitude change. In discussing this process Mitrany indulges his usual proclivity for colorful but vague generalities. His references to the growth of a 'new conscience', 'common habits and interests', 'a collectivity of functional loyalties', and 'an international outlook and public opinion'[13] convey the fact of attitude change but do little to specify the conditions under which change might occur. Fortunately, subsequent research enables us to say something more on this aspect of the learning process, although many questions still remain.

Most studies of attitude change have dealt with national participants in multilateral decision-making processes. Very little has been said about relevant attitudes of secretariat officials or the general public, two other groups of considerable importance in the functionalist scheme. Functionalists have assumed that public opinion would rally behind the cause, once knowledge of the benefits of multilateral cooperation became widely diffused. As for international civil servants, they are among the experts and technicians so central to the functional thesis, the front-line workers in the working peace system.

167

With respect to the latter, we are aware of no systematic studies of attitude change, but the general literature on international secretariats indicates that their attitudes tend to be supportive.[14] This is due in part to vested interest, but it also is fed by idealism, the dynamics of personal involvement, and genuine belief that the organization is performing a useful service. In any given case these elements obtain in such varying mix as may be induced by individual experience with the nitty-gritty of functional cooperation.[15] For many individuals, support is directed mainly toward the goals of the organizational sub-unit in which the person is located. Some agencies are characterized by a high degree of sub-goal dominance, to the great dismay of the director or secretary-general.[16]

There is likewise little data available on public attitudes toward functional international organization. A few cross-national polls on the United Nations are available as are numerous surveys dealing with the European Community. The surveys generally have shown majority opinion supportive of both institutions. Even in the United States where, in recent years, most respondents have indicated that the UN is not doing a 'good job', support for continued U.S. membership has remained high, at about the 75 % mark.[17] European opinion has also been favorable to integration, if not wildly enthusiastic.[18] One careful student of the subject has characterized public opinion toward the community as creating a 'permissive consensus' with respect to further integration. That is,

There was a favorable prevailing attitude toward the subject, but it was generally of low salience as a political issue – leaving national decision-makers free to take steps favorable to integration if they wished but also leaving them a wide liberty of choice.[19]

The 'permissive consensus' that Inglehart found in Europe would probably describe the opinion of most national publics toward most other international organizations, to the extent that any opinion exists at all. If the European Community has been of low salience as a political issue, the United Nations surely is of lower salience, with most functional international organizations lower still. The 'international outlook and public opinion' that Mitrany foresaw may have emerged in the sense that publics will follow their leaders into a great deal of international involvement when the issues are of low political salience. As an active force for international cooperation, however, public opinion is largely non-existent.[20]

We are on somewhat firmer ground in dealing with the attitudes of national participants in the work of international organizations, because of the small but growing body of literature on the subject.[21] The fact of cognitive change is well substantiated. All of the studies show that participants gain greater awareness and a more sophisticated understanding of the multilateral process. Affective change also commonly occurs but not consistently in the direction predicted by functionalists. The studies that have attempted to identify different attitudinal dimensions indicate that affect is multi-dimensional and that experience with international organizations may engender positive affect along one dimension but negative along another. Our own findings show experience to be associated with positive affect toward the UN along a 'general evaluation' dimension and an 'international cooperation' dimension. Yet, experience is associated with negative affect along the 'action commitment' dimension for some groups in our sample, and for nearly all groups on the sovereignty transfer dimension.

These findings are enough to negate the notion of a direct relationship between experience with international organizations and the development of favorable attitudes. The consistently negative attitude change with respect to increased UN authority indicates clearly that participants regard international organizations as vehicles of cooperation, not as agencies for authoritative decision-making. The hopes of those who looked to a gradual relinquishment of national sovereignty in favor of international agencies find no sustenance in our data.

Increased contact may bring greater awareness of the need for international cooperation and perhaps new insights into its possibilities. Yet that same experience is likely to reinforce the preference for leaving authoritative decisions in the hands of the sovereign state. Mutual interest in the accomplishment of specific tasks voluntarily agreed upon by the participants gives legitimacy to cooperative institutions. But governmental or coercive institutions must rest on a broad base of shared values and mutual trust which participation in international organizations apparently does not generate. Instead, participation tends to bringe awareness that more member cooperation – not more institutional authority – is necessary to improved task performance, and that increased authority may only increase the potential for abuse by unfriendly majorities. The differential effect of experience upon these two dimensions of support for international organization may help explain why the very substantial growth of functional cooperation has seen no corresponding decrease in national attachments. Among national bureaucrats and legislators at least, familiarity with international agencies creates no disposition to relinquish even small slices of sovereignty.

The data presented in chapters 3-5, which relate primarily to the

United Nations, leave open the possibility that participation in more specifically functional organizations might engender greater support for those organizations. In fact, this appears not at all the case with respect to sovereignty transfer. In order to test this proposition, questionnaires were sent to a sample of government officials in the United States Departments of Agriculture, Treasury, and Health, Education and Welfare in the summer and fall of 1976. The three departments were asked, respectively, about the Food and Agriculture Organization, the International Monetary Fund, and the World Health Organization. On the question of increasing the authority of the organization, the responses in each case were the same as for the UN questionnaire: the most experienced show the greatest aversion to increased organizational authority, in every case to a statistically significant degree. There were inter-departmental differences on some other attitudinal dimensions, which tends to confirm the finding of departmental differences in response to the 1974 UN questionnaire; but on this issue the same negative relationship is pronounced and consistent[22]

### Difference in attitudinal response

Our research findings also provide clues to understanding individual differences in attitudinal response. Inferences from the questionnaire data, supplemented by extensive personal interviews, suggest that attitudinal differences are intimately related to individual perceptions of where self-interest lies. 'Interest' in this sense may mean personal interests of the respondent, but it also includes interests of the governmental unit or sub-unit with which he identifies, and the interests of his country as a whole. Specifically, we found evidence that attitudinal response to participation in international organizations varied with the norms and goals of the domestic organizational unit, the perceived effectiveness of the international agency, and the substantive nature of the function it performed.

Differences associated with the respondent's organizational unit give substantial support to Allison's maxim, developed in the context of intragovernmental bureaucratic politics, 'Where you stand depends on where you sit.'[23] We found, in the United States responses, that the positive effect of experience upon attitudes is heightened for respondents whose job assignment is in an international affairs sub-unit of the department to which he is assigned. In Norway this same booster effect appears for officials of the Foreign Affairs Department, as compared with respondents from the Departments of Commerce and Foreign Aid. The effect of organizational context stands out sharply when comparing the responses of the three Norwegian Departments on

170

the question of channeling more economic aid to developing countries through the United Nations. Increased experience with the UN makes Foreign Aid officials less supportive of aid through the UN, while officials from the other Departments become more supportive. The Foreign Aid position probably indicates a concern that a larger allocation to the UN might mean a smaller share of Norwegian aid for the Department's client network built up primarily through bilateral channels. Not surprisingly, on the question of increasing Norway's overall aid package, Foreign Aid respondents are substantially more positive at all experience levels than the other two departments.

Another confirmation of the importance of domestic organizational context appears both in personal interviews and in the 1976 mailed survey of three United States government departments. Respondents from the Department of Agriculture, on the average, were noticeably less positive about the FAO than were Treasury or HEW respondents in appraising the IMF and the WHO, respectively. Leaving aside possible differences in the effectiveness of the international agencies, this seemed anomalous because a very large proportion of the Agriculture respondents had substantial foreign affairs responsibilities as members of the Foreign Agriculture Service (FAS). The anomaly was dispelled when subsequent investigation revealed that a primary function of the FAS is to promote the sale abroad of U.S. agricultural products. FAO offers little or no assistance in this activity and, to the extent that the FAO helps promote agricultural development abroad, it might even create additional competition for U.S. products.

The same point may be illustrated by contrasting interview responses of two professionals located in different branches of the National Institutes of Health. One, when asked about the WHO, retorted: 'It doesn't do us a damn bit of good.' He then went on to complain that the WHO would spend money to send someone to a developing country on a research and training grant but wouldn't give him a dime to bring people to the United States, even when better training could be obtained here. (This represents only a limited view of U.S.-WHO relationships. WHO funds are regularly used to send health personnel to the United States for training. U.S. expenditures for international health training and research far exceed the entire WHO budget, however.) WHO, as he saw it, was doing little to further goals important to his work. Another respondent, whose responsibility was to obtain an adequate supply of monkeys for medical experimentation, voiced an entirely different opinion when asked about international organizations. The Pan-American Health Organization (PAHO), a regional branch of WHO, sponsored a primate production program that played a very essential role in American plans for a long-term supply of primates. PAHO facilitated a modest sharing of the financial burden and, more important, enabled the United States to avoid the difficulties of trying to obtain its own supply of primates on a unilateral basis. Because of a useful program directly related to the goals of his organizational unit, this professional had a correspondingly high opinion of international organization.

If attitudinal responses are in part determined by norms and goals derived from the domestic organizational context, another important variable is the perceived effectiveness of the international agency. The UN questionnaire focussed primarily on a single international organization – the United Nations; but personal interviews, as well as responses to the 1976 three-department survey, added a comparative dimension. To some extent, a person's appraisal of the international agency is affected by his attitude toward the kind of function it performs. But discussions with many government officials led us to believe that an organization is also judged on how well it does its job, how efficient it is, how effective in accomplishing its own purposes.

One touchstone of efficiency is the perceived quality and competence of the international secretariat. Negative (or positive) opinions of an international organization were frequently associated with correspondingly negative or positive evaluations of its professional staff. In particular, Agriculture officials who voiced negative views about the FAO commonly coupled their evaluation with specific comments about the overgrown, inefficient FAO bureaucracy.

Another complaint that surfaced frequently was the intrusion of politics into the work of the organization. Usually the reference to 'politics' meant organizational catering to the demands of the lesser developed countries even when considerations of technical efficiency would dictate otherwise. This included decisions about grants of technical assistance funds, selection of administrative and project personnel, location of projects, and other matters that ought to be decided on technical grounds but in fact were not. Occasionally the reference to 'politics' meant the dissipation of energy with extraneous issues, such as the Arab-Israeli question, when the organization should have been concerned with problems within its own field.

Frequently, also, the interviewees drew a distinction between organizations that talk and organizations that do things. International agencies with quite specific, technical functions were frequently mentioned as performing valuable work. Agriculture respondents who denigrated the FAO as too political or too much given to debate might nevertheless laud the work of the Codex Alimentarius Commission, a joint FAO/WHO body engaged in drafting world-wide standards for food products in international commerce. Medical researchers could be only lukewarm about the WHO, yet speak high praise of the International Agency for Research on Cancer – a WHO affiliate located in Lyons, France. Among U.S. Customs Service officials, high marks were generally accorded the work of the Customs Cooperation Council in developing common nomenclature for the uniform classification and valuation of goods by national customs services. Among technical specialists, the international agencies working on specific technical problems tended to win greater approval than organizations identified with higher level political-diplomatic debate.

There is in the interview responses an indication that the substantive nature of the function may also account for differences in attitudes. Some types of functions are inherently easier than others to reconcile with national goals and interests. This point was made by several interviewees in the Department of Agriculture and the U.S. Public Health Service when asked why the WHO was given more favorable ratings than the FAO. 'No one can disagree with efforts to promote better health,' was a common response, 'but all sorts of economic interests come into conflict when agricultural production and marketing are the issues.' Without any awareness of functionalist thought, these government officials were propounding a theory of controversiality much like that of Mitrany: functionalism works best where the functions are least controversial.

Probing of our parliamentary data uncovers other reasons why the international organization experience does not induce the same attitudinal response in all participants. For parliamentarians, at least part of the difference is ascribable to 1) differences in previously held views, interacting with 2) the special characteristics of the international experience, and conditioned by 3) the legislator's relationship with domestic reference groups. U.S. Congressmen who had a relatively intense and lengthy period of participation at the UN General Assembly appeared to experience a convergence of views. Those least favorable at the outset became significantly more positive toward the United Nations, while the Congressmen with initially high opinions of the UN showed little increase in positive affect or, in some cases, change in a negative direction. Congressional participants in other international meetings, generally of a briefer nature, tended to exhibit a reinforcement of previously held views – the positive becoming more positive and the negative more negative. This appeared to be attributable, at least in part, to the influence of domestic reference groups whose effect upon attitudes was more marked when the international experience was less intense and profound. The impact of differing international experience was also evident in the Norwegian data, where delegates to the UN showed more sympathy for the needs of developing countries than did parliamentarians whose participation had been primarily in European regional organizations where developing countries are not represented.

The impact of pre-existing attitudes, the domestic milieu, and the nature of the experience may help account for differences between our own findings and those of Kerr and Bonham, who discovered little or no affective change resulting from participation. To the extent that participants in European regional assemblies are recruited by self-selection, they are likely to have an initially high opinion of European integration. In that event, the convergence effect found by Pool, by Keller and Bauer, by Karns, and in our own study of U.S. Congressmen, could explain the absence of a significant increase in support for integration among the Kerr and the Bonham interviewees.[24]

Differences in domestic milieu could also account for differences in attitudinal response. Kerr's discovery of a strong relationship between party affiliation and delegate attitude points to an essential difference between United States Congressmen and their European counterparts. While there are substantial differences among European party systems, the European parliamentarian is more tied to his party, organizationally and ideologically, than the national legislator in the United States. Distinct party positions on issues are much more likely to be articulated in European parties, and the individual legislator is more dependent upon his party both for election and for political status. In a situation where party positions have a very large bearing on attitudes and preferences, the parliamentarian is much less open to other influences, and perhaps especially impervious to extra-national ones. This would not necessarily account for our finding of increased support for the United Nations among Norwegian parliamentarians, since Norway fits the general pattern of European party systems. The difference here might result from recruitment factors, differences in the nature of the experience, or possibly the lesser salience of UN issues as compared with European integration issues, which could make party positions on the former less constraining for individual parliamentarians. In any event, if circumstances that affect attitudinal change are significantly different, it is quite possible to conclude that delegates to the UN General Assembly undergo a change in the direction predicted by functionalism, but that delegates to European regional assemblies generally do not.

*Appraising the functionalist explanation*

Taking into account all of the evidence in the preceding pages, how can we appraise the capacity of functionalist theories of learning to explain or predict the growth and development of international institutions? Judging on the basis of observed change, functionalist predictions about the learning process have at least a limited validity. The theory scores high on the demonstration effect, as evidenced by the proliferation of international institutions. There is also solid evidence of individual learning but not altogether as predicted. Attitudes are multidimensional, and experience is not associated with favorable opinions of multilateral cooperation along all dimensions. In our own data the theory holds well for both Norway and the United States at the level of general approval. The measures of association are weak but consistently positive. The relationships are not as consistent when action commitment is at issue, and the theory utterly fails at the point of sovereignty transfer. Perhaps one could argue that facing the issue of sovereignty directly is just what functionalism proposes to avoid. The theory makes explicit that the walls of state sovereignty will be most difficult to scale – so burrow under them, get around them, or slip through the cracks in the wall by concentrating on need and function. But, ultimately, functionalism assumes that slices of sovereignty will be willingly relinquished; and our evidence shows the most experienced participants to be the least willing to relinquish it.

When we look beyond the fact of attitude change to the reasons for differences in attitudinal responses, functionalist explanations fare about as well as the functionalist prediction that positive change will occur. That is, some elements of the explanation conform well to the observed facts and others do not. Consider first, the points of congruence. Functionalism postulates that people who participate in functional activities will develop supportive attitudes because they perceive their interests to be well served by functional cooperation. Recast as a conditional statement, this accords with our own observations. Participants do judge an international agency by how well it serves their interests; and, when perceived interests are served, supportive attitudes develop. This reformulation limits the predictive strength of the basic postulate, but the explanation remains largely intact.

We also found evidence that favorable attitudes tend to be most frequently associated with tasks that are relatively non-controversial, technical, organized separately, and left largely to experts in the field. Despite the difficulties of deciding in advance what categories of functions are of high or low controversialtiy, several officials interviewed made precisely this distinction in explaining why, in their opinion, our survey revealed more support for WHO than for FAO. In addition, the international agencies that evoked the most consistent and enthusiastic appraisals were generally obscure, highly technical agencies whose work was in fact left largely to experts. These agencies also were shielded from the ordinary vicissitudes of bloc and power politics by special constitutional arrangements or by virtue of their obscurity and technicality. Prime examples are the agencies previously mentioned – the Codex Alimentarius Commission, the International Agency for Research on Cancer, and the Customs Cooperation Council. The principle of *talking* vs. *doing* also emerged frequently during the interviews, without coaching or cuing by the interviewer. Officials had respect for international agencies that did things, and contempt for agencies that seemed to produce nothing but talk.

When the evidence is summarized in this fashion, it constitutes rather impressive support for a number of functionalist propositions. Much of what Mitrany saw is consonant with what governmental officials see today. A technical, non-controversial task – performed, not merely talked about – will evoke favorable attitudes. When the conditions are met – particularly those relating to the participant's perception that his interests are being served – functionalism as explanation appears quite defensible.

But 'functional' has been defined, even by its proponents, as covering virtually the whole range of economic and social activities; and functionalist assumptions about integrative learning have been proclaimed without careful reference to qualifying and limiting conditions. When the functionalist explanation is applied thus broadly, it falters at two important points, both of which have been repeatedly identified by previous critics of the theory. The first is the assumption that important functions left to the experts will be efficiently performed in the common interest. The second is the assumption that the creation of 'separate and autonomous' functional organizations can generally insulate economic and social activities from the play of politics.

The first assumption is probably less disabling to the explanation than the second, although at the point of recruiting the experts the two problems merge. Experts appear on the functional scene, typically, in one of three settings: 1) as members of national delegations to international meetings; 2) as skilled persons appointed in an individual capacity for a special assignment – for example a technical assistance appointment or service on a special study or advisory committee; or 3) as members of international secretariats. Experts may also be in the service of voluntary groups, but this study has chosen to focus on the intergovernmental aspects of functionalism rather than the non-governmental. When functionalists speak of leaving an inter-governmental task to be carried out by experts, they may have in mind either the national or the individual experts if the task is primarily negotiation or preparation of a report. But if it involves administration of a program, an international secretariat is almost necessarily involved. Thus,

176

'leaving it to the experts' generally means turning it over to an international secretariat to administer.

And herein lies a problem seldom addressed by functionalists: there is no guarantee that an international bureaucracy, any more than a national bureaucracy, will faithfully and efficiently serve the interests of its constituents. Bureaucracies have their own interests, which do not always correspond with the broader public interest. Nor are they always efficient, if comments of our interviewees, published studies of the international civil service, and common sense are to be believed.[25] International bureaucracies respond to pressures of special interests (which may mean the importunings of particular governments) just as do national bureaucracies; and given current methods of recruitment to professional posts, many of the experts are not politically disinterested. The functionalist image of the capable, impartial expert is an ideal type to which real-life experts conform only to a limited extent. The failure of the facts fully to satisfy this assumption does not shatter the functionalist explanation, but it raises some serious caveats.

## The 'politics problem'

The second assumption, that economic and social activities can be effectively insulated from politics, poses a far more serious problem for functionalist explanation. As pointed out in Chapter 1, this is the issue on which both Haas and Sewell (and other critics) find functionalism most seriously lacking. 'Here lies the greatest deficiency in the functionalist argument,' says Sewell, '– its inadequate consideration of the nature and operation of politics.'[26] For Haas also the very essence of the integrative process is political – 'an institutionalized pattern of interest politics, played out within existing international organizations.'[27] Even when dealing with the role of the expert, the functionalist archetype of the non-political actor, Haas' prescription for integration calls for 'experts aware of the political implications of their task' and representative of significant public or private constituencies.[28] Claude, with his usual apt imagery and cleverly turned phrase, makes the same point in somewhat different terms:

The clearest lesson of United Nations experience is that functionalism's assumption of the preliminary separability of political and nonpolitical matters does not hold true – not in this generation, at any rate. We are not vouchsafed the privilege of warming up the motors of international collaboration in a sheltered area of concordant interests, getting off to an easy start and building up momentum for crashing the barriers of conflicting interests that

177

interpose between us and the ideal of world order. The dilemma of functionalism is that its ultimate impact upon politics may never be tested because of the immediate impact of politics upon functionalism.[29]

Let us examine the 'politics problem' more closely. By politics we mean forms of interaction characterized by competing and conflicting demands, with outcomes determined by the influence of the parties. This contrasts with the functionalist model of human relationships in which people's wants are characterized as needs rather than demands, and satisfaction of needs is treated as a matter of problem-solving by technical experts rather than the exercise of influence by political actors. Probably neither of these models adequately describes the whole range of international interactions, but the contrast makes the deficiencies of the functionalist model readily apparent. It begs the whole question of conflicting interests and, by implication, makes distributional equities a matter of technical judgment. Even if the distribution of benefits did not involve competing interests (which, in practice, it assuredly does), it still requires significant value judgments as to who *ought* to get what. Assuming away the interest conflicts, can we also assume that the technical experts are experts on value questions as well as the subject matter of their specialty?

In any event, functionalists cannot successfully write off the phenomenon of competing interests. Every actor, individual or collective, has interests. This includes governments, governmental subunits, private groups, national legislators, diplomatic and political leaders, and even experts and technicians. Although documentation for such an assertion is scarcely necessary, Nau's analysis of fast reactor cooperation in Europe is a revealing study in conflict and disagreement among the experts assigned to the project.[30] The oft-noted competition for UNDP development funds allocated to UN specialized agencies should also put to rest any notion that the experts are above the political fray.

Functionalism of course recognizes that governments will enter into functional arrangements on the basis of perceived interests. There must be common or converging interests of some sort for any arrangement to come into being. But functionalism underrates the strength of the competing interests that emerge in the process of carrying out functional activities, or else overrates the capacity of the functional agency to harmonize and smooth over differences in ministering to the common need. Medical researchers whose grant applications are consistently rejected in favor of less meritorious projects, as they believe, will have a jaundiced view of the grantor agency. If primate programs are

178

bungled, or obstructed by politics, and monkeys are no longer available for medical research, good will toward the organization that sponsors the programs will dwindle. Functional agencies that promote world production of fruit and vegetables (or tobacco, or wheat) will not commend themselves to governmental officials whose agricultural clients sell for less in a glutted market.

Many of our interviewees, of course, were able at least intellectually to disengage the activities of the FAO or WHO in their own special areas from the general programs of the organization. They could admit that the organization wasn't doing much for them but still agree that some worthwhile overall objective was being promoted. But this is not the stuff of which strong loyalties are built. Such faint favor fades when the shoe pinches hard enough.

Furthermore, political leaders in governments are seldom willing to leave an international problem of any magnitude or political sensitivity to technical experts, national or international. How many attempts to deal with economic and social questions have been bedevilled by East-West quarrels, North-South differences, and, in recent years, the Arab-Israeli conflict? Even without such overriding super-issues, conflicts of interest within and between governments are inevitable. How will the development pie be split? Who controls the issuance of SDRs and on what terms? Who gets the high level secretariat appointments? How will the international radio frequencies be allotted? Who will be permitted to develop the resources of the seabed? Such questions could be spun out endlessly; and all identify potential conflicting interests. These are issues that require the input of experts; but no government will wholly abandon policy decisions to the good judgment of experts. Indeed, intra-governmental positions must first be hammered out through an essentially political process of internal conflict resolution. Then the international decision is made in a context of competing demands and influence.

In this situation, so far removed from the functionalist ideal, learning continues to occur. But it is learning not altogether of the kind functionalists predict. Developing countries learn that they may control a parliamentary situation by carefully orchestrated bloc action. Arab states learn to bargain a variety of favors in return for anti-Israeli votes. Soviet leaders learn how to tailor their proposals to win the support of anti-colonial states. The United States learns the limits and possibilities of political arm-twisting in an international agency. Yes, learning occurs. But it is not all calculated to build either a spirit of cooperation or support for expansion of organizational tasks. Even when functional growth occurs, through increased budgets or the creation of new organs, it is generally over the strenuous objection of

179

minorities who happened to lose out in that phase of the political struggle.

Some of the functionalist-predicted learning undoubtedly occurs too. Unfortunately, its policy impact tends to be inversely proportioned to the political importance of issues. As an issue moves up the scale of political salience, decisions are made by political leaders rather than by experts. Political leaders are less exposed to the working of functional cooperation with its presumed attitude-molding effects, and they respond to a different set of pressures. Enter, thus, the high politics/low politics distinction of Stanley Hoffman[31] or the 'dramatic-political actor' somewhat tardily acknowledged by Haas.[32] Decisions are snatched from the hands of the people who might be subject to the positive socializing effects of participation in international organizations, and taken over by leaders operating in a different arena. Integrative decisions may still be made but the motivations will be political, not functional.

If decisions about the substance of functional cooperation are made in a political context, the same is true of institutional arrangements – the area supposedly governed by the principle of technical self-determination. Stanley Hoffmann reminds us that 'the process of political integration is set in motion by political decisions made by states . . . What launched the European integration movement was neither the common climate nor the common ideological and social structure, but the initiative of political leaders (Schuman, Adenauer, de Gasperi) at a time when the western European political constellation was unique.'[33] The same could be said of every other functional organization. The creation of intergovernmental institutions always requires a political act, a conscious decision by political authorities.

Recognizing the political nature of the initial decision to cooperate does not necessarily defeat the theory of technical self-determination. Even Mitrany acknowledges that 'a state's decision to participate inevitably is a *political* act.'[34] But technical self-determination does require that the developing form and processes of a functional organization be decided by experts, or at least decided in accordance with their advice. This in turn rests on an assumption that there are technical standards or rules upon which experts can agree, from which will flow recommendations about institutional development. It also assumes that the decisions will largely be free from the pulling and hauling that accompanies decisions made in a setting of competing interests.

In fact neither of these assumptions wholly corresponds with reality. Sewell has detailed the inadequacy of technical self-determination in explaining the evolution of the World Bank and related agencies,[35] largely because of political factors of which the theory took no account.

Nau has shown how European cooperation in nuclear research and development became possible only after 'political changes created the conditions for overcoming scientific and technological differences.'[36] Other illustrations of political impact on institutional change can readily be cited. Periodic revision of voting quotas in the World Bank and International Monetary Fund have responded to shifts in members' political and economic power rather than to any technical requirements of the situation. When IMF organs proved unwieldy, the industrialized countries organized an informal Group of 10 to conduct private discussions of monetary matters among themselves. The rival 'Group of 24' developing countries was similarly a politically-induced response to problems of decision-making within the IMF. In each case the organizational development came about primarily for reasons of political interest rather than technical efficiency. Mitrany was not altogether wrong in stating that form is affected by function. The problem is that the interaction is reciprocal. Form also affects function. If a proposed institutional change would alter the distributional pattern of rewards and burdens, the issue will flow into the political arena where interest and influence ultimately determine outcomes.

### Dealing with the politics problem

This brief survey of the political context of functional cooperation leads to an inescapable conclusion. If functionalism is to offer a very satisfactory explanation of institutional growth and development, it must be explicitly broadened to include a political dimension. This is radical surgery – but well worth doing. Functionalist thought is consistent with many observed aspects of international life in non-conflict situations. The usefulness of its insights can be substantially enhanced by grafting on political variables.

Giving functionalism a political dimension does not mean that it must be expanded into a complete theory of international behavior. Even on the cooperation side of the ledger, functionalism is not now a theory in any rigorous sense of the term. It is largely a set of insights waiting to be elaborated, refined, and supplied with limiting conditions. As these insights are explored, the political context of multilateral cooperation can be included as a set of conditions placing limits upon the application of functionalist propositions. Political variables can then be built into the theory as, step by step, the nature of the limits is defined.

Haas' restatement of several 'functionalist separability doctrines'[37] provides a good illustration of this approach. Taking the general proposition that 'power is separate from welfare,' Haas reformulates it to state that 'functionally specific international programs, if organizationally separated from diffuse orientations, maximize both welfare and integration.' This statement is consistent with views frequently expressed by the officials we interviewed and, properly operationalized, could be subjected to empirical test.

Haas' entire discussion can be read with profit, but perhaps one more illustration of his approach will suffice. A second 'separability' doctrine is stated as follows: 'Through the process of learning, initially power-oriented governmental pursuits evolve into welfare-oriented action.' This seems a reasonable rendering of Mitranian ideas, which Haas then revises to state: 'When actors realize that their interest would best be achieved by adopting new approaches, and if these approaches involve commitment to larger organizations, then and only then does "learning" contribute to integration.' As thus restated, the proposition is so hedged and qualified that it borders on the tautological (the actors will do it if they want to do it); but at least the revision introduces the limiting condition of interest into what might otherwise be a categorical statement of evolution from power to welfare. It is a step toward defining the limiting conditions imposed by the political context.

This is not the place to chart in detail the possible interface of politics with functional cooperation. The reference to Haas' work is meant only to illustrate what has been, and can be, done. We will, however, suggest one additional area that merits exploration. High priority might well be given to a study of political salience as a limitation upon functional growth. The problem has in the past been addressed in terms of the distinction between 'high' and 'low' politics. We prefer the concept of salience because it projects the image of a continuum in which issues may have degrees of political salience, depending on the nature of the issue, the time and the circumstances. Development of a coherent statement about political salience would require an inquiry into the precise effects of nature, time and circumstances; but even here, we are not without some guidance. Stanley Hoffmann has given a very insightful analysis of 'high politics' limitations upon the functional approach, which he calls the 'Monnet model', as applied to European regional integration. We quote at some length:

> . . . First, when the function which is being 'integrated' involves issues which permit the participants' interest to be calculated (i.e., expressed in material and quantitative terms), which represent only a negligible fraction of the nations' resources, or over which they all have convergent expectations of gain, the 'Monnet model' is entirely applicable. Here – through a decision originally made by the governments – the main actors become the supranational authorities and interested citizens (for instance, the businessmen affected by trade

liberalization) rather than the national government.

Secondly, when the problems can still be calculated, but either represent an important fraction of the nations' resources or affect a well organized interest, or both, and when the nations have conflicting and competing expectations of gains and losses, the difference between a 'fifty-fifty compromise' and a 'solution upgrading the common interests' becomes extremely thin – bargaining partakes both of pressure group conflicts and of interstate disputes . . .

Thirdly, when the functions are concerned with the ineffable and intangible issues of *Grosspolitik,* when grandeur and prestige, rank and security, domination and dependence are at stake, we are fully within the realm of traditional interstate politics . . . The bigger the stakes, the less applicable the method that consists of flooding the common interest with light and leaving the conflicting ones in the dark. For not only is this separation highly artificial and distorting, but the very nature of interstate competition pushes the spotlight back on the conflicting interests.[38]

Hoffmann's account has special reference to the European Community, but it could have a broader application in specifying some of the conditions that create political salience.

Reference to the work of Haas and Hoffmann by no means exhausts all the possibilities for research into the political context of functional cooperation, but it illustrates some of the significant directions that may be pursued. Unquestionably it points the way for all those who advocate that the empirical insights of functionalism be taken seriously. The surest road to increased credibility is for functionalists to stop denying or ignoring the relevance of politics and begin building political variables into the theory.

## The Linkage with World Peace

In addition to its explanation of institutional growth at the international level, functionalism asserts a linkage between functional cooperation and world peace. This includes: 1) building world community, 2) diminishing the significance of the territorial state, 3) alleviating economic and social problems that might give rise to conflict, 4) wielding economic sanctions for peace, and 5) providing a governmental apparatus for the global community.[39]

The functionalist program is obviously a long-run strategy but, like the explanation of institutional growth, the prognosis of peace is based on the premise that the political will be subordinate to the functional.

Unfortunately for the theory, our conclusions about the process of institutional growth do not inspire full faith in the premise. In the short run at least, economic and social cooperation are inextricably intermingled with politics. The practice of functionalism has not observably altered the elements of human nature that make politics in the generic sense so omnipresent and pervasive. Can we nevertheless hope, by ignoring the political and concentrating on the functional, that the most violent forms of political conflict among nations will in the long run go away? We will attempt a response to that question by addressing each of the five contributions to peace enumerated above.

Of the five, the last two items can be written off very quickly. The governmental apparatus is still in the distant future, unless one could grace with the term 'government' the melange of international institutions now providing the organizational superstructure for functional cooperation. Nor do functional agencies wield sanctions that have any significant impact on war and peace. The multilateral lending institutions, including the World Bank and the International Monetary Fund, may impose economic conditions upon their loans, which is a mild form of sanctions, but this is not done in the interest of deterring armed aggression. Even within the European Community, where functional cooperation has reached its greatest height, there is no provision for withholding economic benefits as a means of political coercion. The most one can say is that economic integration, especially the integration of heavy industry, would make internal war within the Community more difficult for any member to undertake. And each would have to regard the disruption of economic ties as an additional cost of engaging in armed conflict with one another.

The promotion of peace through economic and social problem-solving, the third enumerated contribution, is a difficult claim to evaluate. A very long list of existing functional programs could be prepared, ranging from economic development to the global weather watch. The direct economic and social consequences can generally be identified, and these are often beneficial. But what is the impact on world peace? The conflicts that might have occurred but for this web of cooperative activity cannot be identified. The many conflicts, including armed hostilities, that have occurred in spite of it are all too evident. To borrow once more from Claude, the really troublesome political conflicts of our era – such as the Cold War or the Arab-Israeli conflict – 'have shown little susceptibility to being transformed by functionalist programs; on the contrary, they have shown every indication of being able to transform functionalist workshops into political arenas.'[40] We may grant, as a matter of faith, that the functional attack on economic and social problems has helped reduce the amount of conflict in the international system and may do even more in the future. But objectively, in terms of the world's need, the past contribution has been far too little; and judging by the present pace the long-run contribution may well be too late.

Functional cooperation is also supposed to diminish the significance of the territorial state so as to reduce the competiveness that breeds conflict and war. What is the evidence on this score? Certainly the world is becoming more and more interdependent, in the sense that one nation's actions have significant effects upon people in other countries. States have become more permeable, penetrated, interconnected. Faced with multiplying interdependencies, states (and private groups) have turned to international functional cooperation as a means of responding to new problems and opportunities.

Widespread recognition of this condition has been echoed by a rising chorus of voices, both public and private. 'We live in an era of interdependence,' is the opening line of a recent work on world politics by two distinguished political scientists.[41] 'The state is about through as an economic unit,' reports a well-known economist.[42] And from a recent U.S. Secretary of State, himself deeply rooted in the classical tradition:

> Now we are entering a new era. Old international patterns are crumbling; old slogans are uninstructive; old solutions are unavailing. The world has become interdependent in economics, in communications, in human aspirations.[43]

But has either the fact of interdependence or the practice of functional cooperation diminished the significance of the state in any absolute sense? The answer is probably 'no'. Claude points out that the emphasis of many functional agencies upon economic development has had quite the contrary effect. This 'developmental functionalism', as he calls it

> is a state-building enterprise, not a state-undermining project. It is directed towards making national sovereignty meaningful, not reducing it to meaninglessness. It is aimed at assisting states in achieving genuine and effective statehood, not at promoting their merger into larger groupings. Its task is not to help peoples get over the idea of the sovereign, independent state, but to help them realize that ideal . . .[44]

Even outside the realm of development, most intergovernmental agencies do not provide services directly to or enforce regulations upon the peoples of the world. They operate through governments as mediators,

185

which tends to magnify the importance of governments rather than of international organizations. The European Community may be a significant exception to this generalization, but even there we find little evidence of the erosion of national identities or the submergence of the state.

Viewed from a domestic perspective, most governments – under the same kinds of pressures that have spawned rules and institutions at the international level – are trending toward increased budgets, multiplying regulations, and increased intervention in the lives of their citizens. This is hardly the pathway to diminished significance. In the international arena state rivalries persist, with the build-up of national armaments to a level of destructiveness never before known in history. Perhaps the rivalries would be much worse without the meliorating presence of functional international organizations. But apparently a great deal of hot-blooded competitiveness can coexist in the same world with an extremely complex network of functional international cooperation.

*Building community*

The remaining functionalist claim to peace building, and certainly the most important, is the forging of a world community. 'Doing things together in workshop and market place' lays a concrete foundation of shared interests and cooperative habits. Upon this foundation rises a sense of common identity among participants and beneficiaries. Recognition of these commonalities brings the community into being. In this sense we speak of a community of scholars, despite wide geographical dispersion of the scholars. Their common interests make them a community. We have international communities based on religious, business, and professional identifications. One person may be part of many communities, some overlapping the others. With such a broad definition, functional cooperation undeniably creates communities among groups of affected peoples. The question is, how significant are these communities and what is their contribution to world peace?

In the nature of things the answer cannot be very precise. Substantial bonds of community have been forged in Western Europe. This includes a great variety of specialized economic communities, some organized as interest groups and some not. For the public in general, there is broad recognition of the existence of the European community although the mantle rests very lightly. There is a sense of commonality, but for most it is not very salient. For other functional organizations, particularly those at the global level, the groups of people who share the sense of commonality are small. Some, such as international secretariat personnel, may strongly identify with the work of their respective organizations. Most others who identify with a functional activity in some way are likely to have much stronger ties to other communities. For the vast majority of mankind, functional agencies and their work are too obscure, too far removed from daily concerns, indeed too unknown, to foster any sense of community.

Contacts of the transnational, non-governmental variety involve many more people in communities that cut across national boundaries. The multinational business creates important transnational communities of economic interest. Many people may also see themselves bound to fellow human beings through the medium of a worldwide church. International communities of the arts and sciences unite people of different nationalities. The more than 2000 formal non-governmental international organizations testify to the extent and variety of functional communities that exist outside the framework of inter-governmental cooperation.

To what extent do these communities serve as building blocks in the edifice of world peace? We cannot know their potential. We can scarcely appraise with accuracy their actual effect. We do know that a great deal of conflict can coexist with such communities. The force of nationalism, combined with habitual obedience to national political authorities, seems sufficient to bring people into line behind the most jingoistic or aggressive foreign policies of their governments. When political leaders have infused an issue with the urgency of high politics, neither intergovernmental nor transgovernmental communities seem much proof against it. Robert Angell has argued that contacts of the transnational variety have created 'a broadening stream of influence on national policy-makers toward accommodation among nations.'[45] Yet even he refuses to forecast any 'decrease in the number or seriousness of conflicts between nations.' Indeed,

> The clash of national interests, population pressures, ideological rivalries, arms races – these and other sources of friction will for a long time continue to disturb the world. The growth of transnational participation will rarely prevent such conflicts . . .

The most he predicts is that policy-makers may approach conflicts 'with greater appreciation of the problems of their counterparts in other countries and more disposition to exhaust all peaceable means before resorting to violence.'[46]

In this broad and hazy area of community building, data can be amassed by the ton; but the links between functional cooperation and world peace still remain tenuous. After plowing through mounds of data on the International Labor Organization, Haas concluded, '. . . it is difficult to relate the performance of a given organization to a change in values, habits, and institutions in the environment of the system; it is hazardous to argue a direct integrative impact attributable to organizational performance.'[47]

And yet, we would hesitate to assert that the ILO, and other functional organizations, have *not* affected the system in any peace building way. Perhaps Rosenau came close to the truth in his perceptive review of Haas' ILO study. 'I would argue,' he said,

> that progress toward international integration must be measured in terms of small increments and that it is at only a few points along the vast periphery, and not at the center, of world politics that these small increments of integrative experience become part of the patterns of international behavior. Haas's data, considered from this perspective, do seem to be patterned in an integrative direction. The ILO may not have *markedly* influenced the course of events since 1919, and other variables have unquestionably been more potent sources of change; but the findings of this book make it reasonable to presume that, in the absence of such an organization, the international environment would not have been transformed quite as much or in exactly the same way as in fact it was.[48]

Functional cooperation, as one among many variables affecting international behavior, has not turned a war-prone system into a peaceful world order. But here and there, through incremental change along the system's vast periphery, the communities fostered by functional cooperation may constitute small building blocks in a slowly emerging structure of peace.[49]

## Functionalism as Paradigm

When Thomas S. Kuhn popularized the term 'paradigm' in his essay on 'The Structure of Scientific Revolutions',[50] he was concerned mainly with the 'universally received paradigm' characteristic of the physical sciences in modern times.[51] The study of politics, including international politics, is still in a pre-paradigmatic stage by this standard. In keeping with usage within the discipline, however, the present state of affairs might better be regarded as a condition of 'many, often poorly-developed, competing paradigms.'[52] Leaving aside the need for universal recognition, there clearly are approaches to the study of international politics that have paradigmatic qualities, even by Kuhn's definition. Paradigms, he said, are 'universally recognized scientific achievements that for a time provide model problems and model solutions to a community of practitioners'.[53] Paradigms help 'define the legitimate problems and methods of a research field,' 'attract an enduring group of adherents away from competing modes of scientific activity,' and are 'sufficiently open-ended to leave all sorts of problems for the redefined group of practitioners to resolve.'[54]

Neither functionalism, nor any other school of thought, has universal acceptance within the field of international politics today. For two decades after World War II, variants of the 'realist' or security politics model constituted the dominant – but not the sole – paradigm in the field.[55] The central concerns of this paradigm were 'competition for military security and its concomitants, territorial domain, ideological ascendance, and high prestige.'[56] The realist paradigm is now on the decline, although it has not lost all relevance and certainly it retains adherents.

Since the early 1960s, a new major competing paradigm has begun to emerge in the functionalist mold. The new paradigm embraces many variants and specific foci. They include the literature on regional and global integration, the multinational corporation, transnational relations, transgovernmental relations, a great variety of topics now being discussed under the rubric of 'interdependence', and of course the work of avowed functionalists whose focus cuts across all of the other sectors. To call this emerging set of interests and concerns the 'functionalist' paradigm might be presumptuous. Yet Robert Cox treats the transnational approach and the transgovernmental approach as 'derivatives of functionalism': and, manifestly, the neofunctionalist approach to regional integration is a variant of functionalism. One could also contend that the interdependence literature[58] derives from the functionalist perspective and shares a number of functionalist assumptions. Perhaps, as an alternative, the new framework should be labeled the 'interdependence paradigm', of which functionalism is an important variant.

Whatever its label, the new paradigm rejects the state-centric or 'billiard ball' world view in favor of the more complex 'cobweb' model of the international system, involving multiple actors, multiple channels connecting societies, and multiple issues.[59] It gives greater priority to welfare issues than the realist paradigm. It places more emphasis upon the management of cooperative activities, less on the phenomenon of interstate conflict. It focuses on the analysis of concrete problems rather than the development of overarching schemes of global governance. All of these characteristics of the new paradigm are consonant with functionalist perspectives.

Functionalism also poses research questions that fit easily within the

189

new paradigm. Under what conditions are political leaders likely to perceive a 'need' for new ventures in international cooperation? In what issue-areas is this most likely to occur? What kinds of learning result from functional cooperation? To what extent is this learning integrative in impact? What conditions increase the probability of integrative learning? How do technical/welfare issues become politicized? To what extent is politicization incompatible with integration? What is the relationship between functional cooperation and the reduction of conflict? In specific situations? In the international system as a whole? What is the role of non-governmental groups in the integrative process? In what way is policy-making within governments affected by the international networks of functional cooperation? What limits upon functional cooperation are imposed by the political context? Functionalism, as we have characterized it in this study, does not constitute the whole of the emerging paradigm of interdependence: but it has strongly influenced the shape and direction of the whole, and constitutes a significant part of it.

Functionalist thought is by no means proof against criticism, whether as prescription, explanation, prediction or paradigm. But its relevance to the facts of modern international life cannot easily be dismissed. Its prescriptions are attuned to the growing interconnectedness of the world. Its explanations and predictions, despite pressing need for refinement and reformulation, provide useful insights into international cooperative behavior. As a paradigm for the study of international politics, it identifies a subject matter and a set of questions that can lead to fruitful research. As those questions become the subject of careful investigation, the answers may not all be the same as Mitrany might have predicted. But understanding will be advanced and that, after all, is the test of any mode of thought.

# Appendix A: Norway

## 1. Questionnaire Sent to Norway Respondents

*Instructions:* Please place an (X) by the response closest to your own attitude on each statement below.

| | Highly agree | Agree | Undecided | Disagree | Highly disagree |
|---|---|---|---|---|---|
| 1. 'The UN helps to promote a more peaceful, cooperative world.' | | | | | |
| 2. 'The UN, and what the organization in principle stands for, represents the most important "cornerstone" in Norwegian foreign policy.' | | | | | |
| 3. 'Norway ought to be generally more involved in the work of the UN.' | | | | | |
| 4. 'The UN ought to have greater financial resources available.' | | | | | |
| 5. 'Norway ought to channel more of its foreign aid through UN's multilateral programs.' | | | | | |
| 6. 'Norway ought to increase its overall foreign aid package.' | | | | | |
| 7. 'Norway ought to grant trade preferences to the developing countries.' | | | | | |
| 8. 'Norway ought to give increased humanitarian aid to the Palestinians.' | | | | | |
| 9. 'The UN ought to have more authority to enforce its rules upon the member states.' | | | | | |
| 10. 'Anything that strengthens the UN is likely to be good for Norway.' | | | | | |

## 2. Additional Items Presented to Norway Parliamentarians Who Had Been UN Delegates

| | | | | | |
|---|---|---|---|---|---|
| 11. 'My stay at the UN increased my understanding of the organization.' | | | | | |
| 12. 'The UN-stay has led me to become more actively concerned with the UN and UN-related matters.' | | | | | |
| 13. 'I have developed a more positive attitude of the UN and UN-related matters.' | | | | | |

Attendance at International Organization meetings and work time devoted to International Organization affairs as related to Norway civil servants' attitudes, controlling for education, age, and visit to third world.

| Questionnaire Item | International Organization Work Time | | | | | | International Organization Attendance | | | | | |
|---|---|---|---|---|---|---|---|---|---|---|---|---|
| | Education | | Age | | Third World Visit | | Education | | Age | | Third World Visit | |
| | Low | High | Old | Young | No | Yes | Low | High | Old | Young | No | Yes |
| | Tau B | | Tau B | | Tau B | | Tau B | | Tau B | | Tau B | |
| 1. UN is cornerstone for Norway | .163 | .041 | -.004 | .142* | .133 | -.202* | -.043 | .035 | -.046 | .090 | -.011 | -.024 |
| 2. UN promotes peace | -.110 | .140* | .010 | .163* | .032 | .055 | -.108 | .164* | .006 | .128 | .025 | .119 |
| 3. Strengthening UN is good for Norway | -.104 | .102 | -.055 | .200* | .006 | .121 | -.124 | .100 | .015 | .073 | -.013 | .143 |
| 4. Norway should be more involved in UN | .214 | .098 | .106 | .151* | .079 | .101 | .045 | .021 | .049 | .071 | -.098 | .122 |
| 5. Increase UN financial resources | -.090 | .113* | .082 | .157* | .025 | .263* | .109 | .230* | .209* | .240* | .088 | .329* |
| 6. Channel more foreign aid through UN | .162 | .074 | .251* | -.015 | .070 | .196* | -.003 | .074 | .132* | .061 | .023 | .187* |
| 7. Grant trade preferences | .091 | .076 | -.024 | .135* | .039 | .097 | .078 | -.095 | -.028 | -.001 | -.145* | .077 |
| 8. Norway should increase foreign aid package | .094 | .001 | -.020 | .067 | -.042 | .137 | .119 | -.083 | .080 | .015 | -.115 | .095 |
| 9. Norway should increase Palestinian aid | .010 | .049 | -.024 | .130 | .072 | .019 | -.059 | -.009 | .001 | .159* | -.032 | .114 |
| 10. Give UN more authority | -.018 | -.092 | -.166* | .048 | -.099 | -.008 | .104 | -.099 | -.076 | -.084 | -.104 | .020 |
| | N=42 | N=184 | N=114 | N=112 | N=152 | N=74 | N=42 | N=184 | N=114 | N=112 | N=152 | N=74 |

* Significant at .05

NOTE: Italics have been used for emphasis to show the higher (or least negative) coefficient of each pair.

# Appendix B: United States

1. Questionnaire Sent to United States Civil Servants
2. Questionnaire Sent to Members of U.S. Congress Who Had Not Attended the UN General Assembly
3. Questionnaire Sent to Members of U.S. Congress Who Had Been Delegates to the UN General Assembly
4. Content Analysis Rules for Inclusion and Exclusion of Speeches and Other *Congressional Record* Items
5. Content Analysis Rules for Evaluation of Speeches and Other Items on the Favorable-Unfavorable (F-U) Scale.

# 1. Questionnaire Sent to United States Civil Servants

Please place an (X) by the response closest to your own attitude on each statement below.

| | Strongly Agree | Agree | Undecided | Disagree | Strongly Disagree |
|---|---|---|---|---|---|
| 1. The UN helps to promote a more peaceful, cooperative world. | | | | | |
| 2. The UN is important to the United States as a means of carrying out our foreign policies. | | | | | |
| 3. In its own self-interest, the United States should be more willing than at present to make use of the UN. | | | | | |
| 4. The UN should have more authority to enforce its rules upon member states. | | | | | |
| 5. The UN should have greater financial resources to carry out its programs. | | | | | |
| 6. The United States should channel more of its foreign aid through UN programs for economic development. | | | | | |
| 7. The United States should grant trade preferences to developing countries. | | | | | |
| 8. The United States should comply with UN sanctions by not importing chrome from Rhodesia. | | | | | |
| 9. The UN is dominated by small countries whose collective influence is far out of proportion to their resources or real interests. | | | | | |
| 10. Anything that strengthens the UN is likely to be good for the United States. | | | | | |
| 11. The UN is more effective in dealing with economic and social problems than with political and security problems. | | | | | |
| 12. The specialized agencies of the UN perform their tasks more effectively than does the UN itself. | | | | | |
| 13. The specialized agencies of the UN are more useful to the United States than is the UN itself. | | | | | |
| 14. International organizations such as the UN and its specialized agencies are a necessity in today's complex world. | | | | | |
| 15. International secretariats are inherently more inefficient than national bureaucracies. | | | | | |
| 16. The United States should use its influence to end Portuguese colonialism in Africa. | | | | | |
| 17. It is in the United States' interest to promote economic development of poorer countries, even at some present sacrifice to ourselves. | | | | | |

18. How many meetings of international organizations have you attended in some official capacity for the United States?

☐ None  ☐ 6–10
☐ 1 only  ☐ 11–20
☐ 2–5  ☐ More than 20

19. What portion of your time in your present job is concerned with the activities of international organizations?

☐ None  ☐ 25–49%
☐ Less than 10%  ☐ 50–74%
☐ 10–24%  ☐ 75% or more

20. Prior to your present post, did you ever hold a governmental position that involved you in any way with the activities of international organizations?
☐ Yes    ☐ No

21. If your work is now, or in the past has been, concerned in any way with the activities of international organizations, please specify which organizations. (If none, write 'none.' Spell out all organization names.)

_____

_____

_____

_____

_____

Place an (x) in the appropriate boxes or fill in the requested information.

22. Education
☐ Bachelor's Degree
☐ Bachelor's Degree and Some Graduate Study
☐ Master's Degree
☐ Ph.D.
☐ Other (specify)
_____

23. Religion
☐ Jewish
☐ Protestant
☐ Roman Catholic
☐ Other (specify)
_____
☐ None

24. Year of birth

_____
(Year)

25. ☐ Male    ☐ Female

26. Birthplace  _____
(State)          (Country)

27. Please list foreign countries in which you have resided one or more years, with number of years of residence:

a. From age 5 to 21

| Country | Years of Residence |
|---|---|
| _____ | _____ |
| _____ | _____ |
| _____ | _____ |
| _____ | _____ |
| _____ | _____ |
| _____ | _____ |

b. Since age 22

| Country | Years of Residence |
|---|---|
| _____ | _____ |
| _____ | _____ |
| _____ | _____ |
| _____ | _____ |
| _____ | _____ |
| _____ | _____ |

196

28. Excluding military service, in what year did you enter federal government service?
———

29. Please indicate the department and departmental sub-unit to which you are presently assigned.

_____     _____
(Department)                              (Sub-unit)

30. What is your present Foreign Service or GS grade? —————
Thank you for completing the questionnaire. Please return to the above address.

## 2. Questionnaire Sent to Members of U.S. Congress Who Had Not Attended the UN General Assembly

Please place an (X) by the response closest to your own attitude on each statement below.

|  | Strongly Agree | Agree | Undecided | Disagree | Strongly Disagree |
|---|---|---|---|---|---|
| 1. The UN is important to the United States as a means of carrying out our foreign policies. |  |  |  |  |  |
| 2. The UN helps to promote a more peaceful, cooperative world. |  |  |  |  |  |
| 3. In its own self-interest, the United States should be more willing than at present to make use of the UN. |  |  |  |  |  |
| 4. The UN should have more authority to enforce its rules upon member states. |  |  |  |  |  |
| 5. The UN should have greater financial resources to carry out its programs. |  |  |  |  |  |
| 6. The United States should channel more of its foreign aid through UN programs for economic development. |  |  |  |  |  |
| 7. The United States should grant trade preferences to developing countries. |  |  |  |  |  |
| 8. The United States should comply with UN sanctions by not importing chrome from Rhodesia. |  |  |  |  |  |
| 9. The UN is dominated by small states whose collective influence is far out of proportion to their resources or real interests. |  |  |  |  |  |
| 10. The UN is more effective in dealing with economic and social problems than with political and security problems. |  |  |  |  |  |
| 11. I would welcome an appointment to serve as a U.S. delegate to a session of the UN General Assembly. |  |  |  |  |  |

12. Have you participated in meetings of the UN or any other international agency?

☐ Yes      ☐ No

If your answer to question 12 is 'yes,' please state which agency or agencies.

_____

_____

Thank you for completing the questionnaire. Please return to the above address.

## 3. Questionnaire Sent to Members of U.S. Congress Who Had Been Delegates to the UN General Assembly.

Please place an (X) by the response closest to your own attitude on each statement below.

| | Strongly Agree | Agree | Undecided | Disagree | Strongly Disagree |
|---|---|---|---|---|---|
| 1. My experience as a UN delegate significantly increased my understanding of the UN. | | | | | |
| 2. My experience as a UN delegate significantly increased my understanding of foreign affairs. | | | | | |
| 3. I gained a more favorable opinion of the UN as a result of my experience as a UN delegate. | | | | | |
| 4. I have paid more attention to the United Nations since serving as a UN delegate than I did before. | | | | | |
| 5. The UN helps to promote a more peaceful, cooperative world. | | | | | |
| 6. The UN is important to the United States as a means of carrying out our foreign policies. | | | | | |
| 7. In its self-interest, the United States should be more willing than at present to make use of the UN. | | | | | |
| 8. The UN Should have more authority to enforce its rules upon member states. | | | | | |
| 9. The UN should have greater financial resources to carry out its programs. | | | | | |
| 10. The United States should channel more of its foreign aid through UN programs for economic development. | | | | | |
| 11. The United States should grant trade preferences to developing countries. | | | | | |
| 12. The United States should comply with UN sanctions by not importing chrome from Rhodesia. | | | | | |
| 13. The UN is dominated by small countries whose collective influence is far out of proportion to their resources or real interests. | | | | | |
| 14. The UN is more effective in dealing with economic and social problems than with political and security problems. | | | | | |

Thank you for completing the questionnaire. Please return to the above address.

198

## 4. Content Analysis Rules for Inclusion and Exclusion of Speeches and Other Congressional Record Items.

1. Include each speech or other item placed in the *Record* by the Congressman if it makes one or more references to the United Nations, one of its agents, or one of its subordinate or constituent agencies. Specialized agencies, or other inter-governmental organizations that are related but not subordinate to the UN will not be included.
2. A reference to the UN may be either directly or by synonym (such as 'international agency', 'this agency', 'world body', etc.) or by a pronoun having one of the preceding entities as its grammatical referent, as long as the reference to the UN is clear.
3. When general reference is made to agencies or organizations in the plural, the UN being one of the agencies referred to, code the paragraph as though it referred simply to the UN.
4. A short introductory statement preceding an 'other' item placed in the *Record* will not be included as a 'speech' unless it contains significant independent evaluation of the UN. The 'other' item will, of course, be included if it makes reference to the UN.
5. A Congressman's entire discussion of a single subject for a given day will be counted as a single speech, even though his comments may be interspersed with comments of other members of the House or Senate.
6. If a long statement by someone other than the speaker appears to be read by the speaker as part of his remarks (not merely introduced for the record), it is coded as part of his speech. If the statement is simply inserted in the *Record* to accompany the speaker's remarks, it is coded separately as an 'other' item.
7. In the paragraph count, include each paragraph making reference to the UN as in rule 1. When a paragraph appears to end in a colon, include the paragraph immediately following as part of the first paragraph.
8. Comments in any quoted source are attributed to the Congressman speaking or inserting them, unless it is clear from the context that the speaker disagrees with the quoted comments. In that event, the comments should not be evaluated or included in the count.
9. Each article, editorial, etc., in a group of items, introduced simultaneously by the Congressman and appearing consecutively in the *Record*, should be counted and coded separately as long as it contains a reference to the UN.

## 5. Content Analysis Rules for Evalution of Speeches and Other Items on the Favorable-Unfavorable (F-U) Scale.

1. Code each paragraph separately using the following symbols: SF (strongly favorable), F (favorable), N (neutral), U (unfavorable), SU (strongly unfavorable). Then code each speech overall on the same scale.
2. Use common sense in interpreting the plain meaning of the words. Use the other rules only when in doubt.
3. Factual description without evaluation by the speaker is coded N.
4. A paragraph containing both positive and negative evaluation should not be ordinarily coded N. Choose the one that predominates.
5. An evaluative statement appearing at the end of a paragraph or a speech may be given greater weight than a statement appearing at the beginning, when one is negative and the other positive.

6. Greater weight will ordinarily be given to general approval or disapproval of the UN as an institution than to evaluation of a specific activity or action of the UN, when both appear in the same paragraph or speech and one is negative while the other is positive. Consider the context and overall impact of the statement, however.
7. When rules 5 and 6 lead to different conclusions, rule 6 should take precedence.
8. Consider the possibility that words neutral or simply descriptive at face value may carry an evaluative meaning in context. For example, the statement, 'In the UN we provide funds for others to spend', could be taken as implied criticism of the UN.
9. Ordinarily, any combination of two or more positive (or negative) adjectives, adverbs, or attributed characteristics appearing in the same clause will qualify the paragraph for SF (or SU) rating, unless counterbalancing comments are made in another portion of the paragraph. An attributed characteristic may appear in various grammatical forms, including nouns (the world's best hope) or verbs (the UN has usurped . . . implying the UN is a usurper). The modifiers may refer either to the UN directly (an insidious, threatening organization) or to the speaker's attitude toward the UN (I am highly disturbed with the UN).
10. If no modifying adjective, adverb, or value-laden attributed characteristic is present, the paragraph probably will not be coded SF or SU. It may still be coded F or U, however, if the context indicates a favorable or unfavorable view of the UN, i.e., tends to identify it with values that are dear (or repugnant) to the speaker.
11. Approval of a U.S. delegate to the UN (e.g., 'U.S. Permanent Representative Adlai Stevenson made a stirring speech today before the UN Association') does not necessarily indicate approval of the UN.

# Notes

CHAPTER I

1 R. J. Harrison, 'Testing Functionalism', in A. J. R. Groom and Paul Taylor, eds. *Functionalism: Theory and Practice in International Relations* (London: University of London Press Ltd. 1975), p. 112.

2 Functionalism as discussed here should be distinguished from the related but conceptually different bodies of thought in sociology, anthropology, and political science, also referred to as functionalism or structural-functionalism. See, e.g., Robert K. Merton, *Social Theory and Social Structure*, rev. ed. (Glencoe, Ill.: The Free Press 1957); Talcott Parsons, *The Social Sytem* (Glencoe, Ill.: The Free Press, 1951); and Gabriel A. Almond and James S. Coleman, *The Politics of the Developing Areas* (Princeton: Princeton University Press, 1960.)

3 Paul S. Reinsch, *Public International Unions: Their Work and Organization: A Study in International Administrative Law* (Boston: Ginn and Company, 1911); J. A. Salter, *Allied Shipping Control: An Experiment in International Administration* (Oxford: Clarendon Press, 1921); Leonard S. Woolf, *International Government: Two Reports* (New York: Brentano, 1916); Woolf, *The Framework of a Lasting Peace* (London: Allen and Unwin, 1917). Mitrany also built on the work of Norman Angell, Robert Cecil, and G. D. H. Cole, among others, in developing his own statement of the functionalist thesis. For a brief discussion of Mitrany's intellectual antecedents, see Paul Taylor, 'The Functionalist Approach to the Problem of International Order: A Defence,' *Political Studies,* vol. 16, no. 3 (1968), pp. 393-410; and Taylor and A. J. Groom, 'Introduction: Functionalism and International Relations,' in Groom and Taylor, pp. 1-6. For much more extensive treatment of the intellectual foundations of international functionalism see Harold E. Engle, *A Critical Study of the Functional Approach to International Organization,* unpublished Ph. D. dissertation, Department of Public Law and Government, Columbia University, 1957; and Curtis W. Martin, *The History and Theory of the Functional Approach to International Organization,* unpublished Ph. D. dissertation, Department of Government, Harvard University, 1950. A lengthy bibliography of functionalist and related writings is found in Groom and Taylor, pp. 284-337.

4 *American Journal of International Law,* vol. 1 (July 1907), pp. 565-578. Engle finds evidences of the functionalist mode of thought even earlier. He quotes Edgar Saveney, writing a quarter of a century before Baldwin, on the spreading of international cooperation in technical fields: 'In the end', says Saveney, 'the nations would find themselves federated, after a fashion, by the very force of things.' Engle, p. 8.

5 *A Working Peace System: An Argument for the Functional Development of International Organization,* 1st ed. (London: Royal Institute of International Affairs, 1943). More recently *A Working Peace System* and other Mitrany writings have been republished with an introduction by Hans J. Morgenthau (Chicago: Quadrangle Books, 1966). Mitrany's functionalist conception was first elaborated in the William Dodge lectures given at Yale University in 1932, published as *The Progress of*

*International Government* (New Haven: Yale University Press, 1933). Other Mitrany works on the functionalist idea include 'The Political Consequences of Economic Planning', *Sociological Review*, vol. 26, no. 4 (October 1934), pp. 321-345; *The Road to Security* (London: National Peace Council 1944); 'Problems of International Administration', *Public Administration*, vol. 23 no. 1 (Spring 1945), pp. 2-12; 'International Consequences of National Planning', *Yale Review*, vol. 37, no. 1 (September 1947), pp. 18-31; 'The Functional Approach to World Organization', *International Affairs*, vol. 24, no. 3 (July 1948), pp. 350-363; 'Reflections on UNESCO Exchange of Persons Programme', *International Social Science Bulletin*, vol. 2, no. 2 (Summer 1950), pp. 256-261; 'The International Technical Assistance Program, United Nations: Success or Failure?' *Proceedings of the Academy of Political Science*, vol. 25, no. 2 (1953), pp. 145-155; 'An Advance in Democratic Representation', *International Associations*, vol. 6, no. 3 (March 1954), pp. 136-138; 'International Cooperation in Action', *International Associations*, vol. 11, no. 9, (September 1959), pp. 644-648; 'The Prospect of European Integration: Federal or Functional', *Journal of Common Market Studies*, vol. 4, no. 2 (December 1965), pp. 119-149; 'The Functional Approach in Historical Perspective', *International Affairs*, vol. 48, no. 3 (July 1971), pp. 532-543; 'A Political Theory for the New Society', in Groom and Taylor (1975), pp. 25-37.

6  Mitrany, *A Working Peace System*, Quadrangle Books ed., p. 28. Hereafter all references to this work are to the Quadrangle Books edition.

7  *Ibid.*, p. 97.

8  *Ibid.*, p. 31.

9  *Ibid.*, p. 98.

10  *Ibid.*, p. 69.

11  *Ibid.*, p. 98.

12  Michael D. Wallace and J. David Singer, 'Intergovernmental Organization in the Global System, 1815-1964: A Quantitative Description', *International Organization*, vol. 24, no. 2 (Spring 1970), pp. 239-287.

13  For example, the Treaty constituting the European Coal and Steel Community (1951) in its first preambular clause asserts that 'world peace may be safeguarded only by creative efforts equal to the dangers that menace it . . .' The Convention on International Civil Aviation (1944) speaks of the need to 'avoid friction and to promote that cooperation between nations and peoples upon which the peace of the world depends . . .' UNESCO's Constitution (1946) declares 'that since wars begin in the minds of men, it is in the minds of men that the defenses of peace must be constructed . . .' And the World Health Organization Constitution boldly asserts, 'The health of all peoples is fundamental to the attainment of peace and security'. These and other constitutional documents are found in Amos J. Peaslee, *International Governmental Organizations: Constitutional Documents*, 2 vols. (The Hague: Martinus Nijhoff, 1956).

14  See comments on 'developmental functionalism' in Claude, *Swords Into Plowshares*, pp. 405-407; and Claude, 'Economic Development Aid and International Political Stability', in Robert W. Cox, ed., *The Politics of International Organizations* (New York: Praeger Publishers, 1969), p. 57. Claude suggests that the developmental approach, as a 'state-building' rather than a 'state-undermining' enterprise, 'has stood the conventional theory of functionalism on its head'. *Ibid.*, and *Swords Into Plowshares*, p. 406. The shift from functionalism to a developmentalist ideology is also discussed in Cox and Harold W. Jacobson, et. al., *The Anatomy of Influence* (New Haven: Yale University Press, 1973), pp. 404, 425; and Susan Strange, 'The United Nations and International Economic Relations', in Kenneth J. Twitchett, ed., *The Evolving United Nations*, published for the David Davies Memorial Institute of International Studies (London: Europa Publishers, 1971), pp. 116-117.

15 *Yearbook of International Organizations,* 15th ed. (Brussels: Union of International Associations, 1974), p. 533. *Yearbook* figures differ somewhat from those cited by Singer and Wallace, *supra.* note 12, primarily because 2-member organizations are included by the latter but not by the *Yearbook.*

16 See, e.g., Robert O. Keohane and Joseph S. Nye, Jr., 'Transgovernmental Relations and International Organizations', *World Politics,* vol. 27, no. 1 (October 1974), pp. 39-62; C. Robert Dickerman, 'Transgovernmental Challenge and Response in Scandinavia and North America', *International Organization,* vol. 30, no. 2 (Spring 1976), pp. 213-240; Raymond F. Hopkins, 'The International Role of "Domestic" Bureaucracy', *International Organization,* vol. 30, no. 3 (Summer 1976), pp. 405-432; and Lawrence Juda, 'A Note on Bureaucratic Politics and Transgovernmental Relations', *International Studies Notes,* vol. 4, issue 2 (Summer 1977), pp. 1-3.

17 The *Yearbook of International Organizations,* p. 533, shows an increase in the number of formal non-governmental organizations from 1268 to 2470 during the period 1960-1972.

18 A very careful analysis of Mitrany is found in James Patrick Sewell, *Functionalism and World Politics* (Princeton, New Jersey: Princeton University Press, 1960), esp. pp. 28-72. See also Haas, *Beyond the Nation-State,* esp. pp. 3-50; and Ardrew W. Green, 'Mitrany Reread with the Help of Haas and Sewell', *Journal of Common Market Studies,* vol. 8, no. 1 (September 1969), pp. 50-69. Unpublished sources are Engle and Martin.

19 Mitrany assumes that functional cooperation would be limited to 'those things which cannot be done well or without friction, except on an international scale'. *A Working Peace System,* p. 28.

20 See his discussion of needs in *ibid.,* pp. 54-59 and *passim.*

21 The functional approach is to 'shift the emphasis from political issues which divide to those social issues in which the interested nations are plainly akin and collective; to shift the emphasis from power to problems and purpose'. 'The Functional Approach to World Organization', in *ibid.,* p. 164.

22 *Ibid.,* p. 70.

23 *Ibid.,* p. 28.

24 *Ibid.,* p. 56.

25 Learning continues to be a central concept in Haas' reformulation of functionalist theory. See Haas, pp. 12-13, 47-48. It was also an important idea in the work of earlier functionalists, such as G. D. H. Cole and Norman Angell, upon whose work Mitrany built.

26 *A Working Peace System,* p. 79.

27 *Ibid.,* p. 63.

28 'International Cooperation in Action', p. 647.

29 *A Working Peace System,* pp. 72-73.

30 The spreading out of functional cooperation from one area to another is now commonly called a 'spillover' process. Mitrany did not use this term, however, and his meaning is more accurately conveyed by reference to 'technical self-determination', demonstration effects, and attitudinal change. 'Spillover', as applied to the integrative process, is an expression attributable to Ernst B. Haas. Haas defined it as a distinctly political phenomenon that is not easily reconciled with functionalist notions of technical self-determination and noncontroversiality. According to the Haas definition, spillover is a 'political process which results in the accretion of new powers and tasks to a central institutional structure, based on changing demands and expectations on the part of such political actors as interest groups, political parties, and bureaucracies. It refers to the specific process which originates in one functional context, initially separate from other political concerns, and then expands into related activities as it becomes clear to the chief political actors that the achievement of the initial aims

cannot take place without such expansion.' 'International Integration: Regional Integration', *International Encyclopedia of the Social Sciences*, David L. Sills, ed., vol. 7 (New York: The Macmillan Company, 1968), p. 523.

31 *A Working Peace System*, p. 30.

32 *Ibid.*, pp. 73-76.

33 Andrew Green, p. 58, concludes: 'On balance, the best summary of Mitrany's thought is that functional institutions create a sense of community which will create world peace and ultimate development of functionalism into world government'.

The problem of global security raises serious questions about the ultimate authority structure of the functionalist world. Mitrany apparently regards security as 'a separate function like the others'. *A Working Peace System*, p. 76. But if the means of military coercion are 'entrusted to a common authority', *(ibid.*, p. 31) how is this to be reconciled – either practically or philosophically – with his ideal of a cooperative and essentially voluntaristic system? The issue is not explored.

34 Attention is called to Sewell's excellent analysis of the dynamic elements in functionalism, as gleaned from Mitrany and others. Drawing on a wide range of functionalist writings Sewell identifies five ways in which functional activity is said to contribute to the process of peaceful change: It (1) eliminates sources of friction, (2) reorients peoples away from divisive political issues, toward more constructive pursuits, (3) provides a 'training ground of cooperation', (4) operates as an 'invisible hand' creating 'widening circles' of cooperation, and (5) creates international community through a vague 'natural' growth process derived from the organismic analogy. See Sewell, pp. 57-71.

35 Mitrany, *A Working Peace System*, p. 25.

36 *Ibid.*, p. 96.

37 'German aggression was a particularly vicious outgrowth of a bad general system, and only a radical and general change of the system itself will provide continuous security for all.' *Ibid.*, p. 76.

38 'Our social activities are cut off arbitrarily at the limit of the state and, if at all, are allowed to be linked to the same activities across the border only by means of uncertain and cramping political ligatures.' *Ibid.*, p. 82.

39 *Ibid.*, p. 38.

40 *Ibid.*, p. 62. Inis L. Claude, Jr., identifies three basic assumptions about the causes of war that undergird the functionalist prescription. According to this interpretation, war is produced by 1) objective social conditions, such as proverty, deprivation and ill-health; 2) the institutional inadequacy of the state system in dealing with problems of global reach; and 3) the attitudes, allegiances, and habits of thought and feeling fostered by the state system. See Claude, *Swords Into Plowshares*, 4th ed. (New York: Random House, 1971), pp. 378-408. As general propositions, these appear to be an accurate representation of Mitrany's position. One may question Claude's critique of the first proposition, however, in which he attributes to Mitrany a belief that there is 'a direct correlation between national economic backwardness and aggressiveness.' Claude refutes this proposition by pointing out that 'it was advanced Germans, not primitive Africans, who shattered world peace in 1939.' *Ibid.*, pp. 387-388. Claude, to some extent, is attacking a straw man. Mitrany's writings do not assert a direct correlation between 'economic backwardness and aggressiveness' but rather present a much more complex view of the relationship between conflict and social conditions.

41 *The Road to Security*, p. 15.

42 The last point is made somewhat tentatively in *A Working Peace System*, p. 77: 'Possiby they could even be used, very properly and effectively, as a first line of action against threatening aggression, by their witholding services from those who are causing the trouble.' Mitrany becomes more emphatic in *The Road to Security* (London: National Peace Council, 1944), pp. 16-17. 'Economic technical agencies

would be preventive, by their very nature, in a way in which military agencies never can be. Just as it would be their function to give service wherever it was needed, so it would clearly be their duty to deny service where it was not obviously needed and might be abused. And they would have the means to do so without using force.' If aggression occurred, they would be able 'effectively to check it simply by witholding their services at a moment's notice.'

43 For comment on global government as a contribution to peace, see Sewell, pp. 17-18.

44 Claude, pp. 385-387.

45 *Ibid.*, p. 387. Claude, in fact, rejects many functionalist assumptions as theoretically untenable and empirically invalid. See *ibid.*, pp. 387-391, 396-407.

46 'Transnational Participation and International Peace', *International Organization,* Vol. 25, no. 3 (Summer 1971), p. 324.

47 This also seems to be a fair evaluation of neo-functionalism, a variant of functionalism originally elaborated by Ernst B. Haas and subsequently developed by Philippe Schmitter, Leon Lindberg, J. S. Nye, and others in its application to regional integration. Neo-functionalist studies of regional integration have yet to move far beyond the state of conceptualization and model-building toward rigorous formulation and testing of hypotheses.

48 See e.g., Haas, *The Uniting of Europe* (Stanford, California: Stanford University Press, 1958); Haas and Philippe B. Schmitter, 'Economics and Differential Patterns of Political Integration: Projections About Unity in Latin America,' *International Organization,* vol. 18, no. 4 (Autumn 1964), pp. 705-737; Schmitter, 'Three Neo-Functional Hypotheses About International Integration', *International Organization,* vol. 23, no. 1 (Winter 1969), pp. 161-166; Leon N. Lindberg and Stuart A. Scheingold, *Europe's Would-Be Polity* (Englewood Cliffs, New Jersey: Prentice-Hall, Inc., 1970); Lindberg and Scheingold, eds., *Regional Integration: Theory and Research* (Cambridge: Harvard University Press, 1971); J. S. Nye. *Peace in Parts* (Boston: Little, Brown and Company, 1971); James A. Caporaso, *Functionalism and Regional Integration* (Beverly Hills: Sage Publications, 1972).

Haas has since concluded that theories of regional integration, including neo-functionalism, have tended either not to predict very accurately or not to explain very convincingly. In any event, regional integration theories have become obsolescent to the extent that extra-regional forces and actors create interdependencies that cut across regional blocs and groupings. Thus, Haas argues, theories of regional integration 'ought now to be subordinated to a general theory of interdependence.' See Haas, 'Turbulent Fields and the Theory of Regional Integration', *International Organization,* vol. 30, no. 2 (Spring 1976), pp. 173-212.

49 For example, in their Latin-American study, Haas and Schmitter identify three sets of conditions bearing on prospects for spillover from economic to political integration. These include 'background conditions' (size of integrating units, rate of transaction, pluralism, elite complementarity), 'conditions at time of economic union' (governmental purposes, powers of union), and 'process conditions' (decision-making style, rate of transaction, adaptability of governments). J. S. Nye, 'Comparing Common Markets: A Revised Neo-Functionalist Model', *International Organization,* vol. 24, no. 4 (Autumn 1970), pp. 796-835, identifies an even more impressive list of 'process mechanisms', 'structural conditions', and 'perceptual conditions'.

For a good, brief characterization of the neo-functionalist approach, see Caporaso, pp. 30-31, and also the very perceptive analysis in Robert W. Cox, 'On Thinking About a Future World Order', *World Politics,* vol. 28, no. 2 (January 1976), pp. 188-189. 'Neofunctionalism', says Cox, 'was concerned primarily with analysis of the political processes which would transform a less integrated into a more integrated international system. Whereas Mitrany had envisaged a mere addition of problem-solving tasks, neofunctionalism introduced as a key concept the notion of "spillover''. In practice, the tasks of administration are linked, so that if the performance of some particular function becomes organized internationally, this will create the opportunity to raise the question of similarly organizing the performance of related tasks. Perceptive leaders in the internationally integrated sectors could use these linkages among related functions so as to precipitate or take advantage of crises to bring about a step-by-step expansion of internationally performed tasks. As this happened, the various client groups within countries could increasingly focus their interests upon the international agencies carrying out these tasks, thereby expanding the authority of the international institutions at the expense of national institutions.' With European integration in the 1960s increasingly deviating from neofunctionalist predictions, despite attempts to salvage the theory through such conceptual additions as 'spill-back' and the 'dramatic-political actor', neofunctionalism became 'largely a checklist of concepts drawn up in relation to the question as to whether the international system was becoming more centralized.'

50 *Beyond the Nation State: Functionalism and International Organization* (Stanford: Stanford University Press, 1964). Haas' statements on functionalism are found in a number of publications in addition to that just cited. These include, among others, *The Uniting of Europe;* 'The Challenge of Regionalism', *International Organization,* vol. 12, no. 4 (Autumn 1958), pp. 440-458; 'Technocracy, Pluralism, and the New Europe', in Stephen R. Graubard, ed., *A New Europe?* (Boston: Houghton Mifflin Co., 1964), pp. 62-88; Haas and P. Schmitter, 'Economics and Differential Patterns of Political Integration: Projections about Unity in Latin-America', *International Organization,* vol. 18, no. 4 (Autumn 1964), pp. 705-737; Schmitter and Haas, *Mexico and Latin-American Integration* (Berkeley: Institute of International Studies, 1964); ' 'The Uniting of Europe and the Uniting of Latin America', *Journal of Common Market Studies,* vol. 5, no. 4 (June 1967), pp. 315-343; and The Study of Regional Integration: Reflections on the Joy and Anguish of Pretheorizing', *International Organization,* vol. 24, no. 4 (Autumn 1970), pp. 607-646. Our comments are limited primarily to his exposition in *Beyond the Nation State* because it applies functionalism to organizing at the global level, while the other writings deal primarily with regional integration. For a good analysis and critique of Haas' functionalism, particularly as it applies to regional integration, see Michael J. Brenner, *Technocratic Politics and the Functionalist Theory of European Integration* (Ithaca, N.Y.: Center for International Studies, Cornell University, 1969), pp. 3-16.

51 *Beyond the Nation State,* p. 35.

52 His claims are carefully hedged, however. See *ibid.,* pp. 458, 497.

53 Sewell, p. 249.

54 *Ibid.,* p. 43.

55 *Ibid.,* p. 291.

56 'When actors realize that their interest would best be achieved by adopting new approaches, and if these approaches involve commitment to larger organizations, then and only then does "learning" contribute to integration. Learning, further, often involves the redefinition of an earlier conception of self-interest concerning welfare as a result of exposure to a new situation. As new alternatives for action become apparent to the actor, his original notion of his welfare may undergo some change. In this sense, initially unintended consequences of organizational action are assimilated into the perceptive equipment of the actor – in other words, he "learns".' Haas, *Beyond the Nation State,* p. 48.

57 For example, 'What emerges from this turmoil are not so much organs in a nascent world community as new instrumentalities born of the play of international politics. "Instrumentalities" is employed deliberately, for it would seem that IFC, IDA, and the Special Fund, whatever their differences, hold this characteristic in common: they are products of converging shifts in national policies without evidencing any funda-

mental change in position, much less "attitude".' Sewell, p. 291.

58 In fact, he seems to be concerned more with attitudes of governments than of individuals.

59 For a review of this literature, see Peter Wolf, 'International Organization and Attitude Change: A Re-examination of the Functionalist Approach', *International Organization*, vol. 27, no. 3 (Summer 1973), pp. 347-371.

60 B. E. Matecki, *Establishment of the International Finance Corporation and United States Policy: A Case Study in International Organization* (New York: Frederick A. Praeger, 1957).

61 *Ibid.*, pp. 159-160.

62 Benjamin V. Cohen, 'The Impact of the United Nations on United States Foreign Policy', *International Organization*, vol. 5, no. 2 (May 1951), p. 280.

63 *Beyond the Nation-State*, pp. 132-133.

64 *The Political Dynamics of European Economic Integration* (Stanford: Stanford University Press, 1963), pp. 286-87. See also Leon N. Lindberg, 'The Role of the European Parliament in an Emerging European Community', in Elke Frank, ed., *Lawmakers in a Changing World* (Englewood Cliffs, N. J.: Prentice-Hall, 1966), p. 124: 'We have some evidence suggesting that what takes place in the Strasbourg conference hall, the lobbies, the caucus and committee rooms, and the political group offices has contributed to the development of new norms of conflict resolution, to a sense of legitimacy in the institutions (especially the Commissions), to a concept of community "general interest", and to a sense of mutual identification.'

65 Kenneth Lindsay, ed., *European Assemblies: The Experimental Period, 1949-1959* (New York: Praeger, 1960), p. 94. And at p. 80: 'There can be no doubt that the experience of working in an international assembly has indirectly contributed greatly to the knowledge and outlook of many members of parliament. This has already had far-reaching consequences. It has made international cooperation more real and national parliaments more alert to international affairs.'

66 Quoted in J. Allan Hovey, Jr., *The Super-Parliaments: Inter-Parliamentary Consultation and Atlantic Cooperation* (New York: Praeger, 1966), p. 81. Fens continues: 'This is a revolutionary development and has received far too little attention. We have only to recall that the same treaty would never have been ratified unless there had been in each of the parliaments a similar body of opinion prepared to support the adventure of a European Economic Community. Hitherto, it had not existed. That it does today is a tribute to the importance of the European assemblies.'

67 Lindberg and Scheingold, esp. pp. 119-120, 159-162, 293-295.

68 Alger, 'United Nations Participation as a Learning Experience', *Public Opinion Quarterly*, vol. 27, no. 3 (Fall 1963), p. 425.

69 *Ibid.*, p. 422. The quotation is from Ithiel de Sola Pool, Suzanne Keller, and Raymond A. Bauer, 'The Influence of Foreign Travel on Political Attitudes of American Businessmen', *Public Opinion Quarterly*, vol. 20, no. 1 (Spring 1956), p. 169. See also Alger's subsequent discussion of 'Personal Contact in Inter-governmental Organizations', in Herbert C. Kelman, ed., *International Behavior* (New York: Holt, Rinehart & Winston, 1965), pp. 523-547. Much of Alger's data for this article is drawn from his study of UN participation previously cited and from Gary Best, *Diplomacy in the United Nations*, unpublished Ph. D. dissertation, Northwestern University, 1960.

70 Harold K. Jacobson, 'Deriving Data from Delegates to International Assemblies', *International Organization*, vol. 21, no. 3 (Summer 1967), pp. 592-613. The response rate was very low – 28 returns from 179 questionnaires (16%), which makes conclusions from the data highly tentative. Jacobson also surveyed delegates to the International Labor Conference and World Health Assembly in 1966, with an even lower response rate.

71 'Sixty-three percent of those delegates who had never attended an ITU meeting

previously checked that ITU and its activities were "very important" to their state, and 37 percent checked "important". Only 25 percent of the group that had previously attended an ITU meeting checked "very important" while 67 percent checked "important".' *Ibid.*, p. 610. The total ITU sample included just 28 respondents, 12 with previous experience and 16 without, which made controls for other respondent characteristics unfeasible.

72 G. Matthew Bonham, 'Participation in Regional Parliamentary Assemblies: Effects on Attitudes of Scandinavian Parliamentarians', *Journal of Common Market Studies*, vol. 8, no. 4 (June 1970), p. 325.

73 A total of 84 interviews are reported – 18 from the Consultative Assembly group, 21 from the Nordic Council, and 45 from the control group.

74 *Ibid.*, p. 334. Because the issue of political integration is not equally salient in the three Scandinavian countries, Bonham's study might have profited from a comparison of responses by national groups. This would permit some assessment of the importance of domestic political context. The small size of the sample may have rendered such further sample subdivision impractical, however.

75 Henry H. Kerr, Jr., 'Changing Attitudes Through International Participation: European Parliamentarians and Integration', *International Organization*, vol. 27, no. 1 (Winter 1973), pp. 45-83.

76 *Ibid.*, p. 61.

77 *Ibid.*, p. 76.

78 There was a slender bit of evidence in support of affective change in one area. With the exception of French Gaullists, all persons interviewed – delegates and non-delegates – evidenced general support of increased powers for the European Parliament. Among the Gaullists, however, 55 % of the delegates favored increased powers, compared with 36 % of the Gaullist non-delegates. See *ibid.*, p. 72.

79 David A. Karns, 'The Effect of Interparliamentary Meetings on the Foreign Policy Attitudes of United States Congressmen', *International Organization*, vol. 31, no. 3 (Summer 1977), pp. 497-514.

80 One further study of European parliamentarians, not primarily concerned with the effect of attitude change, provides data incidentally bearing on this question. Of 82 national legislators interviewed for the study, 18 had attended the European Parliament. Of these, just four admitted having acquired 'a more "European" orientation.' See Werner Feld and John K. Wildgen, 'Electoral Ambitions and European Integration', *International Organization*, vol. 29, no. 2 (Spring 1975), pp. 447-468, at p. 453.

81 'The European Economic Community and National Civil Servants of the Member States', *International Organization*, vol. 26, no. 1 (Winter 1972), pp. 121-135.

82 *Ibid.*, p. 133.

83 *Ibid.*, pp. 134-35.

84 Keith Smith, 'The European Economic Community and National Civil Servants of the Member States – A Comment', *International Organization*, vol. 27, no. 4 (Autumn 1973), pp. 563-568.

85 *Ibid.*, p. 564.

86 William R. Pendergast, 'Roles and Attitudes of French and Italian Delegates to the European Community', *International Organization*, vol. 30, no. 4 (Autumn 1976), pp. 669-677.

87 *Ibid.*, p. 673. Of 19 respondents who addressed the issue, two indicated increased support, two a lessening of support, and 15 no change.

88 *Ibid.*, pp. 673-674.

CHAPTER II

1 See Mitrany, 'The Prospect of European Integration: Federal or Functional', in Mitrany, *A Working Peace System* (Chicago: Quadrangle Books, 1966), p. 213.

2 Even such specialized agencies as UNESCO, ILO and WHO, frequently referred to as typical functional organizations, have shown signs of being politicized in the most pejorative sense of the term.

3 See Donald T. Campbell and Julian C. Stanley, *Experimental and Quasi-Experimental Designs for Research*. (Chicago: Rand McNally & Company, 1966).

4 *Ibid.*, p. 12.

5 In the case of Norwegian parliamentarians, international organizations 'other than the UN' refer to the North Atlantic Union, the Council of Europe, the Nordic Council, and the Inter-Parliamentary Union. With regard to Norwegian and U.S. civil servants, the non-UN fora include the whole range of major international organizations. For United States Congressmen the other international organizations include the Inter-Parliamentary Union, the NATO Assembly, the OECD, and a variety of UN specialized agencies, special conferences, and suborgans.

6 Hubert M. Blalock, Jr., *Causal Inferences in Non-Experimental Research* (Chapel Hill: The University of North Carolina Press, 1964) p. 13.

7 Campbell and Stanley, p. 12.

8 This does not mean that we are matching the control groups with the test groups in terms of their background characteristics. Rather, we are dealing with natural intact groups, in which group differences are subjected to statistical controls for background characteristics.

    Cambell and Stanley advise against matching test and control groups because it is '. . . usually ineffective and misleading, particularly in those instances in which the persons in the experimental group have sought out exposure to the X.' *Ibid.*

9 Herbert Hyman, 'Problems in Treating Relationships between Two Variables', in Hyman, ed., *Survey Designs and Analysis* (Glencoe: The Free Press, 1960), p. 199. Emphasis added.

10 Campbell and Stanley, p. 5, warn that maturation processes within the respondents, operating as a function of the passage of time, and not specific to the particular X we are investigating, may influence the value of Y. However, this warning is of little relevance to our investigation, since the members of the test group did not become exposed to X all at the same age. Furthermore, in our statistical runs we are controlling for the age factor.

    Our concern for the impact of self-selection can hardly be overestimated, given the problems of control under this design. It should be recalled from our literature review, chapter 1, that both Kerr and Bonham found attitude differences among parliamentarians to be largely due to patterns of self-recruitment among the members of the test groups, rather than the result of the participation in international meetings.

11 Such as, for example, the interviews conducted by Chadwick F. Alger, 'United Nations Participation as a Learning Experience', *Public Opinion Quarterly*, vol. 27, no. 3 (Fall 1963), pp. 411-426.

12 In the socio-psychological literature on attitudes and attitude formation, the analytic distinction between cognitive and affective components is clearly the most common one. See e.g. Daniel Katz, 'The Functional Approach to the Study of Attitude Change', *Public Opinion Quarterly*, vol. 24, no. 2 (Summer 1960), pp. 163-204; Herbert C. Kelman and Raphael S. Ezekiel, *Cross-National Encounters* (San Francisco: Jossey-Bass, Inc., 1970); and William A. Scott, 'Psychological and Social Correlates of International Images', in Herbert C. Kelman, ed., *International Behavior* (New York: Holt, Rinehart & Winston, 1965), pp. 70-103.

CHAPTER III

1 For an explanation of 'type 1' attitudes, see chapter II.

14 – Beyond Functionalism

2 Percentage agreement figures are used to simplify the data presentation. The loss of statistical information thereby incurred seems tolerable.

3 Statistically the two independent experience variables are strongly intercorrelated. The Kendall rank order correlation coefficient (Tau B) is .423, significant at .001.

4 The agreement score differences are very small in the two cases not fitting the hypothesized relationship.

5 See articles by Bonham, Karns and Kerr, respectively, discussed in Chapter I. See also our discussion in chapter II of the self-selection factor as a research design problem.

6 See description of research design in chapter II.

7 One of these is statistically significant at .05.

8 Intercorrelation of questionnaire items confirms the impression that helping developing countries and channeling aid through the UN touch two different attitudinal dimensions. The association between Item 8 (increase foreign aid package) and Item 7 (increase trade preferences) is very strong (Tau B = .539), while the association between Item 8 and Item 6 (increase aid through UN) is much weaker (Tau B = .099).

9 The Commerce Department administers both domestic and foreign trade regulations.

10 By rank order measures, responses to questionnaire Items 1-10 are all positively associated with one another. However, all are negatively associated with Item 11. While most of these negative associations are small, those pertaining to Items 7-9 are quite high. Since these three items concern the question of aid to developing nations and aid to the Palestinians, we may conclude that officials most convinced of majority rule in the UN are least likely to support increased foreign aid allocations.

11 As pointed out earlier, the Commerce Department also regulates domestic trade activities. The Foreign Affairs Department handles only matters related to an international context.

12 In Table 13 the Commerce respondents score slightly higher on Item 7 (trade preferences). However, from our discussion of Hypothesis 2, it should be recalled that among Commerce respondents experience is related negatively to this item, which is the opposite of the relationship found for respondents from the other two departments. The reader may wish to re-examine the explanation offered for this finding in the light of the client concept built into Hypothesis 5.

13 This set of findings shows very clearly that the recruitment process – discussed in chapter II as a potential threat to our research design – does not offer a viable explanation for the more favorable attitudes among Foreign Affairs officials. If it did, the attitudinal differences should be apparent among inexperienced as well as experienced respondents. In fact the difference tends to be the reverse of that indicated by the recruitment or self-selection theory. Our data strongly suggest that the overall attitudinal differences derive from some aspect of the work experience rather than from the recruitment process.

14 By examining visits to the Third World we are tapping the attitudinal effect of a special type of international experience. The findings are consistent with previously reported data on the attitude-experience relationship and give further support to the functionalist notion of 'familiarity breeding favorableness'.

15 See Appendix A where the associations are reported in the form of Tau B coefficients.

16 Although the data used to test hypotheses 5 and 6 (see Tables 13-15) show some 'deviations' from the data pattern in Figure 1, these are not consistent enough to necessitate a reinterpretation of the four dimensions. Furthermore, the small Ns in Table 15 suggest that the data should be treated with special caution.

17 See chapter II for a discussion of civil servants and legislators as 'types' of functionalist actors.

18 In addition to the parliamentarians the Permanent Mission of Norway to the United Nations includes a number of non-parliamentarians. These represent for the most part

large interest groups, such as The National Council of Women, labor unions and employers' federations. Also, the Foreign Affairs Department delegates a number of civil servants to work in conjunction with the non-parliamentarians and parliamentarians, as well as with the Permanent Mission.

19 The Storting consists of 155 members elected for a 4-year term. With 13 delegates per General Assembly session, a total of 52 may serve as UN delegates during one Storting period. As a rule very few members are redelegated, in order to let as many legislators as possible get the UN experience. If we count the total number of UN delegates in the Storting (including those from previous Storting periods who are still members), they represent almost half the Storting membership.

20 In a sense, comparing attitudes of UN-delegates and non-delegates is a more direct probing of the hypotheses to the extent that most of the questionnaire items deal specifically with the UN (Items 1-6, and Item 10). Statistically the two independent experience variables are strongly intercorrelated. The Kendall rank order correlation coefficient (Tau B) is .509, significant at .000.

21 See chapter II.

22 Although not necessarily representative for assignments to other international organizations, in the case of the European Parliament self-recruitment has been shown to be an important factor. Legislators who serve as delegates to this international forum have been found to have favorable attitudes toward further European integration prior to their first arrival for the Parliamentary Session. Both Bonham and Kerr (See chapter I) found self-recruitment among parliamentarians to be an important reason for their participation in regional assemblies.

23 A five-point scale registering agreement and disagreement was used in grouping the data. As in the case of civil servants' attitudes, percentage agreement figures are used in the table presentations.

24 On the basis of personal interviews we have reason to believe that the relatively high agreement score for the UN delegates on Item 9 (Palestinian aid) is due in great measure to comprehensive lobbying on the part of Palestinian representatives at the UN.

25 See Chapter II for our discussion of 'types' of functionalist actors.

26 See our discussion of Bonham's and Kerr's findings in Chapter I.

27 From personal interviews as well as reading of foreign policy debates in the Storting, we find that former UN delegates are more prone to bring up UN-related issues than their inexperienced counterparts.

28 G. Matthew Bonham, 'Participation in Regional Parliamentary Assemblies: Effects on Attitudes of Scandinavian Parliamentarians', Journal of Common Market Studies, vol. 8, no. 4 (June 1970), p. 334.

29 As previously pointed out in this chapter, we have no reason to believe this is the case.

30 See Johan Galtung, 'Foreign Policy Opinion as a Function of Social Position', Journal of Peace Research, vol. 1, no. 2-3 (1964), pp. 206-231, and 'Social Position, Party Identification, and Foreign Policy Orientation', in James N. Rosenau ed., Domestic Sources of Foreign Policy (New York: Free Press, 1967), pp. 161-194. In his studies Galtung uses an index of social rank position which proves to be a powerful predictor of foreign policy orientation. The index is a one-dimensional measure of the 'total rank' of an individual's status-set, counting eight factors: age, sex, income, education, job, job branch, ecology, geography. An individual who is young, male, has high income and education, has a white collar job in the secondary or tertiary industry, and comes from an urban background in the central parts of Norway, is likely to be highly knowledgeable of, have a strong interest in, and be opinionated on foreign policy issues. These individuals Galtung calls 'topdogs' (vs. 'underdogs') located in the 'center' (vs. 'periphery'). His findings suggest that foreign policy issues which are old, moral, and/or absolute are more likely to be accepted in the periphery, and that

recent, pragmatic/gradualist issues are more likely to be accepted in the center. Support for multilateral cooperation would generally tend to fall in the category of recent, pragmatic/gradualist issues, and 'center' individuals should thus be expected to be most supportive of this. By examining the attitudinal effect of all eight factors on legislators' views of the UN, we discovered only partial support for this prediction. For purposes of our analysis and data presentation we decided to retain only those four factors which seemed to exert some noticeable degree of attitudinal impact. The remaining four factors – sex, income, job branch, and geography – were left out from the analysis, partly because they overlap with the other factors (e.g. income and job-branch are highly intercorrelated with education), partly because they do not show any attitudinal effect one way or the other (sex and geography).

31 Active participation in international labor meetings by the Norwegian Labor Party is a manifestation of this party's internationalist platform to contribute to the promotion of social democratic principles and ideas.

32 The relationships between responses and age, LDC-visit, and party affiliation proved somewhat less consistent and less statistically significant. A possible reason for this is that the UN experience exerts a muting effect on these attributes.

33 When linked with experience at international organizations other than the UN, the observed attitudinal effect of the 'collective attribute' does not emerge. Cf. our previous observation that these are for the most part European regional organizations with little or no representation from the Third World.

34 Perhaps the reason is that the dimension of international cooperation constitutes a more recent, pragmatic/gradualist type of issue than the remaining dimensions included in our questionnaire, thus in a sense confirming Galtung's premise. See footnote 30 for comment on Galtung's line of reasoning.

35 See Chapter 6 for a discussion of this face of functionalist thought.


CHAPTER IV

1 Current telephone directories for Agriculture and Commerce were not available. Respondents from these agencies came entirely from the special lists.

2 A total of 832 questionnaires were mailed, of which 26 were returned undelivered. The return rate of 56 % is based on the delivered questionnaires.

3 See chapter III.

4 Each respondent was asked to list by name the international organizations with which his work was concerned.

5 Using chi square on a 2 x 2 table, the differences are significant at .01 for the first and third pairings on Item 2. All reference to statistical significance of findings is made with full recognition that the deficiencies of the mail-questionnaire sample make generalization to any larger population risky.

6 See articles by Bonham, Kerr, and Karns, discussed in Chapter I.

7 Of those responding to this item, 9 strongly agree, 33 agree, 11 are undecided, 16 disagree, and 3 strongly disagree.

8 Four strongly agree, 18 agree, 9 are undecided, 27 disagree, and 4 strongly disagree.

9 The association between experience and increased support for international cooperation does not extend to support for UN-sanctioned international coercion. Two questionnaire items probed this attitude dimension. (1) The United States should comply with UN sanctions by not importing chrome from Rhodesia. (2) 'The United States should use its influence to end Portuguese colonialism in Africa'. (Events in Portugal made this question redundant shortly after the questionnaire was mailed). On both items, the respondents who had attended no international organization meetings and had no work-time devoted to IO affairs have higher agreement scores than the more experienced respondents. However, those with United Nations experi-

ence score higher than those without, and current IO Bureau and USUN officials score still higher. Respondents from international affairs sub-units have significantly greater agreement on both items than other respondents. Respondents from the State Department have higher agreement scores than any other executive department. Thus organizational unit rather than international organization experience appears to be the more important source of variance in response to these two statements.

10 Of 54 relationships for the UN support items (3 items, 9 departments, 2 experience measures), 33 were negative and 21 positive. For the two aid and trade items, 28 were positive and 8 negative.

11 One other interpretation of these responses is at least plausible. For most respondents, experience with international organizations means organizations other than the United Nations. In a situation of limited resources these officials may see UN demands competing with needs of the international organizations (IMCO, WHO, FAO, etc.) with which they have a more direct relationship. Hence, a reluctance to approve more resources for the UN.

12 Andrew K. Semmel found a similar negative relationship between length of diplomatic experience and support for strengthening the UN among State Department officials interviewed in 1970. He also found that officials in sub-units concerned with bilateral diplomacy (the State Department Bureau of European Affairs and the United States Mission to Italy) were more in favor of strengthening the UN than officials in sub-units concerned with multilateral affairs (IO Bureau and the U.S. Mission to the UN). Both of the interview items on which Semmel's conclusions are based deal with increased UN authority; 1) 'expand the range of independent authority of the Secretariat and especially . . . the Secretary-General'; and 2) give the UN 'limited power to impose nonpunitive taxes on its member states'. In substance they are fairly close to our 'sovereignty transfer' item. However, members of the U.S. Mission to the UN were more favorable to both proposals than members of the IO Bureau, which does not comport with our findings. His sample of the Mission was small, however, including just nine interviews. See Semmel, 'Some Correlates of Attitudes to Multilateral Diplomacy in the U.S. Department of State', *International Studies Quarterly*, vol. 20, no. 2 (June 1976), pp. 301-324; esp. pp. 309, 314, 317.

13 Some 65 % of respondents from international affairs sub-units devoted 10 % or more of their work time to international organization activities, compared with 29 % for other respondents.

14 Significance level is better than .01 in each case, using chi square. In this instance, as in all others where chi square is used in this chapter, the data are reduced to a 2 x 2 table and calculations assume just one degree of freedom.

15 See chapter 1.

16 Nearly all of the Commerce respondents were assigned to an international affairs sub-unit within that department.

17 We have noted, for example, the relatively negative attitude of Treasury respondents and the more positive attitude of State Department respondents toward the United Nations.

18 Semmel, *op. cit.*, p. 319, offers evidence that organization characteristics affect attitudes toward multilateral cooperation. His study is limited to the Department of State, however, and examines different organizational subunits within the Department. He concludes that 'a foreign policy participant's working group or specific task location tends to be a better predictor of policy preferences than does either his social background or the career attributes of the department or of the Foreign Service as a whole.' Semmel's findings would support an inference that, as between departments, departmental differences might also engender differences in attitudes.

19 For all respondents in the general survey group, the Kendall tau B coefficients produced when items 4 (IO necessary), 8 (trade), and 9 (promote Development) are

15 – Beyond Functionalism

rank ordered with meeting attendance, are, respectively, .051, .017, and .071. For the younger age group they are .218, .107, and .165; and for the group with residence in a developing country they are .113, .149 and .143. The differences are consistent and statistically significant, but far from spectacular.

20 A factor analysis of the questionnaire items produced loadings on three factors. The first corresponded to our general evaluation dimension, and the third factor combined the sovereignty transfer and UN action-commitment items.

21 At least two conservative Republicans on the House International Relations Committee, E. Ross Adair and H. R. Gross, have declined the opportunity to serve in New York. See comments in David A. Karns. 'The Effect of Interparliamentary Meetings on the Foreign Policy Attitudes of United States Congressmen', *International Organization,* vol. 31, no. 3 (Summer 1977), pp. 499, 508.

22 Ibid., p. 502.

23 This explanation follows categories discussed in Donald P. Warwick, 'Transnational Participation and International Peace', *International Organization,* vol. 25, no. 3 (Summer 1971), p. 307. In commenting on the 'socialization' approach to the study of the effects of transnational participation, he suggests three major sources of variation: '1) the prearrival characteristics of the participant, 2) the character of his transnational experience, and 3) post-return conditions related to his transnational experience.'

24 Karns, p. 500, observes with special reference to interparliamentary meetings: 'Critics of the expense can easily find cases of probable waste. For example, many trips last about a week, but only two or three days are occupied with business sessions. Then the congressional delegates, and their spouses, together with their foreign counterparts take a trip to some area in the host country like Banff, Acapulco, or Hawaii, at taxpayer expense. This portion is vacation. However, during interviews many delegates were able to document valuable results of the joint vacations, including lasting friendships. That not all of the friendships were international is an interesting latent function of their transgovernmental activity.'

25 Before-and-after data derived from content analysis of speeches is presented later in this chapter. The reader is also referred to Karns, who analyzes before-and-after voting behavior as evidence of attitude change. As discussed in chapter 1, Karns finds a slight tendency toward more 'internationalist' voting following the experience of attendance at international meetings, although sub-group changes – in both positive and negative directions – are more pronounced.

26 See e.g., Julius Turner, *Party and Constituency: Pressures on Congress* (Baltimore: The John Hopkins Press, 1951); rev. ed., with Edward V. Schneier, 1970; Duncan MacRae, *Dimensions of Congressional Voting* (Berkeley: University of California Press, 1958); David B. Truman, *The Congressional Party: A Case Study* (New York: John Wiley & Sons, Inc., 1959); Herbert McClosky, Paul Hoffman and Rosemary O'Hara, 'Issue Conflict and Consensus Among Party Leaders and Followers', *American Political Science Review,* vol. 54, No. 2 (June 1960), pp. 406-427; Lewis Froman, *Congressmen and Their Constituencies* (Chicago: Rand-McNally, 1963); Froman, 'The Importance of Individuality in Voting in Congress', *Journal of Politics,* vol. 25, No. 2 (May 1963), pp. 324-332; Froman, 'Inter-Party Constituency Differences and Congressional Voting Behavior', *American Political Science Review,* vol. 57, no. 1 (March 1963), pp. 57-61; Warren E. Miller and Donald E. Stokes, 'Constituency Influence in Congress', *American Political Science Review,* vol. 57, no. 1 (March 1963), pp. 45-56; John Jackson, 'Some Indirect Evidences of Constituency Pressures on Senators', *Public Policy,* vol. 16 (1967), pp. 253-270; Wayne Shannon, *Party, Constituency and Congressional Voting* (Baton Rouge: Louisiana State University Press, 1968); Cleo Cherryholmes and Michael Shapiro, *Representatives and Roll Calls: A Computer Simulation of Voting in the Eighty-eighth Congress* (Indianapolis: Bobbs-Merrill, 1969); Aage Clausen, *How Congressmen Decide: A Policy*

*Focus* (New York: St. Martin's Press, 1973); John W. Kingdon, *Congressmen's Voting Decisions* (New York: Harper and Row, 1973); Morris P. Fiorina, *Representatives, Roll Calls and Constituencies* (Lexington, Massachusetts: D. C. Heath Company, 1974); John E. Jackson, *Constituencies and Leaders in Congress: Their Effects on Senate Voting Behavior* (Cambridge, Massachusetts: Harvard University Press 1974); and Donald R. Matthews and James A. Stimson, *Yeas and Nays: Normal Decision-Making in the U.S. House of Representatives* (New York: John Wiley & Sons, 1975).

27 Most notably research in the early 1960s by Leroy N. Rieselbach. See Rieselbach, 'The Basis of Isolationist Behavior', *Public Opinion Quarterly,* vol. 24, no. 4 (Winter 1960), pp. 645-657; 'The Demography of the Congressional Vote on Foreign Aid, 1939-1958' *American Political Science Review,* vol. 68, no. 3 (September 1964), pp. 577-588; *The Roots of Isolationism* (Indianapolis: Bobbs-Merrill, 1966). But see also Neil Heighberger, 'Representatives' Constituency and National Security', *Western Political Quarterly,* vol. 26, no. 2 (June 1973) pp. 224-235; H. Wayne Moyer, 'House Voting on Defense: An Ideological Explanation', in Bruce M. Russett and Alfred Stephan, eds., *Military Force and American Society* (New York: Harper and Row, 1973); Robert A. Bernstein and William W. Anthony, 'The ABM Issue in the Senate, 1967-1970: The Importance of Ideology', *American Political Science Review,* vol. 68, no. 3 (September 1974), pp. 1198-1206; and Barry Bozeman and Thomas E. James, 'Toward a Comprehensive Model of Foreign Policy Voting in the U.S. Senate', *Western Policical Quarterly,* vol. 28, no. 3 (September 1975), pp. 477-495.

28 E.g., the works, cited above, by Turner, MacRae, Miller and Stokes, Jackson, Shannon and Clausen.

29 Miller and Stokes.

30 As Clausen points out, p. 41, there are a number of different dimensions of international involvement; and the study by Heighberger indicates that the kind of international involvement associated with high defense spending is likely to be supported by Congressmen with quite the opposite characteristics from those suggested above.

31 Information on constituency characteristics is found in *Congressional Districts in the 1970's* (Congressional Quarterly, 1973) and the U.S. Department of Commerce, *Statistical Abstract of the United States, 1974* (Washington: U.S. Government Printing Office, 1975). Constituency data is used with full recognition of its weakness as a valid indicator of actual influences on Congressmen. The effective constituency to which the legislator responds may be a somewhat different group of people than the actual or legal constituency. Constituencies are not homogeneous, and an average statistic may conceal more than it reveals. Moreover, constituency characteristics as such exercise no influence on congressional behavior; they must be mediated by other variables of which an analysis such as this takes little account. See Clausen, pp. 155-159, for a further elaboration of the weaknesses of census-type data as used for this purpose. Nevertheless, such data has been of value as a predictor of congressional behavior for other purposes and will be used here despite the foregoing caveat.

32 Background and experience data on individual members is taken from the *Congressional Directory* and *Who's Who in America*. ADA scores are found in '1973 ADA Voting Record', *ADA World,* vol. 29, nos. 2 and 3 (February-March 1974), pp. 5-12. In most of our analyses, Senators and Representatives are treated as a single group of Congressmen, despite the fact that data on Senators is aggregated by state, while data on Representatives is aggregated by the usually smaller Congressional district. Senators are a small proportion of the respondents, however, and sample statistical runs for the combined group did not prove markedly different from results obtained for House members alone. For the sake of the larger N, therefore, it was decided to treat them all as 'Congressmen' except when specifically comparing House and Senate responses to the questionnaire.

33 The 'previous occupation' variable is dichotomized to distinguish only business from non-business.

34 For geographic region, the respondents are dichotomized as 'South' or 'other'.

35 The word 'change' is used for convenience of expression, with full realization that we are comparing static groups rather than measuring before-and-after responses.

36 See pp. 110-11, *supra*, for a discussion of how delegates are selected. At two per year, the total number should have been 44. However, in the interest of comparability, a decision was made to include each member of Congress only once during the time period, and then only if he had no prior experience as a UN delegate. Because of this rule, John Sherman Cooper was not included for his 1968 assignment because he had served in 1949, and Mike Mansfield was included as a House member in 1951 but not when he served as a Senator in 1958. Senator John Pastore served as a third Congressional appointee in 1955. Senators Sparkman (1950), Pastore (1955), and Allott (1962) were appointed as UN delegates although they were not members of the Senate Foreign Relations Committee.

37 Kerr makes a very good argument that more information may lead to more interest, *op.cit.*, pp. 67-68.

38 There are obviously many variables that may affect a person's attitudinal response to a new experience. Warwick, in his discussion of the 'socialization approach' to the study of transnational participation, suggests three major sources of variation, including the pre-arrival characteristics of the participant, the character of his experience, and relevant post-return conditions. See *supra*, n. 23. Kelman emphasizes the importance of the character of the experience. He observes, '. . . it is the joint occurrence of friendly behavior toward the other and genuinely new information about him that makes favorable attitude change possible.' Providing new information is necessary but not sufficient. 'To change hostile or neutral attitudes into friendly ones,' the new information must be provided 'in the context of a positive interaction between the people giving and receiving the information.' *Journal of Social Issues,* vol. 18, no. 1 (1962), pp. 85, 86.

39 The hypothesis of attitude change through personal experience with the attitudinal object finds ample basis in the social-psychological literature as well as in functionalist theory. The distinctions between cognitive and affective dimensions of attitudes are in fact drawn from social-psychological works. See, e.g., William A. Scott, 'Psychological and Social Correlates of International Images', in Herbert C. Kelman ed., *International Behavior* (New York: Holt, Rinehart and Winston, 1965), pp. 72-77. Such writers frequently distinguish a third 'behavior' or 'action' component of attitudes. See Harry C. Triandis, *Attitude and Attitude Change* (New York: John Wiley and Sons, 1971), p. 61. Social-psychological theories of attitude change through role-playing are also relevant here, since delegates to the General Assembly find themselves playing roles that, at very least, imply acceptance of the legitimacy of UN processes and require frequent justification of national positions in terms of UN norms. See Theodore M. Newcomb, Ralph H. Turner, and Philip E. Converse, *Social Psychology: The Study of Human Interaction* (New York: Holt, Rinehart and Winston, 1965), pp. 108-109.

Cognitive dissonance theory, utilized by Karns, provides a further rationale for attitude change. New experiences may bring perceptions of the UN at variance with previous cognitions, creating inner tensions or pressures that are relieved through attitude change as the individual strives to satisfy his functional need for attitudinal consistency. See Karns, pp. 504ff., and Leon Festinger, *A Theory of Cognitive Dissonance* (Stanford: Stanford University Press, 1957); Jack Brehm and Arthur Cohen, *Explorations in Cognitive Dissonance* (New York: John Wiley and Sons, 1962); Charles A. Kiesler, Barry E. Collins, and Norman Miller, *Attitude Change: A Critical Analysis of Theoretical Approaches* (New York: John Wiley and Sons, 1969); Chester

A. Insko, *Theories of Attitude Change* (New York: Appleton-Century-Crofts, 1967); and Robert Abelson, *et. al.*, ed., *Theories of Cognitive Consistency* (Chicago: Rand McNally, 1968).

40 Cost considerations precluded coding of all materials by more than one person, although five different coders were used at different times during the project. One additional reliability check was made, based on the assigned numerical values. Two coders each did all of the speeches for one prolific Senator. They differed on some of the individual scores, but the differences almost completely concelled each other out. For one coder, the average was 275; for the other it was 276. See appendix for a detailed statement of the coding rules. The initial coding was on a five-point scale, including 'strongly favorable' and 'strongly unfavorable' options. The data were later collapsed to a three-point scale.

41 Milton Rokeach, *Beliefs, Attitudes and Values* (San Francisco: Jossey-Bass, Inc., 1968), p. 138, questions 'whether it is ever possible to obtain a behavioral measure of a given attitude-toward-object that is uncontaminated by interaction with attitude toward situation.'

42 Fortunately, the direction of the distortion imposed by extrinsic events is not likely to be consistent over the 20-year period from which speeches are drawn. Hence, an unwarranted inference of change in the predicted direction during one year may be counterbalanced by a similarly grounded inference of change in the opposite direction for another year. This should leave room for the hypothesis to apply, that is, for changes in the predicted direction to outnumber all other cases. Furthermore, the vagaries of extrinsic events need not greatly distort the average scores for 'before' and 'after' speeches because, with exceptions of the earliest and latest years, each year is at once a 'before' year for some Congressmen and an 'after' year for others.

43 A difference of means test (t-test) for correlated data, one-tailed for comparing the years immediately before and after participation, and two-tailed for the first and third years before, was applied to this data. The before-and-after differences were significant at the .01 level (t = 2.41, N = 43); differences for the two 'before' years were not significant at any acceptable level of confidence. This strongly suggests that the before-and-after differences are unlikely to be attributable to chance. The generalizability of this finding is, of course, limited by the fact that these congressmen are scarcely a random sample of the larger population of past and potential future participants in international organizations.

44 The total number of speeches was ascertained by counting items listed in the index to the *Record* under the heading of 'Remarks' by each Congressman. For uniformity and simplicity (and probably at the expense of accuracy) items having multiple page references were nevertheless tallied as a single speech.

45 Using chi square, the difference between the before-and-after years was significant at the .01 level.

46 The differences between the two time periods as reflected in Table 23 are significant at .01 (chi square). Using absolute numbers of speeches rather than percentages, the figures are much the same for the two sets of paired years. For the two years prior to the UN experience, 18 Congressmen delivered more UN speeches in the subsequent year, 17 gave fewer, and 8 delivered the same number. For the years immediately before and after, 27 showed an increase, 7 remained the same, and 9 recorded a smaller number of speeches.

An interesting sidelight emerges when the number of United Nations speeches is compared with the number of separate paragraphs in which a reference to the UN is made. As indicated in the text above, the mean number of speeches for the years immediately before and after UN participation increased from 4.1 to 6.0. The mean number of paragraph references, however, increased from 17.6 to 31.4. The increase in speeches is of the magnitude of 50 %, but the increase in paragraph references is nearly 100 %. Thus speeches about the UN not only were more numerous during the subsequent year; they also were longer.

In addition to speeches, a count was also made of other materials inserted in the *Congressional Record* at the request of the members of Congress. As followers of the *Record* know, this embraces a wide variety of materials – letters, editorials, speeches delivered outside the halls of Congress, reports by Congressmen to their constituents, excerpts from books and magazines, and what-have-you. Such insertions in the *Record* were not very sensitive to changes in Congressional attitudes. The average number of items for the year before was 6.7 per Congressman, while the average for the year after was 8.0. Change is somewhat more marked when paragraph references to the UN rather than whole items are used. The average numbers for the years before and after were 45 and 64, respectively.

47  The one congressman who disagreed with the statement was interviewed in July 1974, and offered a very practical explanation. At the time of his appointment as a UN delegate he had been chairman of the House Subcommittee on International Organizations and Movements. He subsequently relinquished that post and therefore had less occasion to follow UN issues. Three others interviewed on an 'opportunity sample' basis were unanimous and emphatic that the experience had increased their awareness of the United Nations and UN-related matters.

48  The probability that this before-and-after difference represents only chance variation is less than .01, based on a chi square calculation. By contrast, differences between the two years preceding the UN experience are negligible.

49  This observation is based on a one-tailed t-test for correlated data. A two-tailed test was applied to the two prior years, where no change – or only random change – was anticipated. The mean score for the third year before UN participation was 237. The two-tailed probability for the two prior years was .82, suggesting only chance variation. In each case, mean differences were computed from the F-U averages of Congressmen who spoke in either year. Thus $N = 27$ for the two prior years ($t = 0.23$), and N-33 ($t = 2.39$) for the before-and-after years. To repeat a cautionary note sounded above, such tests of significance may give some basis for estimating the probability that differences are attributable to chance, but the generalizability of these conclusions to other groups of participants in international organization will be affected by the representativeness – or non-representativeness – of this sample of participants.

50  Analysis of non-speech items showed a similar trend, but such material was not as sensitive to shifts in Congressional attitudes as were speeches. For the before-and-after years, 17 Congressmen changed in the predicted direction (more favorable), 11 showed a less favorable average, and 3 remained the same.

51  Data from the survey supports this conclusion. Of ten former delegates who responded to the mailed questionnaire, six 'agreed' and two 'strongly agreed' with the statement, 'I gained a more favorable opinion of the UN as a result of my experience as a UN delegate.' Two were 'undecided' and no one disagreed. One of the 'undecided' Congressmen had shown a rather dramatic shift in favor of the UN as measured by the content analysis data. A personal interview with him revealed that the UN experience had worked an equally dramatic change in his conduct. He now was 'fighting the budget battle' for the UN, participating in a program to acquaint members of Congress with the organization, and generally more engaged in consideration of matters affecting the UN.

52  Specifically, the proportions experiencing favorable change in affect are Democrats 58 %, Republicans 64 %; high ADA ratings 56 %, low ADA ratings 75 %; urban constituencies 50 %, less urban constituencies 62 %. Other indicators show a similar negative relationship between prior year F-U scores and positive change in affect: Congressmen with advanced academic degrees 54 %, those without such degrees

218

78 %; well-educated constituencies 43 %, less well educated 67 %; and high proportion of foreign stock 46 %, lower proportion 67 %.

There is another relationship of interest. Delegates who share the incumbent President's political party affiliation are more likely (71 %) to experience favorable change in attitude than those of the opposite party (50 %). This variation, if attributable to other than chance factors, may reflect differences in the nature of the experience. It probably is not related to differences in prior attitudes, because the average F-U score for both groups is an identical 229.

53 Taking F-U scores for the prior year as one variable and, as a second variable, the difference between F-U scores for prior and subsequent years (prior year scores minus subsequent year scores), a Kendall tau (beta) coefficient of .50 for two variables is obtained. This is a rather strong relationship and further confirms the proposition that low F-U scores for prior years are likely to be associated with favorable change in affect toward the United Nations in a subsequent year.

54 Karns, p. 508, n. 25; and Philip J. Runkel and Joseph E. McGrath, *Research on Human Behavior: A Systematic Guide to Method* (New York: Holt, Rinehart and Winston, 1972), pp. 39-40.

55 See Karns, p. 508 and n. 25.

56 Bauer, Pool and Keller, p. 173.

57 Chadwick F. Alger, 'United Nations Participation as a Learning Experience', *Public Opinion Quarterly,* Vol. 27, no. 3 (Fall 1963), pp. 422, 425.

58 Karns, p. 12.

59 *Ibid.*

60 Or possibly it means that controlling for more than one variable at a time with only 43 or fewer cases produces Ns so small that a valid and reliable test of the theory is not possible.

CHAPTER V

1 Comparative research in the study of politics has in recent years developed into a special discipline with a number of basic methodological requisites, such as rules for randomization and specification and emphasis on the use of non-culture-bound concepts. For an instructive discussion of the concerns and requisites of comparative research, see Robert Holt and John Turner, eds. *The Methodology of Comparative Research* (New York: The Free Press, 1970), chapter 1. See also Adam Przeworski and Henry Teune, *The Logic of Comparative Social Inquiry* (New York: Wiley-Interscience, 1970).

2 International cooperation, especially within the UN, has enjoyed strong and rather stable support in the Storting during the entire post-war period. While Congressional support for the UN was high during the first two decades of the Organization's existence, this support has declined in recent years.

3 The difference in sampling techniques is reflected in our findings about the civil servants' reported involvement with international organization activities. In the U.S. sample 13.4 % of the officials spend more than 50 % of their work time on international organization activities, while the figure is 25.2 % for the Norway respondents.

4 A fifth possible source of divergent responses from the two national groups may inhere in the questionnaire instrument rather than the characteristics of the samples. Although the questionnaires are quite similar in wording and format, there are slight differences; and even the same words may carry a different conceptual load in the two political settings. For instance the question of increasing the financial resources of the UN may have different meanings in the political contexts of the two member nations. The United States has traditionally been by far the largest financial contributor to the

UN, while at the same time probably having experienced the biggest political setback of any member nation.

5 A cross-national survey from 1961 shows that 75 % of Norway respondents rated the UN record to date as 'good', while only 57 % of U.S. respondents were of the same opinion. The poll, taken by the Canadian Institute of Public Opinion and reported in *The Montreal Star*, February 22, 1961, may of course have given somewhat different results in the 1970s, although we have reason to believe that the UN is still held in higher esteem in Norway than in the United States.

6 The findings are mixed on the question of sovereignty transfer. While the youth factor turns out to be insignificant in the U.S. data, it clearly does not promote greater willingness to favor sovereignty transfer in the Norway data.

7 To avoid unnecessary duplication of data presentations we have omitted the tables where experience with international organizations other than the UN serves as the independent variable. These findings do not differ a great deal from the attitudinal pattern reported in Table 4.

CHAPTER VI

1 *Report of the Commission on the Organization of the Government for the Conduct of Foreign Policy* (Washington, D.C.: U.S. Government Printing Office, 1975), p. 27.

2 See the very perceptive discussion of 'Realism and Complex Interdependence' in Robert O. Keohane and Joseph S. Nye, *Power and Interdependence* (Boston: Little, Brown and Company, 1977), pp. 23-37.

3 Keohane and Nye, speaking primarily in analytic rather than prescriptive terms, suggest that world political reality sometimes reflects realist assumptions, while at other times it fits their model of complex interdependence. *Ibid.*, pp. 23-24, 36.

4 For a good statement of the case against world government, see Inis L. Claude, Jr., *Swords Into Plowshares*, 4th ed. (New York: Random House, 1971), pp. 411-432. See also the very trenchant comments of Willmoore Kendall, *Contra Mundum* (New Rochelle, N.Y.: Arlington House, 1971), pp. 625-632.

5 For example Falk identifies nine 'principal types of world order that seem relevant to the future'. Richard A. Falk, *A Study of Future Worlds* (New York: The Free Press 1975), pp. 174ff. Most of them could be treated as variations of the functionalist, state-centered, and world government models, however.

6 See for example the strategy employed by European functionalists in their efforts to achieve integration, as described in Amitai Etzioni, 'European Unification: A Strategy of Change', *World Politics*, vol. 16, no. 1 (October 1963), pp. 32-51.

7 Falk, p. 152. Falk's discussion of the 'fallacy of premature specificity' has much in common with the functionalist refusal to specify organizational details in advance: 'There is some temptation to become enthralled with the intricacies of constitutional forms whenever proposals for new world order arrangements are made. This temptation should be resisted because it undermines the credibility of the basic recommendations and encourages a static mood toward the future. It is impossible to anticipate, from this vantage point in time, the details of institutional structure that would be agreed upon once the requisite political consciousness emerges that would engender a revolution in world order. Despite a measure of interplay, the mechanics of administrative management are an outgrowth of political consciousness rather than its source. Though sympathetic to the functionalist approach, Falk does not style himself as functionalist.'

8 A.J.R. Groom, 'The Functionalist Approach and East/West Cooperation in Europe', *Journal of Common Market Studies*, vol. 13, no. 1 and 2 (1975), p. 24.

9 *Ibid.*, pp. 21-60.

10 Strange, 'The United Nations and International Economic Relations', in Kenneth J.

Twitchett, ed., *The Evolving United Nations: A Prospect for Peace?* (London: Europa Publications, 1971), p. 116.

11 James Patrick Sewell, *Functionalism and World Politics* (Princeton, N. J.: Princeton University Press, 1966), p. 286.

12 *Ibid.*, pp. 43-44.

13 *A Working Peace System* (Chicago: Quadrangle Books, 1966), pp. 63, 79; and 'International Cooperation in Action', *International Associations*, vol. 9, no. 9 (September 1959), p. 647.

14 See, e.g., *The International Secretariat of the Future* (London: Royal Institute of International Affairs, 1944); Egon F. Ranshofen-Wertheimer, *The International Secretariat: A Great Experiment in International Administration* (Washington: Carnegie Endowment for International Peace, 1945); Philip C. Jessup, 'The International Civil Servant and His Loyalties', *Journal of International Affairs*, vol. 9, no. 2 (1955), pp. 55-61; Alexander Loveday, *Reflections on International Administration* (London: Oxford University Press, 1956); Georges Langrod, *The International Civil Service* (Leyden: A. W. Sythoff, 1963); Sydney D. Bailey, *The Secretariat of the United Nations*, rev. ed. (New York: Frederick A. Praeger, 1964); Leon Gordenker, *The UN Secretary-General and the Maintenance of Peace* (New York: Columbia University Press, 1967); Arthur W. Rovine, *The First Fifty Years of the Secretary-General in World Politics, 1920-1970* (Leyden: Sijthoff, 1970); Mark Zacher, *Dag Hammarskjöld's United Nations* (New York: Columbia University Press, 1970); Brian Urquhart, *Hammarskjöld* (New York: Alfred A. Knopf, 1972).

15 Support for agency norms and goals does not mean that international officials discard their national loyalties. Most undoubtedly retain them. Some may even pursue national causes in ways inimical to the purposes of the international organization. For the most part, however, such multiple loyalties are reasonably compatible. See, e.g., Bailey; Jessup; Harold Guetzkow, *Multiple Loyalties: Theoretical Approach to a Problem in International Organization* (Princeton, N. J.: Princeton University Center for Research on World Political Institutions, 1955); Roger Pethybridge, 'Soviet Nationals at the United Nations', *International Relations* (April 1965), pp. 709-720; David A. Kay, 'Secondment in the United Nations Secretariat: An Alternative View,' *International Organization*, vol. 20, no. 1 (Winter 1966), pp. 63–75.

16 See, e.g., Robert W. Cox, 'The Executive Head: An Essay on Leadership in International Organization', *International Organization*, vol. 23, no. 4 (Autumn 1969), pp. 205-230; and Norman J. Dufty, 'Organizational Growth and Goal Structure', *International Organization*, vol. 26, no. 3 (Summer 1972), pp. 479-498.

17 See, e.g., American Institute of Public Opinion, *The Gallup Opinion Index*, Princeton, N. J., Report No. 126 (January 1976); Report No. 123 (September 1975); Report No. 117 (March 1975); Report No. 81 (March 1972); and *The Gallup Poll*, vols. 1-3 (New York: Random House, 1972), especially pp. 1705, 1733, which report cross-national polls on the United Nations from a dozen different countries. See also, League of Women Voters Education Fund, *Public Opinion on the UN! What Pollsters Forget to Ask* (Washington, D.C., July 1977). Mimeo.

18 See, e.g., Ronald Inglehart, 'An End to European Integration?' *American Political Science Review* vol. 61, no. 1 (March 1967), pp. 91-105; Richard L. Merritt and Donald J. Puchala, ed., *Western European Perspectives on International Affairs* (New York: Frederick A. Praeger, Publishers, 1968), esp. pp. 283-317; Inglehart, 'Public Opinion and Regional Integration', *International Organization*, vol. 24, no. 4 (Autumn 1970), pp. 764-795; Inglehart, *The 1973 European Community Public Opinion Surveys: Preliminary Findings* (Geneva: University of Geneva, 1974); and Robert J. Shepherd, *Public Opinion and European Integration* (Westmead, Eng.: Saxon House, D. C. Heath Ltd., 1975), esp. pp. 93-126, 227-238.

19 Inglehart, 'Public Opinion and Regional Integration', p. 773. The strength of Euro-

pean sentiment among the younger generation led Inglehart to believe that public preferences might in the future become more than permissive, i.e., 'an increasingly effective long-term influence on decision makers . . . basically favorable to supranational integration.' *op.cit.* p. 795.

20 The experience of Norway in rejecting entry into the European Community and the generally negative attitude of the British public both before and since British entry suggest that public opinion, if the issue is sufficiently salient, may even be a force working against international cooperation. And, as Norway proved in this case of unusual political salience, publics are not always tolerant of whatever international involvement their political leaders are willing to lead them into. On the other side of the ledger, Robert Cooley Angell in his study, *Peace on the March: Transnational Participation* (New York: Van Nostrand Reinhold Company, 1969), concludes that 'policy-makers are being subjected increasingly to a stream of influence from elites toward accommodation among nations, a stream that derives in part from the growing amount of transnational participation with positive effects on these elites.' See pp. 26, 188 and *passim*. His elite groups consist of people who have resided abroad for educational, business, military or governmental reasons, including participation in governmental and non-governmental organizations. They represent specialized publics rather than general public opinion.

21 See Chapter 1.

22 HEW returned 250 of 316 deliverable questionnaires, for a 79 % return; Agriculture returned 248 of 321 for 77 %; and Treasury returned 157 of 228, 69 %.

23 Graham T. Allison, *Essence of Decision: Explaining the Cuban Missile Crisis* (Boston: Little, Brown and Company, 1971), p. 176.

24 See Chapter I.

25 See, e.g., *A Study of the Capacity of the United Nations System* (The Jackson Report), 2 vols, U.N. Document DP 5, 30 September 1969; Joint Inspection Unit, *Report on Personnel Problems in the United Nations* (Bertrand Report), U.N. Document A/8454, 5 October 1971; and Seymour M. Finger and John Mugno, *The Politics of Staffing the UN Secretariat,* The Ralph Bunche Institute on the United Nations, The Graduate School and University Center of the City University of New York (December 1974).

26 Sewell, p. 43.

See also Michael J. Brenner, *Technocratic Politics and the Functionalist Theory of European Integration* (Ithaca: Cornell University Press, 1969), p. 134. Speaking of the British decision to seek entry into the Common Market, Brenner says: '. . . We discovered that interest groups were only marginally involved, that their influence was limited to secondary matters, that bureaucrats in the economic ministries rarely acted in the manner of technocrats single-mindedly pursing the goal of economic advancement, that political leaders carefully guarded their powers of decision, and that considerations arising from the realm of planning and welfare were clearly subordinate to concerns of "high politics" in the final determination of policy. Taken together, these critical judgments suggest that Functionalism's major shortcoming is its failure to recognize the relative independence of political authority and to give sufficient weight to the strictly political factors that impinge upon the decisions made at that level of government. Functionalism does not of course entirely exclude from its theory the "political component", but it does reject the idea that there exists a distinct political function or an autonomous world of "high politics" as we found it.'

27 Ernst B. Haas, *Beyond the Nation-State* (Stanford, California: Stanford University Press, 1964), p. 35.

28 *Ibid.*, p. 49.

29 Inis L. Claude, Jr. *Swords Into Plowshares* 4th ed. (New York: Random House, 1971), p. 399. Mitrany has responded to this criticism by saying that the potential

disruptive effects of politics are no excuse for not trying. What, after all, is the alternative? Will states 'join in some political union where they refuse limited and mutually beneficial cooperative arrangements?' Better to seek partial arrangements, wherever possible and despite their shortcomings, than to reach for the moon or attempt nothing. See Mitrany, 'The Functional Approach in Historical Perspective', *International Affairs,* vol. 47, no. 3 (July 1971), pp. 538-539.

30 According to Nau, the discussions revealed 'acute personal and national differences concerning both the scope and implementation of a common program.' He continues, 'To be sure, scientific competition at this stage is expected, and even necessary, in order to define the technical dimensions of a development project. But this competition, even in a national context, is not wholly an objective process; it also involves an investment of personal and professional capital on the part of the individual scientists. In a transnational context, these personal and professional stakes are magnified by the presence of more widely varying social and cultural backgrounds. The scientific community of each country is rooted in an environment influenced as much by the traditional goals and institutions of that country as by the universal requirements of scientific investigation. Accordingly, each community covets the opportunity to impress the particular make-up of its own research tradition upon the composition and character of the common program.' Henry R. Nau, 'The Practice of Interdependence in the Research and Development Sector: Fast Reactor Cooperation in Western Europe', *International Organization,* vol. 26, no. 3 (Summer 1972), pp. 499-526. The subject is further elaborated in Nau, *National Politics and International Technology* (Baltimore: Johns Hopkins University Press, 1974).

31 E.g., Hoffmann, 'Obstinate or Obsolete? The Fate of the Nation-State and the Case of Western Europe', in Hoffmann, ed., *Conditions of World Order* (Boston: Houghton Mifflin Co., 1968), pp. 110-163.

32 Haas, 'The "Uniting of Europe" and the Uniting of Latin America', *Journal of Common Market Studies,* vol. 5, no. 4 (June 1967), pp. 315-343.

33 Stanley Hoffmann, 'Discord in Community: The North Atlantic Area as a Partial International System', *International Organization,* vol. 17, no. 3 (Summer 1963), p. 529. Recent research has also documented the essentially political nature of decisions by Britain, Denmark, and Norway about entry into the Common Market. See Robert J. Lieber, 'Interest Groups and Political Integration: British Entry into Europe', *American Political Science Review,* vol. 66, no. 1 (March 1972), pp. 53-67, esp. pp. 56, 66-67; and Peter M. Leslie, 'Interest Groups and Political Integration: the 1972 EEC Decisions in Norway and Denmark', *American Political Science Review,* vol. 69, no. 1 (March 1975), pp. 68-75.

34 Mitrany, 'A Political Theory for the New Society', in A. J. R. Groom and Paul Taylor, ed., *Functionalism: Theory and Practice in International Relations* (London: University of London Press, Ltd., 1975), p. 37, n. 27.

35 Sewell, pp. 245-297.

36 Nau, 'The Practice of Interdependence', pp. 521-522.

37 Haas, *Beyond the Nation State,* pp. 47-50.

38 Hoffmann, 'Discord in Community', pp. 530-531.

39 See discussion in Chapter I.

40 Claude, *Swords Into Plowshares,* p. 404.

41 Keohane and Nye, *Power and Interdependence,* p. 3.

42 Charles Kindleberger, *American Business Abroad* (New Haven: Yale University Press, 1969), p. 207.

43 'A New National Partnership', speech by Secretary of State Henry A. Kissinger at Los Angeles, 24 January 1975, Department of State *Bulletin,* vol. 72, no. 1860 (February 17, 1975), p. 197.

44 Inis L. Claude, Jr., 'Economic Development Aid and International Political Stability',

in Robert W. Cox, ed., *The Politics of International Organizations* (New York: Praeger Publishers, 1970), p. 57.

45 Angell, p. 188.

46 *Ibid.*, p. 186.

47 Haas, *Beyond the Nation-State*, p. 431.

48 James N. Rosenau, 'Transforming the International System: Small Increments Along a Vast Periphery', *World Politics*, vol. 18, no. 3 (April 1966), p. 544.

49 Sewell has another view of functionalism's shortcoming as creator of 'peace bearing community'. He argues that the functionalist emphasis on *'interest'* as the basis of community formation fails to take account of the need for *purpose* and *commitment* which create a sense of obligation to the community. He states, 'Community formation by independent political units involves ascendance from the plane where interests interesect to a more permanent juncture of commonly accepted responsibilities . . . (T)he functionalist argument itself takes no account of the necessary shift in levels.' And, 'by what process does it anticipate an elevation from the level of converging ad hoc interests of independent political units to one characterized by a foundation of obligation? We must conclude that it hardly confronts the question.' Sewell, pp. 312-327; quotations at pp. 319-320, 327.

50 Chicago: The University of Chicago Press, 1962; 2nd ed. 1970. Citations are to 1970 edition.

51 *Ibid.*, p. 13.

52 Jack C. Plano and Robert E. Riggs, *Dictionary of Political Analysis* (Hinsdale, Ill.: The Dryden Press Inc., 1973), p. 55.

53 Kuhn, p. viii.

54 *Ibid.* p. 10.

55 See Keohane and Nye, p. vii; Donald J. Puchala and Stuart I. Fagan, 'International Politics in the 1970s: The Search for a Perspective', *International Organization*, vol. 28, no. 2 (Spring 1974), p. 248.

56 Puchala and Fagan, p. 248.

57 Cox, 'On Thinking About Future World Order', p. 189.

58 E.g., Keohane and Nye; Richard N. Cooper, *The Economics of Interdependence: Economic Policy in the Atlantic Community* (New York: McGraw-Hill, 1968); Cooper, 'Economic Interdependence and Foreign Policy in the Seventies', *World Politics*, vol. 24, no. 2 (January 1972), pp. 159-181; Edward L. Morse, 'Transnational Economic Processes', in Keohane and Nye, *Transnational Relations and World Politics* (Cambridge, Mass.: Harvard University Press, 1972), pp. 23-47; Lester R. Brown, *World Without Borders: The Interdependence of Nations* (New York: Random House, Inc., 1972); Richard N. Rosecrance and Arthur Stein, 'Interdependence: Myth or Reality', *World Politics*, vol. 26, no. 1 (October 1973), pp. 1-27; Peter J. Katzenstein, 'International Interdependence: Some Long-Term Trends and Recent Changes', *International Organization*, vol. 29, no. 4 (Fall 1975), pp. 1021-1034; Alex Inkeles, 'The Emerging Social Structure of the World', *World Politics*, vol. 27, no. 4 (July 1975), pp. 467-495; Ernst B. Haas, 'Turbulent Fields and the Theory of Regional Integration', *International Organization*, vol. 30, no. 2 (Spring 1976), pp. 173-212. See also Kenneth N. Waltz, 'The Myth of Interdependence', in Charles P. Kindleberger, ed., *The International Corporation* (Cambridge, Mass.: M.I.T. Press, 1970), pp. 205-223.

Some of the sources cited take issue with the notion of interdependence, either because of its fuzziness or because of its asserted inapplicability. Inkeles finds it necessary to differentiate several subconcepts – interconnectedness, dependence, integration, and convergence. Rosecrance and Stein see increased interdependence in the recent past but raise questions about future prospects. Waltz denies the existence of any long-range trend toward greater interdependence.

224

There is also a vast literature on dependency or dependence theory, which focuses on a highly asymmetric form of interdependence verging in some cases on absence of actor autonomy. This is generally treated in the context of developed-developing country relations. For a recent collection of statements on this subject see James A. Caporaso, ed., 'Dependence and Dependency in the Global System', a special issue of *International Organization,* vol. 32, no. 1 (Winter 1978).

59 See discussion in Keohane and Nye, pp. 24-29, and comments in Puchala and Fagan.